I loved *The Cantaloupe in the*

SIRI

Melanie Shankle has definitely done something jolly with this book.

SIR ANTHONY STRALLAN, *Downton Abbey*

I feel that I have been misrepresented as the villain of this book. You'll be hearing from my attorneys.

THE ANTELOPE

I haven't worn that rust-colored velour jogging suit in at least ten years.

CHARLES MARINO, father of Melanie Shankle

Why did you send me this book, and how did you get my address?

JEN HATMAKER, author of *7*

I don't read many books, but when I do . . . I read Melanie Shankle.

THE MOST INTERESTING MAN IN THE WORLD

This book is the big one, Elizabeth.

FRED SANFORD, owner of *Sanford and Son*

Clear eyes, full hearts; with this book you can't lose.

COACH TAYLOR, former coach of the Dillon Panthers

This book is good, but I still don't understand the problem with having an antelope hanging in your living room.

PERRY SHANKLE, husband of Melanie Shankle

Melanie wrote a book?

EVERYONE WHO WENT TO HIGH SCHOOL WITH
MELANIE SHANKLE

I wish I had Melanie's imagination and storytelling abilities!

C. S. LEWIS

Melanie Shankle's delightful book exceeded my great expectations.

CHARLES DICKENS

I only wish Melanie had been around to write some of the New Testament.

THE APOSTLE PAUL

This book is the funniest book you will ever read. It will absolutely change your life for the better. Why are you waiting? Buy it right now.

GULLEY, best friend of Melanie Shankle

Quit bugging me about helping you come up with fake funny endorsements.

SOPHIE HUDSON, author of *A Little Salty to Cut the Sweet*

# THE ANTELOPE IN THE LIVING ROOM

# The Antelope
## in the
# Living Room

The Real Story of Two People Sharing One Life

- a memoir -

# Melanie Shankle

Tyndale House Publishers, Inc.
Carol Stream, Illinois

Visit Tyndale online at www.tyndale.com.

Visit the author's blog at thebigmamablog.com.

TYNDALE and Tyndale's quill logo are registered trademarks of Tyndale House Publishers, Inc.

*The Antelope in the Living Room: The Real Story of Two People Sharing One Life*

Designed by Ron Kaufmann

Edited by Stephanie Rische

Published in association with William K. Jensen Literary Agency, 119 Bampton Court, Eugene, Oregon 97404.

All Scripture quotations, unless otherwise indicated, are taken from the Holy Bible, *New International Version,*® *NIV.*® Copyright © 1973, 1978, 1984, 2011 by Biblica, Inc.™ Used by permission of Zondervan. All rights reserved worldwide. www.zondervan.com.

Scripture quotations marked NLT are taken from the *Holy Bible*, New Living Translation, copyright © 1996, 2004, 2007, 2013 by Tyndale House Foundation. Used by permission of Tyndale House Publishers, Inc., Carol Stream, Illinois 60188. All rights reserved.

**Library of Congress Cataloging-in-Publication Data**
Shankle, Melanie.
 The antelope in the living room : the real story of two people sharing one life / Melanie Shankle.
  pages cm
  ISBN 978-1-4143-8554-9 (sc)
 1. Marriage. 2. Love. 3. Families. I. Title.
 HQ503.S43 2014
 306.81—dc23                                                    2013030341

Printed in the United States of America

20   19   18   17   16   15   14
 7    6    5    4    3    2    1

## TO PERRY.

As Eula Goodnight says to Rooster Cogburn,
"Livin' with you has been an adventure any woman
would relish for the rest o' time. . . .
I have to say you're a credit to the whole
male sex, and I'm proud to have ya for my friend."
Thanks for the best adventure a girl could have.
I'm so glad God gave me you. I love you
more than I can say.

# Contents

# The Importance of Being Antelope: A Prologue

When I was writing my first book, *Sparkly Green Earrings*, I realized there were so many more stories about our family that I wanted to tell. However, most of those seemed to involve my relationship with my husband, Perry. So I began to think up an outline for a second book with an eloquent title along the lines of *Dadgum, Y'all, Marriage Can Be Hard*.

(I also considered *Big Louis Vuitton Purse with Matching Wallet* based on the number of pairs of sparkly green earrings I received after my first book was published.)

Ultimately, according to vast market research in the form of two people I asked, neither of those seemed to be the catchiest title, so *The Antelope in the Living Room* was born. I've done my best to tell real stories of two people sharing one life, including the things we sometimes try to ignore. The veritable antelopes in the living room of life.

A few months after I turned in the final manuscript for this book, my publisher began to send me various cover options. I'd sent them a drawing I really liked to give them an idea of what I had in mind, and when I saw the first few cover options, I was really excited to see they had incorporated exactly what I had envisioned.

Until I showed them to Perry.

He looked them over and said, "Well, it looks good, but that's not an antelope."

"What do you mean it's not an antelope? Look at those antlers!"

He sighed deeply. "Yes, that's the problem. Antelopes don't have antlers. They have horns."

"Oh. Okay. But I like the antlers! I think they make it look so pretty!"

"Pretty enough to make your entire book a fraud?"

Seriously. This is my life. Who's going to read this book? Jim Fowler?

I replied, "No, of course I don't want the entire book to be discredited by a fraudulent depiction of an antelope for the two readers who will know the difference. I certainly don't want anyone to feel bamboozled."

(I didn't really say bamboozled, but I wish I had. It's a great word.)

He suggested, "Why don't you just send them a picture of the actual nilgai antelope hanging in our living room and let them use that?"

"For the same reason I'm sad it's hanging in our living room. It's ugly. I need my book cover to be pretty."

That's how we ended up spending the next several hours on Google looking at pictures of various antelopes. Ultimately I decided I could forsake my beloved deer image for a kudu, because in my opinion they have the prettiest horns of all the antelopes.

I e-mailed Tyndale and said, "Um. Apparently I requested a deer for the cover of my book instead of an antelope. According to Perry, this bit of carelessness will create a scandal the likes of which the publishing industry has never seen. Can we please exchange these duplicitous antlers for a kudu? You will find a picture attached."

(Moments like these I feel certain that their job is so much easier when they're helping Tony Dungy with a book. I bet he has never once brought up the difference between a deer and an antelope and required their cover artists to deal with this type of wildlife minutiae.)

But the whole thing is a beautiful illustration of our marriage. Perry pays attention to detail. He likes things to be correct. He will measure something down to one-eighth of one-eighth of an inch. Meanwhile, my life philosophy is basically "Eh, close enough" as I nail holes in the wall, all devil-may-care. He believes in rolling the tube of toothpaste from the bottom up to get every last drop of Colgate, like he's some kind of fluoride addict, while I like to squeeze right from the middle of the tube.

And while I believe it is civilized to leave the toilet seat down as a courtesy to other family members, Perry seems to take some sort of sadistic pleasure in leaving it up, thereby creating a potential middle-of-the-night obstacle course that causes me to go scrambling in search of a towel.

Antelope? Deer? Tomato? To-mah-to?

Yet God led us to each other, with all our differing opinions and systems for hanging clothes in our closet and our feelings about salting the tortilla chips and his love of the outdoors and my love of air-conditioning and sheets with a high thread count. We made a promise before God, our families, and our dearest friends to work through all these differences, right before eating pork tenderloin medallions on small rolls and some sort of thing called *Brie en croute*, otherwise known as fancy cheese with crackers.

And somehow we make a good team in spite of it all. Maybe we're actually a great team because of all our differences. We each balance out the other's extremes even though we don't always agree.

Particularly on what constitutes a pretty book cover.

# Introduction:
# Erring on the Side of Love

DR. SEUSS ONCE SAID, "You know you're in love when you can't fall asleep because reality is finally better than your dreams." And that's nice and all. But then you get married and reality isn't always that great because maybe somebody snores or is kind of weird about "staying within our household budget," and your dreams start to look pretty good by comparison. Because marriage can be the biggest blessing and the most significant challenge two people ever take on. It's the joy of knowing there is someone to share in your sorrows and triumphs and the challenge of living with someone who thinks it's a good idea to hang a giant antelope on your living room wall.

The days are filled with laughter and compromise. And then there are days filled with silence and anger. But at the end of it all, you're two people God has joined to journey through life together. For better or for worse. In hunting season and in health.

A few weeks ago, I spent most of the day at my best friend Gulley's house. It was one of those rare, gorgeous Saturdays in Texas when the weather is absolutely perfect. We'd spent our time catching up on life while the kids ran around the yard and did their best to see if there was a way one of them could end up in the ER before nightfall. It's like their hobby to see which of them can make us yell first, "WHY DID YOU DO THAT? YOU'RE GOING TO KILL YOURSELF!"

As day turned to evening, Gulley invited us to stay for dinner. So I called Perry to let him know that was the plan, and he said he'd meet us at Gulley's in the next hour or so to help with the grilling of the meat. Because nothing really brings men together like building a fire and cooking on it. I'm pretty sure that's in the book of Proverbs.

And since it was after five o'clock by that point, and since nothing wears you out quite like watching your children try to push each other off a trampoline, Gulley and I sat out on the swing in her backyard and began to reflect on life in that way you do with your best friend.

The past week had been full of various political rants in the news, and seeing as we'd already covered our latest thoughts on *The Bachelor* and how we felt about colored skinny jeans, our conversation turned to these controversial topics. I was feeling pretty good about life and began a whole discourse on how all we need is love. Just like the Beatles told us in 1967.

I said I felt like maybe I'd been too harsh in the past. Too black and white. Too quick to judge someone before thinking about how they might feel or what they've been through. I'm sure by this time I was waving my hands wildly in that way I do when I feel strongly about something, and I concluded this whole diatribe by saying, "I want my next forty years to be about love. If I err, then let me err on the side of love. May it be said of me that I always erred on the side of love."

Gulley nodded and we toasted to erring on the side of love,

feeling pretty good about ourselves and our new magnanimous take on life. Then I looked up and saw that Perry had arrived. So we made our way back into the house to figure out what we needed to do to get dinner started.

I kissed him on the cheek as I walked into the living room, and he asked, "What were y'all talking about out there on the swing?" Feeling good about my new resolution, I replied, "I was telling Gulley that I've decided maybe I've been too hard on people in the past. From now on, I'm going to err on the side of love."

(Please picture me saying that like I'm Gandhi. I felt like I'd never been more profound.)

Perry looked right at me and without missing a beat said, "That's the dumbest thing I've ever heard."

Well, I bet no one ever talked like that to Gandhi.

But that's marriage. You are two very different people who aren't going to agree on everything. There are times you might feel like the person you married is dead inside because they want to quote the apostle Paul after you've just declared that you want to err on the side of love. And sometimes those moments will lead to a fight in the middle of your best friend's living room that causes her and her husband to find an excuse to leave the room.

Hypothetically speaking.

Marriage is a constant push and pull of thoughts and ideas and values and arguing over whether $100 is too much to pay for a pair of jeans. (It's not.) But it's also the most literal example of how iron sharpens iron.

When I look back on the sixteen years Perry and I have been married, I can see the places where we've made each other better. There are parts of us etched into each other like the rings in the trunk of a tree. We've grown, we've changed, we've been forever marked. And ultimately, we are so much better together than either of us would be on our own.

Sometimes we err on the side of love, and sometimes we think that's a dumb idea. But we are in this thing together for the rest of our lives—not just for better or for worse, but for better AND worse. No one else drives me crazier, makes me laugh louder, or causes me to fall in love all over again when I least expect it.

And that's what this book is about. The times that brought us together and the times we were falling apart. The days that we wouldn't trade for anything in the world, and the days that he hung an antelope on my wall.

Welcome to the story of a real marriage. Dead animals and all.

# CHAPTER 1

# Warm Heart, Cold Salad Bowl

EVERY YEAR on our wedding anniversary, smack-dab in the middle of the hottest month of the year, I know with all certainty that I was out-of-my-mind in love with Perry to marry him at noon in August. In Texas. And not just anywhere in Texas, but in South Texas, where the devil has been known to remark, "Man, it is really hot. Can someone find me a double-wide with a window unit and an extension cord so I can plug in my oscillating fan?"

I'd always envisioned a December wedding complete with twinkle lights, poinsettias, and Christmas trees decorating the church sanctuary. My bridesmaids would be dressed in dark-green taffeta dresses with huge bows on the backs, because this was a late '80s/early '90s daydream, which meant they'd also have enormous hair and bushy eyebrows. In a perfect world, they'd have delicate wreaths of baby's breath encircling some type of elaborate updo and green satin shoes dyed to match their dresses. For years I'd kept a picture torn from an issue of *Bride* magazine that featured a December bride with her hands tucked in a white fur muff with red roses cascading from it like a waterfall. Never mind the fact that in Texas it rarely gets cold enough for a pair of mittens; I wanted to look like Anna Karenina on my wedding day.

However, when Perry finally proposed on April 24, 1997, after two (long) years of dating, I said, "YES!" before he could even get the words out of his mouth. A woman with a stash of contraband bridal magazines hidden underneath her couch is a woman quick to abandon the dream of a wedding with a winter-wonderland theme.

Prior to our relationship, Perry hadn't had many serious girlfriends because he believed his time was better spent hunting deer and making homemade ammunition. Contrary to popular belief, a deer blind with no indoor plumbing isn't really the best place to meet a nice single girl—or even a trashy single girl, for that matter—and thus he went through his late teens and early twenties with a Ford truck and a .257 Roberts as his primary companions.

This may explain why he felt a hunting blind was a perfectly acceptable gift to give me for my twenty-fourth birthday. Fortunately for him, we'd been dating for only about three months, so I accepted the gift with great enthusiasm instead of making him leave on the spot. Looking back, I should have set the gift bar a little higher from the beginning, because he had no way of knowing the small tin of popcorn he got me the following Valentine's Day was going to send me into tears and hysteria. It wasn't so much that I didn't enjoy the festive, cinnamon-flavored popcorn as that I reached the bottom of the tin only to discover there was no velvet ring box.

It's not his fault. All those John Hughes movies I watched throughout my formative teen years would have set up any guy for failure. Who can compete with Jake Ryan, the Porsche, and the final birthday cake scene? It's not possible.

(That movie may or may not also have been responsible for my slight obsession with hair adorned with baby's breath. So classy.)

One night, early in our relationship, we were at my apartment after attending a wedding shower for some of Perry's friends. There is nothing that makes a single girl start to dream about new linens and china patterns like a wedding shower. Because everyone knows that's what marriage is all about—the new household items. It didn't matter that I had no idea how to prepare an actual meal; a new set of Calphalon cookware would change all of that. Perry stood at the door, wrapped his arms around me, and whispered words he would live to regret for the next two years: "For what it's worth, I know you're the girl I'm going to marry."

With that statement I began to mentally plan a wedding. A wedding that wouldn't take place for another two years because Perry left a crucial word off the end of his statement. What he should have said to the crazy lady with starry-eyed visions of ivory silk shantung in her head was, "For what it's worth, I know you're the girl I'm going to marry SOMEDAY," but he didn't know that because it's not a lesson you learn when you spend a large majority of your young adult years with a bunch of guys competing to see who can get their truck stuck in the mud.

When the day finally arrived that an actual proposal of marriage came and the follow-up question from Perry was "How soon can we get married?" I whipped out the wedding planner I'd secretly purchased months before (okay, years before) and said, "Let me call the church." The answer, according to church availability, was August 16, and the rest is history. Instead of looking like a Russian ice princess on my wedding day, I spent my reception with the glow of a woman wearing fifteen layers of petticoats in 120-degree weather.

Love is not only blind but also indifferent to extreme temperatures.

Organizing a wedding in three and a half months isn't the easiest task, so it totally paid off that I'd been planning it in my head for twenty-five years prior to the actual day. All I had to do was substitute a bouquet of lilies for the white fur muff covered in roses, which I was willing to do, because did you read the part about getting new cookware?

At some point in the midst of the wedding-planning festivities, I dragged Perry to several department stores and local boutiques to register for gorgeous place settings of fine china and sterling-silver utensils that, to this day, we've used all of three times—one of which was when I made dinner and discovered that all our regular forks were dirty and we were out of plastic ones. So I pulled out the sterling, and honestly, it did give the Cheesy Cheeseburger Hamburger Helper a certain sophistication that had previously been missing.

These days, whenever we attend a wedding, we sit back with our three plates of cake and four glasses of house wine and watch the bride and groom take to the dance floor for their first dance. We get all sentimental, look deeply into each other's eyes, and say, "Those two fools have no idea what they're getting into. They don't deserve those new dishes. You know who deserves some new towels? We do. We've survived over a DECADE of marriage, and we've earned those towels."

When you're a young, bright-eyed fiancée, you have no idea what color towels you want for your bathroom because chances are you're moving into his apartment, and anything will be a step up from the thirty-year-old towels he stole from his parents' house before he moved out, the concrete blocks that serve as an entertainment center, and the neon Bud Light sign that he and his fraternity brothers swiped during what has become a legendary night in college.

The exception is if you marry a man whose mother served as his interior decorator and helped him purchase all new dishes and linens when he initially moved into his bachelor pad. If this is the case, you may want to reevaluate whether or not you want to spend the rest of your life with a man who let his mother pick out his sheets. It's like the old saying goes: "The hand that picks the sheets rules the world."

Of course, maybe I'm just a little bitter because we're down to a mere three dinner forks in our Country French flatware pattern. It's the price you pay when you eat on paper plates most nights and throw them in the trash, forgetting not everything is disposable.

But all those years ago, I was one of those fools who agonized over choosing all the right items to celebrate our new life together, especially the bedding. I walked around the department store exclaiming, "It needs to be pretty, but not too feminine! It should have a masculine influence because, Honey, I want our bedroom to reflect both our personalities!" How could I have known our bedroom would have plenty of his personality, thanks to all the boxer shorts and socks left lying around on the floor as part of his decorating style—Early American Frat House?

There was no need to choose that over-the-top-masculine navy-plaid Ralph Lauren comforter to convey that a man lived on the premises because the stack of *Texas Trophy Hunters* magazines next to the toilet broadcast that message to any visitor who had the misfortune of using our downstairs half bath, which was the size of a phone booth but without the charm and intimacy.

(If you were born after 1992, I want to explain that a phone booth is something from ye olden days. It was a small glass enclosure with a phone inside that you could use to call someone if you had a quarter or a friend willing to accept a collect call.)

(The phone booth was necessary because there was no other way to make a call if you weren't at home. At the time, iPhones were just a glimmer in Steve Jobs's eye. We couldn't have imagined a world where we would have a device we could carry in our pockets that would give us access to unlimited information and lots of funny videos about cats.)

Perry knew the registering process wasn't about him, because otherwise we'd be at Home Depot or Academy instead of Scrivener's picking out delicate crystal welcome bowls and eating lunch in a tearoom that served chicken salad on a leaf of lettuce with a side of consommé. He just went along for the ride because he instinctively knew his role in this whole affair was to smile and nod at everything I selected, even when everything in him wanted to scream, "We don't even eat shrimp, so why do we need sterling shrimp forks at $75 apiece?"

The great irony of selecting expensive merchandise for your parents' friends to purchase for you in exchange for some free champagne and carved beef tenderloin is you're selecting things for the life you think you are going to live, when in reality there is no way to know what that life will really entail. Based on my registry selections, I had big dreams of a future filled with formal dinner parties requiring twelve full place settings of china and linen napkins. The reality is the last time we had people over for dinner, I served salad from a bag on paper plates and handed them some Viva paper towels to wipe their mouths. Formal dining for us means we put the dogs outside.

Perry and I were two different people coming from two totally different backgrounds. I'd spent the majority of my formative years believing there was no finer meal than a Big Mac spread out on the paper wrapper it came in. He grew up with grandparents with a staff they referred to as "the help" long after it was politically incorrect, and a mother known to make him eat Arby's roast beef sandwiches on fine china at her dining room table because "only stray dogs eat out of bags."

It's no wonder we were a little confused about what our life together would be. He wanted to break free from the formality of his childhood, while I envisioned a life reminiscent of the Ewing family, where we would walk in at the end of a long day, pour ourselves a drink from a crystal decanter, and toast to another day of swindling Cliff Barnes out of his share of the business.

The only problem with this scenario was we didn't own an oil company. Or a ranch. And neither of us really enjoys the taste of whiskey or bourbon or whatever it was Sue Ellen used to inhale straight from those crystal decanters.

(At the time of this writing it had only been a few months since the death of Larry Hagman [aka J. R. Ewing]. I'm not kidding when I say it felt like a piece of my childhood had died. A piece with very large eyebrows.)

During our engagement, I lived in a delightful little apartment complex for the bargain price of $395 a month, all utilities included. I was essentially paying a dollar per square foot. It was a tiny apartment, but did I mention the part about all utilities included? For a single girl living barely above the poverty line, it was a little piece of heaven. I could set the air-conditioning at sixty-five degrees and leave it there all day. I wrapped myself in a down comforter all year long, drank hot chocolate, and pretended it was winter while I watched with the rest of the world to see if Ross and Rachel were ever going to get together.

I quickly noticed within a few days of moving into my little apartment that I was the only resident under the age of eighty-two. I'd inadvertently stumbled onto some sort of semi-assisted-living arrangement reminiscent of *Melrose Place* for the elderly. All the apartments were situated around a common courtyard area with a pool and a landlord who constantly tended to the plants while wearing a surgical mask and toting around her oxygen tank. From time to time she'd pull the mask away from her face long enough to take a hit of her cigarette or yell at one of the residents for parking their Cadillac too close to her hedge of red-tip photinias.

Needless to say, I stood out in this land of Geritol, and they were fascinated with me. There were nights I would go out and arrive home long after the ungodly hour of ten thirty. Perry would walk me to my door, past all the clotheslines hung with large girdles, and we would see thirty-two sets of miniblinds throughout the courtyard pop open as they watched the only entertainment they considered better than *Walker, Texas Ranger*.

Lee Vernon was the neighbor I knew the best. Mainly because I had to walk past her apartment every time I went to my car, and she spent most of the day sitting in a lawn chair right out-side the door with her oxygen tank and her Chihuahua named Penny. Within two days of my move into the complex, she knew everything about me and, most important, everything about Perry. I suspect she had some sort of CIA connections, based on the amount of information she was able to gather about us in such a short amount of time.

I soon learned she was the eyes and ears of Village Oaks. She knew everything about everyone and would tell you about it whether you wanted to know or not. It became part of my after-work ritual to stop by Lee's apartment and catch up on the latest gossip, which usually included juicy information about whose Social Security check had yet to arrive in the mail or who the Bradford widow was trying to seduce. I determined the main reason she always sat outside in her lawn chair was to ensure she didn't miss anything. It was reminiscent of how the paparazzi camp out whenever there's a chance they might spot Britney walking barefoot out of a 7-Eleven or Kim Kardashian buying diapers for baby North (make it stop), except she was waiting to see if Dorothy Nowacek and Evelyn Moore were going to get into a fight over eminent clothesline domain.

Lee was the first person to find out Perry and I were engaged. He proposed to me in my apartment, and as we left for dinner, we shared the news. By the time we returned, everyone in the complex had heard about our newly engaged status and celebrated by staying up late to watch *Murder, She Wrote* while intermittently peeking through their miniblinds to see how late he'd stay at my apartment.

Since my parents lived out of town, and since I wanted to see if I could make five hundred square feet seem even more claustrophobic by packing the place with silver gift-wrapped boxes filled with breakable items, I arranged for all our wedding gifts to be delivered to my apartment. Every day when I'd return home, there was a porch full of boxes waiting for me. I'd carry them into my apartment while being careful not to trip over the punch bowl set with matching cups that I was using as a doorstop. (Incidentally, that was the last time it was used for anything.)

Lee appointed herself watchdog of all my delivered gifts. She had a clear view of my second-floor apartment from her lawn chair and kept lookout all day to make sure one of her fellow senior residents didn't try to make off with a shiny new toaster oven, because everyone knows those octogenarians love nothing more than some toast.

One day I had to work late and then I met some friends for dinner, so I didn't get home until after midnight. When I walked up the steps to my apartment, I was relieved to see I didn't have any packages to be hauled in. I fell into bed and slept until the shrill ringing of the phone woke me at 6:00 a.m.

Reaching past the boxes of new towels, I grabbed the phone and sleepily said, "Hello?"

The raspy voice on the other end said, "Honey, it's Lee. I got worried when you weren't home at your usual time last night, so I picked up all the packages that got delivered yesterday and brought them down to my place. You know these people around here won't hesitate to steal something."

Yes, I have no doubt I was living in an apartment complex that served merely as a front for an elderly crime ring specializing in pawning stolen wedding gifts to pay for their denture cream and support-hose habit.

Lee continued, "Honey, you can come down here and get these gifts whenever you want. I'll be here all day."

I had no reason to doubt the validity of her statement, so I rolled over and went back to sleep. When I finally woke up around

10:00 a.m., I threw on some clothes and went to retrieve the gifts. I walked down the stairs, marveling that she'd managed to make it up to my apartment, collect the gifts, and get them back to her place—all while toting her oxygen tank. It made me shudder to think about what a precarious journey it must have been.

Lee was stationed outside her front door as usual, but she stood when she saw me coming and led me inside to get the packages. There were about three or four things sitting in her living room. As I picked them up to carry them upstairs, she told me I'd need to come back down because there was one more gift in her refrigerator.

Her refrigerator? Did someone send me a ham? Did Perry register for a selection of Hickory Farms smoked meats when I wasn't looking? I walked back down to her place, and she brought the box out of the refrigerator. Sure enough, it was a big cardboard box with the words "Refrigerate immediately" stamped all over it. I couldn't imagine what was in there.

I thanked Lee for taking care of my gifts and then ran upstairs with the package because the curiosity was killing me. Normally I waited until Perry and I were together to open a present (or at least that's what I told him, but in my defense, he really didn't show the enthusiasm I was looking for whenever we received another crystal vase or a set of steak knives), but I couldn't wait to see what this was, not to mention there was no way the whole thing would fit inside my refrigerator.

As I delicately ripped open the box, I continued to speculate about what might be inside. Maybe some bacon? Imported caviar? The first installment in a membership to a cheese-of-the-month club? (Please God, let it be a membership to a cheese-of-the-month club.) I pulled out the tissue paper to reveal a perfectly refrigerated wooden salad bowl with matching tongs.

Apparently someone had packed and mailed their gift using whatever box they had on hand. Thanks to Lee, our new wooden bowl had remained perfectly chilled all night long.

Bless it.

I'd finally found someone as enthusiastic about our wedding gifts as I was and vowed that when the time came for Perry and me to pour the first drinks from our new crystal decanter, we would make a special toast to Lee. Unfortunately, we didn't receive a crystal decanter, so the only toast we ended up making was the kind we could make in our shiny new toaster oven.

Which really worked out, because I believe that bread covered in butter and grape jelly is actually more festive than whiskey anyway.

# CHAPTER 2

# The Art of Kissing Frogs

I FEEL LIKE I SHOULD BACK UP. Because at least two of you might be wondering how Perry and I ended up together.

But first I need you to know that I spent most of my teens and early twenties with an approach to dating that resembled playing a competitive sport. I could have won a silver medal for my flirting abilities and taken the gold for my skills in pursuing the absolutely wrong guy.

And I would have taken last place in protecting my heart. Because I spent a lot of time being in love with the idea of love and not putting nearly enough thought into whether or not the object of my affection was worth it.

It didn't help matters that Danny Zuko and Sandy Olsen from *Grease* influenced most of my thoughts on love and relationships during my formative childhood years. I mean, is there a worse example of changing who you are to make someone love you? Even if the whole thing is done to incredibly catchy songs, you have to know it probably isn't going to work out long term.

But I loved the drama of it all. The red Candie's shoes. The tight black leather pants. The fun house. And, mostly, the chance to say, "Tell me about it, Stud" while dramatically putting out a cigarette with the toe of my shoe.

And then as I grew older, more mature, I decided I wanted to be Scarlett O'Hara. Because that's healthy.

Scarlett and Rhett had passion and fireworks. They ran hot and cold. And they were completely and totally dysfunctional. She wanted him only when she realized she couldn't have him. And I did my best to follow her example for many years. I realize it's probably shocking to learn this just managed to create a lot of heartache for all involved parties.

A big part of the problem was that I had no idea who I was or what I wanted out of life. Or maybe it was that I knew those things but was too insecure to admit them.

During my sophomore year of college, I sat next to a girl who eventually became one of my dearest friends and asked her what she was majoring in. She answered, "Sports management, but all I really want to do is be a wife and a mother." I was shocked that she actually said it out loud. It's one thing to think it, but on the outside, weren't we supposed to act like we aspired to be important businesswomen who speak Japanese and wear suits? Or was that just me?

On the inside, all I really wanted to be was a wife and a mother. Which is great. There's nothing wrong with wanting to be a wife and a mother, and there's nothing wrong with wanting to be an important businesswoman who wears business suits and speaks Japanese, although you should know that Japanese is an extremely hard language to learn and you might possibly make a D in your second semester. And for the love of cherry trees, or *sakura*, as they call them in Japanese, they have three separate alphabets. Or maybe that's just what they tell naive girls from Texas to see if they'll actually believe it.

(To this day the only tangible thing I got from struggling through two semesters of Japanese is to understand that "*Domo arigato*, Mr. Roboto" translates to "Thank you very much, Mr. Roboto.)

(I'd say that was tuition money well spent.)

The problem was that I was looking for a man to complete me. It was all very Jerry Maguire-ish before *Jerry Maguire* ever came out, and we'd all be better off if we leaned more toward *Bridget Jones's Diary* and found someone to love us "just as you are." I was filled with fear and insecurity about what was waiting for me in the real world, and I thought if I could skip over that whole single-career-girl thing and get straight to the house and the minivan and the 2.5 kids, then life would be a lot better. I would be complete and whole and secure. The problem was that I wasn't seeking God in any of this, which led to a series of bad decisions, including a messy broken engagement.

Because here's the thing: I was a bit of an emotional, insecure wreck, and marriage wasn't going to change that. After sixteen years of being married, I can safely say that marriage tends to amplify whatever junk is in your life, because you have someone who may or may not point it out to you and call you on it, but you have to love them anyway because you've pledged to be bound to them until death do you part. Plus, hypothetically speaking, you may have a child who looks just like that person and yells out, "See ya later, losers!" when you drive by a line of cars stuck in traffic, which is God's way of helping you remember why you fell in love with him in the first place.

At some point, I found myself at the bottom of my pile of issues and disappointments and began to realize that only God could heal me and make me feel whole. So I let him. It was a gradual process, but I just kept letting go and then letting go some more. Ultimately, when God brought Perry into my life, it was just as a good friend.

We met through Breakaway Bible study at Texas A&M. Perry hosted a small prayer group in his apartment, and my friend Jen dragged me there one night because she knew I was at a point where I desperately needed to be surrounded by good influences. After my broken engagement a few months earlier, I was raw and hurting and broken.

When I walked in the door that evening, feeling shy and insecure, Jen introduced me to Perry. He was sitting in the corner of the living room, wearing the equivalent of Ray-Ban Aviator sunglasses, yet they weren't sunglasses because they had clear frames. As he began to explain the purpose of the meeting to me in intricate detail, I just nodded at him, trying to figure out why anyone would wear glasses that looked like sunglasses yet provided no protection from dangerous UV rays. It was a mystery that turned out to be a result of his lack of interest in going to the optometrist.

Since we'd just met, I had no idea that the detailed explanation was part of his charm. To this day, he loves nothing more than to lecture on a variety of topics. A few of his more classic offerings are "Why You Should Always Lock the Back Door," "Tools

Should Never Be Left Out on the Back Table," and my personal favorite, "The Importance of Turning the Closet Doorknob the Right Way." They never get old. And by never getting old, I mean that if I have to hear them one more time, I may pack my bags and move into a hotel for the weekend. Or a year.

Anyway, there was something about Perry that intrigued me. He was different from other guys I'd met—more sure of himself or something. And he had a heart for God that I hadn't seen in many other guys. It's shocking the things I don't remember from college, but I remember every minute of that first meeting. I remember what he said and what he prayed, and looking back, I think that was God's gift to me because he knew this man was going to be my husband and these were things I'd want to remember.

We both left Texas A&M a couple of months later as acquaintances. He moved back home to San Antonio, and I moved in with my parents in Houston while I looked for a job. And the job I eventually found landed me in San Antonio. It was a sales job helping people invest their retirement benefits in a variety of mutual funds, and I feel like now is a good time to apologize to anyone who was a victim of my lack of expertise. Nothing like a girl who failed Personal Finance 301 in college to help you plan your financial future.

After a few lonely months in San Antonio, I called my friend Gregg, who had been the leader for Breakaway. He listened to me as I cried about how miserable I was in this new city where I knew no one, and he reminded me that Perry Shankle had also ended up here.

And so, in an act of social desperation, I called Perry. We made plans to meet at a local restaurant later that week. When I told my best friend, Gulley, I was going to meet a friend, her initial response was to exclaim that I didn't have any friends in San Antonio. Then, after I filled her in on who it was, she said, "I can see it now. Mrs. Perry Shankle."

I replied, "Umm. I don't think so. He's not my type."

Prophecy has never been one of my gifts.

The truth was he intimidated me a little. He was so good and strong and just seemed like more than I deserved. God probably had a good girl all picked out for him. A girl who did things like sing in the church choir and play Putt-Putt golf.

But against all odds, we became best friends over the next several months, which was exactly what I needed. I wasn't trying to impress or be something I wasn't—I was just me. And Perry liked me for me, not because I tried to transform myself into some version of what I thought he wanted. Which is a good thing because sixteen years would be a long time to keep up that kind of charade and might also require me to get up and go hunting at 5:00 a.m. in the freezing cold.

I still had moments when I felt like maybe he was too churchy or spiritual for me, but then there came a day when all my fears were relieved. He'd driven me down to his family's ranch to spend the day, and we were in his Ford Bronco crossing a pasture, when all of a sudden a huge group of wild hogs went running across the road. And Perry loudly exclaimed about the size of the male anatomy of one of the hogs in graphic detail. I'll spare you the exact words because I think it might cause controversy, but suffice it to say it sealed my love for him in some weird, inexplicable way. He became real and a little salty—two qualities of which I'm a big fan.

And so after months of friendship and just genuinely falling in deep like and eventually love, we had the DTR talk. Otherwise known as Defining the Relationship.

I was ready because God had brought me to a place where my security and worth were found in him. Perry didn't complete me. He complemented me and made life more fun, but I didn't have that same sense of desperation I'd had for so long. (Although there were still times I could fall back into old patterns. I don't want you to get the impression I'd conquered it once and for all. Old habits die hard and all that.)

I'm not one to offer advice, because that requires, you know, wisdom on a particular subject. And I was no poster child for how to really live a great single life. But here's what I learned along the way.

Someone can look great on paper; your friends may love him; he may have the best job, a cool car, and not wear jean shorts—but that doesn't mean he's the one. (I really did have a list of qualities I wanted in a husband written out in one of my many journals and *no jean shorts* was number four on the list along with number six, *must know how to dance*. And number eight, *he cannot have a mustache*.)

(So I essentially ruled out being married to Kid Rock.)

And while all those shallow qualities I listed on paper are obviously essential to finding someone who is socially competent and well groomed, what you really need is someone you'd want next to you in battle, someone who can make you laugh even in the tough times, someone who will encourage you to be the best that you can be. Because, apparently, marriage is like being in the army.

I think it can be easy to settle for less than you deserve just because less is right in front of you and the best may still be unseen. But I guarantee there are many women in marriages who are so lonely that they long for their single days when at least they had the hope of finding someone who would understand them, love them, and care for them.

Looking back now, I can see that being single gives you the freedom to do whatever it is you want to do without having to answer to anyone else. If I could change anything, I wish I would have embraced it more instead of wishing it away. When it's all said and done, it seems like a mere blip on the radar of life, and it's hard to imagine a time when the most romantic thing in your day didn't involve someone telling you they don't mind eating leftover chili for the second night in a row. I'm not kidding. I adore a man who is willing to eat leftovers two nights in a row.

And you know what I realize now? That we're all waiting on something, no matter where we are in life. It's the human condition. Being married and having kids is wonderful, but I guarantee that every person who is reading this has some secret desire in their heart that they would like to see fulfilled. I have so many things in my life to be thankful for, but there are other things that I dream about and hope for, and honestly, I don't know if those things will ever come to pass or not.

So I try to keep my eyes on the one who knows everything in my heart and trust that he knows what's ultimately the best for me and will bring all things to pass in their time. He hasn't let me down yet, because like it says in 1 Corinthians 2:9, "No eye has seen, no ear has heard, and no mind has imagined what God has prepared for those who love him" (NLT). He knows what's best for me.

He certainly did the day he brought Perry into my life. In all my wildest dreams, I couldn't have imagined him because, honestly, he still surprises me almost daily.

# CHAPTER 3

# White Lace and Promises and Cake

I'm GOING TO GO ahead and tell you the only reason I agreed to and was able to plan a wedding in three months was because Pinterest didn't exist yet. For the love. What fresh scourge hath Pinterest wrought on our society?

(I believe Shakespeare first said that.)

(Actually, I said it. Right after I saw another pin of cupcakes made to look like melting snowmen.)

I don't know how a bride these days ever manages to wade through the myriad of hairstyle options and wedding favors and whether or not to have her bridal portrait taken in the back of an old vintage truck or in a field of sunflowers. I would have had to put my head between my knees and stay that way for the rest of my life had I known about all those things. It took me a full two weeks just to decide if I wanted the baked Brie or a fruit plate at my reception. The option of cookies iced with my new monogram would have sent me into a seizure.

I am not a woman equipped to handle a world where I have to hold a small chalkboard with our wedding date written in some sort of handcrafted calligraphy.

And all the pressure to come up with creative ways to ask your friends to be bridesmaids and then sending out save-the-date cards? You want to know how I did that back in ye olden days of 1997? I called them on the phone (probably a phone with a cord that couldn't find the nearest Starbucks if its life depended on it) and said, "Hey, make sure you put August 16 on your calendar because I'm getting married and I'd love for you to be a bridesmaid."

That was it.

No chalkboard. No balloons filled with white and silver confetti. No creative photos of my new diamond ring or Photoshopped pictures of a bubble coming out of my mouth that read, "I said yes!"

Not to mention the whole "trash the dress" phenomenon. The other day on the news I saw a feature about a girl who set her wedding dress on fire WHILE SHE WAS WEARING IT and then ran into the ocean as someone photographed the whole thing. Trust me when I say this is a terrible idea. The future just called and said thank you for not giving yourself third-degree burns in exchange for some edgy photographs.

Looking back, I feel like our big day was just a hair shy of the lack of pomp and circumstance when Nellie Oleson married Percival in *Little House on the Prairie*. In the late '90s, none of us knew it was even an option to get a portrait made in your wedding dress while sitting on a mattress in a river somewhere. It was a simpler time.

We had the church and the reception site booked within twenty-four hours. (It's easy to pick a wedding date when met with the stipulation that it can't be during hunting season. Perry has always been a romantic fool.) And then, just two days into our engagement, I was offered a new job. A great job in pharmaceutical sales. A job I couldn't turn down even though it meant I was about to spend seven weeks of my three-month engagement out of town at training meetings learning about the respiratory system and various medications and how to spend your days taking doctors to play golf.

So the next three months consisted of my flying home on various weekends to attend wedding showers and parties, check on wedding details, and then fly back to various nongarden spots all over the United States for another grueling week of training and getting up early and sitting all day in a "classroom," which was basically just a fancy term for a hotel room with tables and chairs instead of a bed and a nightstand with a lamp bolted down on it.

There came a point in this process when I was so exhausted I could barely function. Unfortunately, this came on the morning my training class was meeting with a Department of Public Safety officer for mandatory defensive driving tests.

The officer had us file into a plain, white-walled room and lined us up to check our driver's licenses. And when he walked up to me, he informed me that I wouldn't be able to complete my driving course that morning because I was clearly still drunk from the night before.

"Umm, officer? I didn't drink last night."

"Young lady, it's obvious you did. Your eyes are bloodshot, and you can barely focus. It appears you're having a hard time just standing up."

Yes. I call this particular affliction 7:00 a.m. Some would say it's embarrassing, but I just say it's an excuse to explain why I can't commit to any activity that begins before 8:00 a.m. I have an early-morning disability. It's a real thing, even if it's only in my head.

The good news is, I was able to convince him that, yes, while I wasn't fit for public consumption, I was okay to drive, and he let me take the test. The bad news is, I still had two more weeks of training left. By the time I got home for good, a week before my wedding, I had a full-blown case of bronchitis. And what bride doesn't appear even more radiant when she sounds like a six-pack-a-day smoker?

So I hauled myself into the doctor's office to get every antibiotic known to man because I didn't want Perry to think he was marrying an octogenarian named Hazel who came complete with an oxygen machine. Although I never would have fit in better at the Village Oaks apartments. I was one large girdle and a *Murder, She Wrote* episode away from finally being one of them.

By Friday night it was time for our rehearsal dinner, and thankfully I was feeling like a human being again. And there is nothing like the adrenaline that comes with knowing everyone you love is on their way into town to celebrate one of the biggest days of your life with you. I could have lifted a bus off the ground.

A few weeks earlier, I'd called my Me-Ma and Pa-Pa to see if they were going to be able to make the trip. They were both in their late eighties at the time, and I knew the four-hour journey might be too much for them. But Pa-Pa answered the phone with his usual "BIG MEL!"

We talked for a while, and he assured me that he wouldn't miss the wedding for the world. Then he asked me if I wanted to talk to Me-Ma or, as he called her, "my cook." I said I did, and as he handed the phone to her, I overheard her ask, "Who is it?"

And he replied, "Heck if I know!"

So basically he'd just spent ten minutes reassuring someone he didn't know that he wouldn't miss her wedding for love or money.

But that Friday morning my aunt and uncle called to let me know they'd packed up Me-Ma and Pa-Pa and were indeed on their way to San Antonio to see their oldest grandchild get married.

The whole day was a flurry of hugs and friends and family. It was filled with the excitement that comes only a few times in life, when you know you're on the precipice of a whole new beginning. Perry and I sat at our rehearsal dinner that night, surrounded by everyone we loved, and I know neither of us had ever felt more grateful, because not only had we found each other, but we'd also been given the gift of some of the best friends in the world who had taken the time to come celebrate with us and occasionally point out that they knew it was true love when they saw a picture of me dressed in camo and holding a gun.

Because listen, sometimes a girl has to do what a girl has to do to reel in Mr. Right Who Wears Snake Boots and Makes His Own Ammo.

The next morning dawned bright and early. I hadn't slept much at all the night before because one of my special talents is the inability to sleep before any type of life occasion. This explains why I've spent most of my birthdays, Christmas mornings, and final exams in a blank, yawning stupor with bags under my eyes.

But I had an appointment to get my hair styled at 8:30 a.m., which made me seriously question what genius thought a noon wedding was a good idea. My other talent is committing to things that seem like a great idea at the time and regretting it later. The irony is that Perry had almost called the noon wedding a deal breaker when his mother told him he and his groomsmen would have to wear morning coats and possibly gloves, and I talked him into doing it at that ungodly hour with the promise he could wear a plain black tuxedo. Can you imagine what the Dowager Countess of Grantham would have to say about that? Americans are so crass. Was this a wedding or a barbecue?

In case you don't know (Because I didn't. I had to research "morning coats." And this was in the days before Google existed. So I guess I just looked in the encyclopedia under "wedding attire." How did we live like that? It's so primitive.), a morning coat is basically a coat with tails but usually in a nice shade of gray. Think Prince William or Harry at a formal daytime affair. And yes, it's a dapper look if you are the future king of England, but if you're a good old boy from South Texas who rarely has on anything dressier than a Columbia fishing shirt, it's a little much. Especially the version that calls for a top hat. I really didn't want a groom that resembled the evil magician on *Frosty the Snowman*.

Anyway, I headed over to the beauty shop so my hairdresser could attempt to make my hair look like a picture of Paulina Porizkova that I'd torn out of one of my many *Modern Bride* magazines, because apparently I decided my wedding day was a good day for my hair to be as close to God as possible in a configuration of curls and bobby pins that defied gravity and several basic laws of science. A few of my bridesmaids met me at the salon, and then we all headed to the brides' room at the Methodist church to finish putting on our makeup and eat delicate little sandwiches filled with cucumbers, because people on church committees believe that's what brides are supposed to eat on the big day. I would have preferred a Frito pie made with chili straight from the can because I am very sophisticated. And also because I have a stomach made of iron. But I had to settle for a half a cracker with a delicate spoonful of chicken salad. It was totally satisfying.

The next few hours were a blur of navy bridesmaids dresses, complete with big bows in the back, and passing out bouquets and posing for somewhere in the neighborhood of sixty-four hundred pictures. The whole thing felt like an out-of-body experience. I'd always been the bridesmaid, not the bride. And it was surreal to be the one dressed like Italian Bride Barbie, waiting for the moment to walk down the aisle.

Finally, the wedding coordinator signaled that it was time. She ushered my bridesmaids out of the room, leaving me alone with my dad. Clearly, this was one of those moments that inspired God to invent waterproof mascara, because all of a sudden it hit me. I looked at my dad—my dad who has always set the standard for all that is good and right and true, who has always loved me unconditionally and provided for me even when it included ridiculous things like giving me the money to road trip in an RV all the way to Florida with a bunch of other college girls to watch Aggie baseball—and realized that I was leaving his roof for a new roof with my new husband.

I mean, yes, technically I hadn't lived under his roof in years. But he'd continued to be my provider and protector even though I was living two hundred miles away. And now I was really leaving, taking a new name, starting a new life.

And it took everything in me not to cry my eyes out. I knew Perry was absolutely the man for me, but there is something incredibly poignant about leaving behind the old and familiar and heading to the new. Even when the new is exciting and shiny and full of amazing possibilities and the hunter green bath towels you think you want because you don't know any better.

I hugged my dad and told him how much I loved him. I hope I thanked him for everything, but I honestly can't remember. So, Dad, if you're reading this (which I know you will be since you have to because you're my dad), thank you for everything. Including the wedding. It was amazing, and you're welcome that it was at noon and I saved you the expense of an open bar.

The music began to play in the sanctuary, and I heard the soloist start to sing "You Are Awesome in This Place," which is a song I knew I'd have sung on my wedding day when I'd heard it more than a year before during an Easter church service, because it exemplified everything I wanted my wedding day to be.

*You are awesome in this place, Mighty God.*
*You are awesome in this place, Abba Father.*
*You are worthy of all praise.*
*To you our hands we raise.*
*You are awesome in this place, Mighty God.*

After all the bad dating decisions I'd made over the years, the relationships that didn't work out, the tears I'd cried, the enormous mistake of almost marrying the wrong person, I looked at Perry standing at the end of the aisle, waiting for me, and I'd never felt more sure that God had traded my ashes for beauty. And I wanted him to be exalted in that sanctuary because he had done this—he had given me the incredible gift of a man who loved me for exactly who I was at age twenty-six. Which was significantly better than who I'd been at twenty-two but not nearly as stable as I hope I am now. (With the exception of the days when PMS takes over and I have to pop Midol pills like they're Skittles.)

When I was little, I used to watch *The Sound of Music* on TV every year like it was a religious event, because this was back in the day when we didn't have VCRs or DVDs and could only watch our favorite movies one time a year during a very special network broadcast as if we were cave people. I regret to inform you that my sister and I used to anxiously await each year's showing of *The Wizard of Oz* as well, and I would lay out an old yellow blanket on the floor of the living room and demand that she follow me around on her hands and knees so she could be Toto to my Dorothy. And occasionally bark.

It's a wonder she still speaks to me. But in my defense, she was known to bite on occasion, so it wasn't completely out of the ordinary to cast her as a dog.

But back to *The Sound of Music*. I'd watch it every year and swoon in all my little-girl swooniness over the scene where Maria walks down that long aisle to Captain von Trapp with her gorgeous train trailing behind her. I may have even wished I could have a chorus of nuns sing "How Do You Solve a Problem like Maria?" even though that would have been a little awkward since my name isn't Maria. So between that and the fact that I rose at dawn as a ten-year-old to watch Lady Diana Spencer marry Prince Charles in a cream puff of a dress, it's safe to say I'd always dreamed of a dramatic walk down a long aisle.

Which was part of the reason I loved the Methodist church we chose for our wedding. The center aisle was incredibly long, and while we are normally fans of the nondenominational, more contemporary church service, you have to know that their modern folding chair configurations with no center aisle, some fake greenery to hide the sound equipment, and an enormous set of drums behind a Plexiglass screen don't lend themselves to dramatic wedding ceremony moments.

But as I walked down that long center aisle at noon on Saturday, August 16, 1997, no walk had ever felt so long. My legs were shaking, my cheeks hurt from smiling, and my eyes were on overload as I mind-over-mattered myself not to cry and ruin my eye makeup. It's no wonder Princess Diana got Prince Charles's name wrong during their vows; I could barely remember my own name by the time I got to the front of the church.

Yet there I was. Standing before God and everyone, taking Perry's arm, and hearing my dad give my hand in marriage. The preacher began to speak, and all I could think about was how heavy my bouquet felt and that this was really happening. The next thing I knew, I was looking into Perry's eyes as I heard the words, "I now pronounce you husband and wife."

Which I believe is the wedding day equivalent to "Please fasten your seat belts. We are about to take off."

# CHAPTER 4

# The Day After

A FEW YEARS AGO I walked out on our back porch one evening to feed our dogs. When I moved the large can that holds the dog food, a small snake slithered out from under it. I ran back into the house screaming, "THERE'S A SNAKE! A SNAKE! A SNAKE ON THE PORCH!"

Perry looked up at me calmly from where he sat on the couch and asked, "What kind is it?"

Hi. Have we met?

In what realm of his imagination did he believe that I was going to see something that was clearly a reptile and stop to examine it more closely? I'm pretty sure that's exactly what I asked him before ending with, "It's as if you don't even know me."

And that pretty much sums up marriage.

I hope you've enjoyed this book.

The end.

The day after our wedding, we'd "only just begun to live . . . ," in the words of the Carpenters. And we'd also gotten a glimpse into how crazy each other's families could be as we'd planned a wedding, made toasts, and experienced one domineering family friend order us to "CUT THE CAKE RIGHT NOW" because he was ready to go home but didn't want to leave without his share of dessert since he'd bought us a ten-dollar wedding gift and had it coming. If the purchase of four napkin rings doesn't earn you a piece of chocolate cake, then I don't know what does.

We still had rice (or the more politically correct and environmentally friendly birdseed) in our hair from the day before, and our wedding rings were shiny and new with nary a scratch as we boarded a flight to the Bahamas for our honeymoon. I'd already been caught slightly off guard after the reception when we'd driven away in a darling vintage Rolls-Royce, waving good-bye to all our friends and family, and Perry asked the driver if he'd mind making a detour by our new town house because he'd forgotten to pack a bag to take to the hotel where we were staying that night.

The driver pulled up to our new home, and Perry ran inside while I waited in the car. (It seemed like the best option, considering I was still wearing a wedding gown and a veil and didn't exactly blend into the surroundings.) And then I watched my beloved new husband come running back to the car carrying one of those plastic grocery sacks tied in a knot. I'm almost embarrassed to tell you what was in the bag.

A pair of boxer shorts and a toothbrush.

We were heading to a hotel room at four o'clock in the afternoon, my husband was wearing a tuxedo, and all he thought he needed for the next twenty-four hours was a pair of boxer shorts and a toothbrush. He didn't even attempt to pretend that maybe we'd go out to dinner.

God love him.

I guess that's what happens when true love waits.

So the next morning, Perry made the walk of shame in his wrinkled rented tuxedo as we left the hotel in time to go back to the apartment and grab the suitcases we needed for our honeymoon trip before heading to the airport. But at least his teeth were brushed. And he had on a fresh pair of underwear.

We got settled into our seats, enjoying the fact that Perry's godmother had managed to get us upgraded to first class, and I pulled out the large novel I'd bought specifically for the trip. Meanwhile, Perry pulled out two Cabela's catalogs. He flipped through them while I opened my book and immediately became engrossed in the story.

(I wish I could remember what I was reading. It's not really important, but it seems like I would know.)

(This is what fifteen years and the forties do to your mind. The old memory isn't what she used to be. Along with many other things.)

(Had I known then how much would change, I would have worn my bikini on the plane. It was the last time I was ever that thin.)

After about five minutes, he put the Cabela's catalogs in the seat-back pocket in front of him, turned to me, and said, "Well, I've finished those." I put down my incredibly interesting (even though I can't remember it now) book and asked, "Did you bring anything else to read?"

And he uttered words I'll never forget: "No. I don't really like to read."

Oh, my word. I have married a stranger. Possibly an illiterate stranger.

How did I not know he didn't like to read? We'd been together for two years. It seems like that would have come up. I guess I spent all my time being dazzled by his charm and his wit and how cute he looked in his jeans and boots.

So I put down my book because I was a new bride and felt the need to provide him with some sort of in-flight entertainment. We worked on the airline magazine crossword puzzle for a little bit and made a poor attempt at sudoku, because what in the world? You could give me from now until the edge of never and I couldn't tell you how to fill in all those numbers. I know it's supposed to be good for the brain, but not if it causes your brain to explode. That seems counterproductive.

We spent our honeymoon on the Exuma islands in the Bahamas. Perry chose it specifically because it is known for its bonefishing. I agreed to it because it involved sand and the ocean. And so I spent my days lying on the beach while Perry caught fish and topless Europeans ran over to examine his latest catch. (My retinas still haven't recovered from all the freedom people felt to display what God gave them in spite of size and shape. They had body joy like I've never seen.) We ate lobster every night and drank rum punch and lived like kings. Kings who had to go back to reality in six days, but kings nonetheless.

After a few days we decided to rent snorkeling equipment so we could explore all the coral reefs that were practically right outside our hotel room. The first day, we swam out to a private plane that had crashed years before, where multitudes of rainbow-hued fish had since claimed the wreckage as home. We found huge conch shells, giant starfish, and all kinds of incredible things.

It was fun, but every time we got to the edge of the wreckage, we could see where the ocean dropped off and became that deep, dark blue. This was in the days before I had seen *Finding Nemo* 1,842 times and knew what a terrible place the drop-off really is, but even so I knew it was eerie, and just thinking about it right now makes me want to curl up in the fetal position. Eventually a barracuda made his way to where we were swimming, and because we value our limbs, we decided to call it a day.

The next day we decided to stick closer to home. There was a big bay of water that had huge rock formations on either side, creating a cove. After spending the morning lying in the sun, we decided to put on our snorkeling equipment and swim out to a big coral reef we could see in the distance. We started swimming and soon realized it was farther away than it originally looked, so we stopped to tread water and discuss whether or not we were going to keep heading out.

About that time, a small boat appeared out of nowhere and pulled up next to us. The elderly man who was driving said, "You kids probably need to head back to the shore. There's a twelve-foot hammerhead shark that's been swimming around this cove all morning."

Umm, yeah, you know those scenes in cartoons where the characters literally run on top of the water? That's about what we looked like. Between that and the fact that he referred to us as "You kids," it was like we were living in an episode of *Scooby-Doo*. We turned tail and swam like we'd never swum in our lives. And when we finally got to the edge of the water, we collapsed on the beach, panting for air. Then we looked out to wave our thanks to the man in the boat. But he was gone.

(Please insert a Duh Duh DUN sound here.)

I'm telling you, there is no way he could have gotten the boat out of that cove by the time we swam to the shore. And as we strained our eyes to catch a glimpse of him in the distance, all we saw instead was a huge, shadowy figure about twelve feet long swimming right in front of the coral reef we had been heading toward.

I don't know how many other times in my life I've been saved from certain peril by guardian angels, but I have no doubt that on that day in August of 1997, Perry and I were guided by an angel wearing an enormous fishing hat. Because everyone knows the best angels enjoy appropriate accessories. Gabriel might have been wearing a hat when he told Mary she was with child.

I'm just glad neither of us was eaten by a shark on our honeymoon because DOWNER. I realize that every year during Shark Week on the Discovery Channel some professor of sharkology will say that most of the time a shark isn't interested in eating you—it's just tasting you. Oh yeah? Tell that to the girl who used to have a left leg. Something tells me she doesn't find solace in the fact that the shark was just confirming she wasn't a wounded seal. Sharks have sharp teeth and will EAT YOU ALIVE if given the chance. I firmly believe this to be true no matter what the "experts" try to make us believe. Don't try to tell me a shark has "feelings." All it feels is HUNGER.

We made it home from our honeymoon with all limbs intact and agreed that we were ready to settle into our little town house, unpack our wedding gifts, and get ready to resume real life as grown-up married people. Even though neither of us had any idea what that looked like.

Two days after we returned from our honeymoon, Princess Diana was killed in that tragic car accident in Paris, and Perry made the unfortunate discovery that I possess a remarkable ability to sit in front of the TV for a week straight and cry for someone I don't even know. By the time the actual funeral procession was broadcast, I think he was ready to stage an intervention. Perhaps the tipping point was when I suggested maybe we could go get Harry and Wills and raise them as our own.

I just wasn't sure Prince Charles was going to be able to raise them with the warmth and tenderness that Diana would have wanted. Although it now appears he did a lovely job, for no other reason than the fact that Prince William chose the lovely Kate Middleton as his bride. I'm slightly obsessed with her, too, but that's material for an entirely different book. A book that might put me on some sort of watch list in the UK. Let's just say she has now joined a prestigious list that includes Sandra Bullock, Jennifer Aniston, and Connie Britton, which I refer to as the Celebrities Who Would Be My Best Friend if We Ever Met list.

Anyway, eventually all the media coverage on Princess Diana settled down, and I began to focus on more important matters, like getting out of my bathrobe and cooking dinner and doing laundry and not crying. Because apparently I equated marriage to time traveling back to June Cleaver's house, even though the only set of pearls I owned were fake ones I'd bought at Stein Mart and we had wood floors so I couldn't have vacuumed them even if I'd been so inclined.

I was eager to use all my new cookware and serve dinner on our new dishes set neatly on our new place mats. I'd received several cookbooks at various showers and spent the evenings poring over them, dog-earing pages for things that sounded good. I went grocery shopping and bought things like saffron and paprika. I'd never felt more like a grown-up in my whole life.

And for the most part, the cooking went really well. With the exception of the night I made bite-size quiches and tried to pass them off as a main dish. I don't know why I didn't realize how tiny they were going to be, given the size of the muffin tins I baked them in, but I knew I was in trouble the minute I pulled them out of the oven. Perry isn't the type of guy who would consider a full-size quiche consisting merely of spinach and eggs to be a real meal under the best of circumstances, much less a plate full of twelve tiny quiches that I placed in a circle around the perimeter like they were about to perform in some sort of mini-quiche rodeo.

Then there was the night my sister, Amy, was visiting and I decided to show off and make jambalaya. Which was all good and fine, until it almost killed Perry.

We were sitting around the table, enjoying our dinner and visiting, when it became clear he was choking. Pretty much only because he was giving us the international sign for choking. Apparently, a round slice of sausage had gotten caught in his throat. It was approximately thirty seconds later that my sister and I made the unfortunate discovery that neither one of us possessed an adequate working knowledge of the Heimlich maneuver.

Actually, I realized I lacked sufficient Heimlich-maneuver skills while my sister, who probably knew how to do the Heimlich since she was a teacher and trained in CPR, fled the scene because she was afraid Perry was about to throw up and she didn't want to see it.

No one will ever accuse either of us of keeping calm heads in a crisis situation. We were like Lily Tomlin and Jane Fonda in *Nine to Five*.

After Perry realized he wasn't going to be able to save himself on the back of a kitchen chair, I dialed 911. And an ambulance came. And paramedics rushed in the house. And we all had to go to the hospital so they could administer some type of medicine to relax his throat muscles.

I also may have asked if I could have a sedative for myself.

If I recall, this earned me a dirty look from my beloved husband. But he had no idea the stress I was under. It's not every day that you prepare a meal that almost kills your husband and then simultaneously discover you lack the skills to save him. Talk about NEW WIFE FAIL.

Obviously, he recovered from the experience. We discovered shortly thereafter that he had some acid-reflux issues that had caused scarring on his esophagus, which led him to choke easily. So we got that little problem taken care of, because calling 911 during family dinner is kind of a downer. Not to mention expensive.

And honestly, if I have any advice for a newlywed woman, it would be to set the cooking bar a little lower, and not just because you might accidentally kill your husband. In my enthusiasm for married life, I created an expectation that I would provide hot meals every night, and I regret it to this day. I should have been like my friend Jamie, who served her husband nothing but cereal in Styrofoam bowls. When she finally branched out and made a casserole one night, her husband wept with gratitude, whereas Perry thinks a casserole is cheating because it combines all dinner ingredients in one pan instead of being cooked separately. He likes to see all the various food groups represented on his plate like he's a registered dietitian or something.

I blame myself. I made him rotten. Learn from my mistake, young women of America. Just because your Italian grandmother cooked three hot meals a day her entire life doesn't mean we have to do the same. That's why Chinese takeout was invented.

The other discovery I made now that Perry and I were sharing a home was that he likes to change clothes throughout the day. Workout clothes, work clothes, sitting-around-the-house clothes. His life consisted of more wardrobe changes than Cher's show in Las Vegas. And that, combined with the tragic fact our little townhome only had a coin-operated laundry facility, created some logistical laundry issues.

I am of the belief that laundry is something you do once a week. Most of my clothes at the time were work-related business suits that I sent to the dry cleaner, so washing clothes once a week was more than sufficient. However, Cher informed me that he really needed his laundry done at least every three days or he'd run out of clothes. To which I replied that he had two options.

1. He could go buy more boxer shorts and socks.
2. He could do his own laundry.

For reasons that still puzzle me, he chose to do his own laundry. And he still does it to this day. If there is anything I got absolutely right in marriage from the very beginning, this would be it. In fact, Gulley's grandmother Nena was so inspired by my laundry coup that she informed Grandaddy after fifty-five years of marriage that she was no longer doing his laundry. I set her free from the bondage of the washing machine. I had no idea I would become a catalyst for laundry liberation among senior citizens.

And between you and me, I bet Kate Middleton makes William do his own laundry. Which is just one of the many reasons I know we'd be friends.

# CHAPTER 5

# Young Love and
# Old Love and a Rat

A FEW MONTHS AGO Gulley and I decided it might be fun to have a garage sale. Mainly because neither of us had ever actually had one and had no idea that by the time it was all over, our combined earnings would average out to approximately forty-five cents an hour.

But we both had a lot of junk we'd accumulated over the last ten to fifteen years (ironically, some of these things were once wedding presents), and the prospect of having a garage sale gave us incentive to do a massive clean out of our respective homes. So for several weeks I made regular trips to Gulley's house with all my unwanted items, and we began to prepare for the big sale.

The Saturday of the sale arrived bright and early. Two things I never am—bright or early. Especially at the same time. Fortunately

Perry made a run to Shipley's to get us all fresh donuts, or we may not have survived.

While we were setting our wares out on the curb and the driveway, Gulley discovered a long-forgotten engagement portrait of her and her husband, Jon. They were wearing matching khaki shorts with denim shirts and loafers in their best imitation of a 1997 Gap commercial. Best of all, they were leaned in for a kiss, and Gulley's leg was kicked up in the back the way I used to pose my Barbies when they kissed Ken.

The picture was enormous and framed in a gilded frame. Her mother had given it to her years ago because there was a time when that seemed like a good thing to hang in their little newlywed love shack. But sixteen years later that time had long passed, so we put a price tag on it for $1,000 and titled it *Young Love*.

And then we sat back to watch the reactions of our garage-sale patrons.

It was a fascinating study in human behavior. Some people clearly realized it was a joke, but then there were others (and I probably would have fallen in this category myself) who stared at it for a long time trying to figure out why this picture of two unknown people in denim shirts was worth $1,000. I could tell by their faces that they were wondering if they were passing up some incredible find just because they didn't have any sort of art education.

By the end of the day, no one had even tried to haggle with us over the price of *Young Love*. There were no takers. I can't imagine why. Did they not see the denim shirts?

But that portrait started this whole conversation between Gulley, Jon, Perry, and me about Young Love. In those days of engagement portraits and newlywed years, everything is so new. You're on your best behavior. When you have an argument, it feels like the end of the world. You can't eat or sleep until it's resolved. You might belt out Faith Hill's song "It Matters to Me" as you drive around the block crying. You think you need to turn off the TV at night so you can have long, meaningful discussions about current events. You still believe it's a good idea for your husband to go home with you every time you visit your family because you're worried about what people will think if he doesn't, even though it means he's going to be bored for three days straight and may end up going to the mall by himself in a desperate attempt to find something to do.

(This actually happened. It's the first and last time I've ever seen Perry in a mall.)

Young Love is sweet. And naive. And a little exhausting.

Then there's Old Love. Old Love is the comfortable shoe of relationships. You know each other. Each of you is a little more worn and not as pretty and new as you used to be. And yes, you are going to get irritated beyond all reason when he insists on recording *Drury Outdoors: Wildlife Obsession* when you need the space on the DVR for the new episode of *Parenthood*, but you get over it because that's just how he is and you know that. He's been that way for sixteen years. And before the advent of the DVR, he used to record over your VHS recordings of *Friends*. So technology has done nothing except provide you with a new reason to be annoyed.

And when you fight, you no longer feel the need to dramatically slam out of the house and screech out of the driveway and drive around the block like you're planning to actually go somewhere. You can still eat and believe that you could go DAYS without talking to him and be fine. Because history has proven that it will all work out eventually. That's Old Love.

At some point during the Young Love portion of our marriage, maybe a month or so into our new life together, Perry and I got into a conversation about something that has been long forgotten (obviously it was a matter of great importance), and I just couldn't let it go. We had beaten this dead horse until it was way past time to call it a lost cause. Yet I still wanted to discuss and cry and share all my feelings because that's what Young Love does. Perry (always the voice of reason) finally said, "It's late. I'm going to bed. If you want to keep crying about this, then you can follow me upstairs and we'll talk about it there, but I'm tired and I want to go to sleep."

And with that, he got up and headed up the stairs. I was stunned. Here I was in the midst of a good crying jag, and he rudely interrupted me with practical considerations such as going to sleep. The more I thought about it, the madder I got, so I picked up our poor, defenseless (and I should mention ONLY) cordless phone sitting next to me and threw it at the wall. (This was light-years before the iPhone. I'd never throw my phone now because it contains the key to my entire life.) It bounced off the wall and crashed to the floor, spewing batteries and battery covers everywhere. It was like Scarlett O'Hara had taken over my body.

I heard Perry's footsteps as he made his way back down the stairs, peeked his head around the corner, surveyed the tele-communications damage, and calmly said, "Well, that is the most white trash thing I've ever seen anyone do." And, with that, he headed back up the stairs.

That statement pretty much ended the discussion, but we learned two important things that evening. One, do not get into any kind of heated argument at ten thirty at night when you're both tired and unreasonable, and two, when you are a poor newly-wed, it's best not to throw your only cordless phone.

Oh, and three, if you're a woman who is prone to throwing

things in fits of anger, it works out really well if you've married a man skilled in Sheetrock repair.

I haven't thrown anything else since. Not because I don't want to be white trash, but because our stuff is nicer now and I'd hate to break anything. That's part of transitioning to Old Love. Not to mention that all we have now are iPhones and they tend to not do well when thrown against a hard surface, as evidenced by all the times I've accidentally dropped mine.

Plus, as a general rule, Old Love realizes that throwing things usually doesn't solve the problem. And could also result in a nasty rotator-cuff injury because, well, you're not in your twenties anymore.

While we're on the subject, Young Love typically doesn't live in a very nice home because Young Love is usually poor and just paid for a bunch of presents for bridesmaids and groomsmen. But, on the upside, you'll probably never again have a sugar bowl without a crack in it or nicer towels than you do at that moment, so enjoy those things while they last.

About a month or so after we got married, some friends of ours invited us to join them at their beach house for a weekend of fishing. This was an older couple, and by older I mean that they were probably not even in their forties at that point, but they seemed old to us because we were twenty-six. And when you're in your twenties, anyone over thirty seems ancient. It's a wonder they can even get around without walkers.

So Perry and I drove down to the coast, looking forward to a fun weekend. And it was. We ate good food and laughed and talked with friends and then woke up at an ungodly hour on Saturday morning to go fish because someone started an ugly rumor a million years ago that fish bite best in the morning.

At some point everyone decided it might be fun to leave the calm, still bay water and head out to where the waves were breaking to look for trout. I didn't really care one way or the other because YOUNG LOVE—I was just pretending I liked to spend all day out on a boat. The truth was, it was a good opportunity to work on my tan, and if I could make my new husband happy by holding a fishing pole at the same time? Bonus.

Unfortunately, prior to this point in my life, I had no idea that I tend to struggle with seasickness. (This will come up again later in the book.) (No pun intended.) But this quickly became evident as we anchored the boat in the waves and I smelled our live bait and began a desperate attempt to MIND-OVER-MATTER the fact that I was in desperate need of a yuck bucket.

Earlier in the day we'd had a discussion about newlywed life. And I commented that one of the high school girls we mentored had asked me if Perry and I just snuggled on the couch all day long telling each other how much we loved each other. Our older friends laughed at this, and we all agreed that the reality of marriage looks a lot different than you imagine as a swoony sixteen-year-old girl.

As soon as I realized I could no longer use my Jedi mind tricks to fight seasickness, I ran for the edge of the boat and began to empty my digestive system of everything I'd eaten since 1982. There I was. A fresh, new bride. Yacking right in front of my new husband. Our friend Bobby glanced my way and motioned at me with his thumb as he told Perry, "Now that's a pretty good picture of marriage right there."

Yes. His delicate bride wiping her mouth before another wave of nausea hit and she cursed the day eating a bag of Cheetos seemed like a good idea.

Perry later confessed that he was really tempted to just put me in a life jacket and let me bob in the water next to the boat because the fish were biting and he hated to leave a good spot just because I was clearly about to die. It's a good thing common sense prevailed, because otherwise this would be a short book. A short book entitled *That Time I Killed My New Husband*.

During the first six months of our marriage, Perry and I were fortunate enough to live in a townhome at a reduced rental rate in exchange for Perry's serving as the property manager. This worked out because he was a youth minister at the time and, in case no one has ever told you, no one is in youth ministry for the money.

It was a nice little place. Two stories with two bedrooms and two baths. Of course, there was a time when the two bedrooms created their own set of issues.

We'd moved my queen-size bed into the master bedroom and put the twin bunk beds from Perry's childhood room in the second bedroom, because when I call it a bedroom, I'm being generous. It was actually more like a large closet with a window. The problem arose when Perry decided my queen bed wasn't good for his back and he was just going to sleep in the other room in one of the bunk beds.

You know what isn't good for a new bride? Hearing that her husband already wants to sleep in a different room. I was sure it was a sign of bad things to come. He was already tired of me, but I wasn't going down without a fight (Young Love!), so I moved into the guest room with him and slept on the top bunk.

(Doesn't this make you wish you were married to me? Hello, neurotic and insecure.)

(Also, you know what isn't as fun at twenty-six years old as it was at ten? Climbing a ladder to get into bed at night.)

So that's how we ended up at Discount Mattress making our first major purchase together in the form of a king-size bed with firm support. It was shortly thereafter that we also realized the key to a good night's sleep was that we never share covers. Because Perry said I sleep under enough blankets to suffocate a normal person, and to that I said he was welcome to find his own solution. Which he did. In the form of the twin floral comforter I used all through college. He still sleeps with it to this day.

For those of you doing the math at home, that means he sleeps with a bed covering that's well over twenty years old. So much for that plaid Ralph Lauren number I'd so painstakingly chosen when we registered.

Anyway, we'd been sharing a room for a few months when I discovered that Perry talks in his sleep. And he doesn't just mumble. He makes loud declarations about things. There were nights he woke me up to ask if I could see the blue iguana coming out of our wall, or if I knew that there was a clown outside our window. You know, things that might send a person into an adrenaline-fueled reaction that leads to insomnia for the rest of the night.

And that's why I didn't really pay any attention to him the night he woke me up to ask if I'd just seen something small and furry run across our bedroom floor. I figured it was just another one of his sleep-talking ravings, and frankly, I was tired of getting all worked up about false iguana sightings and clowns wielding knives.

But a few mornings later, Perry woke up at the crack of dawn, which he unfortunately likes to do, and went into our kitchen to discover a family of possums huddled in the corner like the Little Match Girl, except they were possums. You didn't read that wrong. Possums. In our kitchen.

To make it worse, that's when he told me he hadn't been asleep when he saw something small and furry run across our bedroom floor a few nights earlier. Which meant there might have been possums. In our bedroom. And let's be honest, possums in the kitchen are tragic enough, but in the bedroom? That's enough to cause a full psychotic episode. I know this to be true because that's what I had.

At times like this, it comes in handy that living with Perry is akin to living with Bear Grylls. He knows how to handle odd situations that most people never encounter. So he herded the possums out into the great outdoors and repaired a small opening under our kitchen cabinets that appeared to be their portal into our home.

The possum invasion was still fresh in my mind a couple of days later. Naturally, I'd scoured the entire kitchen with bleach, but there's just a sense of discomfort that lingers when you know you've shared your food preparation space with an animal that belongs to the phylum Rodentia.

(I really don't know if possums or the more formal, opossums, fall into the rodent phylum. But if they don't, they should, with their beady little eyes and tails that I can't even think about without wanting to dry heave. I can abide many things, but a hairless tail isn't one of them.)

So I became concerned a few nights later when I heard a noise coming from the kitchen. Perry was out late playing basketball with the guys, because that was back when he was young and could do that kind of thing without tearing his meniscus or throwing out his back. I was home alone, and that meant I had to deal with the noise differently than I normally handle these types of situations. By which I mean I couldn't yell for Perry to come handle it.

I tiptoed over to the entrance of the kitchen and flipped on the lights, hoping to scare away whatever it was. And that's when it happened.

Something threw a half-eaten piece of toast at me. A half-eaten piece of burned toast. I can still see the toast when I close my eyes. I can still hear the screaming that happened inside my head. It was like *Friday the 13th* and *A Nightmare on Elm Street* all rolled into one, except with toast instead of a murderer wearing a bad sweater.

Right at that moment, Perry walked through the front door and I went into total FREAK-OUT mode about the noise and being assaulted by a piece of half-eaten toast. To which he replied, "That's weird. We don't even eat toast."

Yes. That's the weird part.

Not the fact that something THREW, nay HURLED, a piece of toast at me. And I may not know if possums belong to the phylum Rodentia, but I knew there was no way they were capable of throwing toast. For starters, they're basically blind.

So Perry set a trap that night and caught a rat. Not a mouse. Not a cousin of Stuart Little. A rat. A rat with a penchant for burned toast. Or maybe he hated the burned toast, and that's why he threw it at me. And, oh, it was an angry rat. It hissed at Perry and jumped on the side of the cage like it wanted to attack.

Needless to say, we started looking for a new place to live the very next day. Because possums are one thing, but when a rat shows up, it's time to move. Or burn the place to the ground. It's your call.

But as for me and my house, we began searching the real estate listings the next day. Because there are some things that even Young Love can't handle.

# CHAPTER 6

# The Great House Search

AT SOME POINT during my teenage years, I decided it would be a dream of mine to buy a house with my future husband that would be the home we would live in forever. The house where we'd raise our family and mark doorways with kids' heights and open presents on Christmas morning and create a whole host of magical memories.

Maybe it was because my parents divorced when I was nine, and by the time I left for college, the only places that really felt like home were my grandparents' homes. Or maybe it was because I became slightly obsessed with the movie *Father of the Bride* and wanted a hypothetical daughter to have her wedding reception in the backyard of the house where she grew up.

Of course, now that I have an actual daughter, she's repeatedly told me that ALL HER FRIENDS have gotten to move to new houses and she's the ONLY ONE who has to stay in the same old house. So in my desire to fulfill my lifelong dream, I may be inadvertently raising a child who will become a wandering gypsy.

The rat incident was the perfect opportunity to begin the hunt for the perfect house since the only other option at that point was to live in a tent outside. The only problem was that we were poor. And houses tend to cost money and require things like insurance and property taxes and down payments because GAH, being a grown-up is hard.

But the six months of living virtually rent-free had given us a chance to save some money, so I began to search the Sunday newspaper for open houses and promptly fell in love with several homes way out of our price range, because frankly, our price range was depressing. I wasn't completely sure our price range was going to be able to afford us the luxury of indoor plumbing.

And after several tearful weeks where Perry would keep having to reel me back into reality, we decided it might be best to find a Realtor to help us in our house search. We ended up with the kindest, most patient Realtor ever. He didn't even laugh when we told him our budget, even though he agreed it might be tough to find everything we were looking for at that price point.

Over the next month or so, we looked at a series of houses that were each more depressing than the last. Some of which might have been located next door to a crack house. We discovered that people like to call a large closet a "third bedroom" and that "updated kitchen" just means it was updated sometime after 1953. And every time we found something remotely promising, it already had a contract on it.

But finally the day came when our Realtor, Robert, called me and whispered furiously, "I'm listening to a deal falling through in the next cubicle on a great house. We need to get over there RIGHT NOW." He gave me the address, and I grabbed Perry and forced him into the car, yelling, "STEP ON IT! I'LL EXPLAIN ON THE WAY!" like we were the Duke brothers, and we screeched out of the parking lot of our rat's nest.

We pulled up in front of the little cottage house, and I knew in my heart it was the one. It was yellow with mint green trim and hideous landscaping, but I could see the potential. And it was in a neighborhood where I'd dreamed of living but didn't think we could ever afford.

I don't know if we'd even seen the third bedroom before I was asking Robert how you put a contract on a house. I knew we wanted it, and we'd seen enough "diamonds in the rough" with blue shag carpeting circa 1973 to know it was going to go fast. Robert advised us to offer an extra $100 in addition to the asking price because it would be a nice gesture. Hey there, Big Spender. We would like to offer you tens of thousands of dollars and this crisp $100 bill.

Apparently it worked because the owners received three offers within the hour and they chose ours, even though it wasn't the highest. They just thought we seemed like a sweet young couple and wanted us to have the house. I could cry right now thinking about it.

It was as if God had handpicked that house for us, and it became ours beyond reason and logic and financial limitations. Of course, given the fact that they had "Save the Whales" stickers on every window, they might be horrified to know that their former walls are now host to several mounts of dead animals. But Perry had on his Birkenstocks the day we looked at the house, and you can't tell me that didn't work in our favor. The only thing better would have been if I were wearing some sort of patchouli oil and a "Meat Is Murder" T-shirt.

A month later we signed all the papers and officially became adults saddled with a thirty-year mortgage. God bless America.

We moved into our new little house, overcome with gratitude that it was ours. Sure, you couldn't run the microwave unless you turned out all the lights in the house first, and the kitchen countertops that were some kind of glittered laminate pattern circa 1972 didn't match, and the washer and dryer were right next to the stove in the tiniest kitchen ever, but that was all part of its charm. We knew we could make it ours in time.

And so we spent the next several months hanging crown molding and painting walls and trying to make those glittered countertops seem a little less like something out of *Saturday Night Fever*. It was a lot of work but totally worth it, because I knew it was the house I'd been waiting for since I was seventeen years old. It was going to be our safe haven from the storms of the world. A place where we would love and laugh and fight and dream and seek God's will for our lives.

And repaint the kitchen at least thirteen different times.

# CHAPTER 7

# We Make Dave Ramsey Sad

I MADE A D IN PERSONAL FINANCE 301 in college. And I passed Business Math 201 only because I guilted my poor professor into passing me after I told him a sob story about how I needed to know my final grade before Christmas break so I could go ahead and inform my parents that I wouldn't graduate on time due to failing an essential course.

(What I neglected to tell him was that I already knew I wasn't going to graduate on time due to the aforementioned D in Personal Finance and my desire to spend one more football season at Texas A&M.)

(I'm also going to admit to you that I graduated while on scholastic probation. And honestly, I'm good with that. I've had to show my college transcript shockingly few times throughout my adult life.)

(Which is good since the university currently has my transcript on lockdown due to outstanding parking tickets from 1992.)

Based on this information, it's safe to assume that I have never known what people mean when they talk about their checkbook being balanced. And I spent most of my early twenties with the security of knowing the bank just took money out of my dad's account whenever my personal account ran out of money.

(Listen, I'm not proud. But I was in my early twenties, and nobody ever talks about how smart people in their twenties are.)

But once Perry and I got married and took on this mortgage for our cute cottage house, a new financial day dawned. We no longer had disposable income to spend on things like cute tops from Banana Republic. And Perry has always loved himself a new shirt from Banana. Or maybe that's me. Either way.

On a related note, I got my first bonus from my new job in pharmaceutical sales after Perry and I had been married about three months, and I promptly drove to Ann Taylor and blew the whole thing on this red wool suit because WE WERE RICH. Except we absolutely were not. I had no business spending that money on a suit, but I felt like I deserved it. And it was red! And the jacket was a peacoat! And it looked just like something Rachel would wear on *Friends*!

Justification is a delicate art form.

I still own that suit, by the way. Not that I will ever wear it again, because the skirt is short enough to offend Kim Kardashian, but I felt so grown up when I bought it. It was like I had arrived, with my wool suit with shoulder pads. And also like we'd have to eat ramen noodles for several weeks until we both got paid again.

Anyway, it appeared that, based on our premarital counseling, responsible married couples are supposed to sit down with their checkbook and have meetings wherein they create a budget using a pie chart. And we tried to do that, but it just made us both hungry for pie.

The truth is, we are not now, nor have we ever been, good budgeters. Perry and I both tend to have a little bit of an impulsive personality: act first, think later. This makes us fun at parties but not the people you want in charge of anything you actually care about. The difference between us is that I will later toss and turn all night worrying that we might end up living on the street, whereas Perry always believes everything is going to be just fine.

I'd always heard that the two biggest issues in marriage tend to be finances and in-laws, but it wasn't until we bought our house and really had to watch how we spent our money that I realized how true that was. And the problem was, whenever we had a little money left over to spend on something frivolous, you could guarantee we'd never agree on how to spend it.

What? We could put it in savings?

How is that fun?

Perry was happy with the entertainment center we'd inherited from his grandfather. Why on earth did we need to buy an armoire for our TV? And I didn't feel like a game feeder on the back of Perry's truck was a necessary expense. Why do you need a contraption to throw corn out on the road while you hunt? Isn't that why God gave us hands?

Gulley and her husband, who were much more financially responsible than we were, had devised a system where they each got a certain amount of "mad money" every month that they could spend on whatever they wanted. Perry and I agreed that seemed like a good idea, so we attempted to emulate the mad-money idea—with little to no success. Mainly because neither of us really agreed on what were necessary expenses versus frivolous expenses. My makeup was necessary. As were new jeans. And he maintained that hunting gear was essential to our survival since it put food on our table. Which, technically, is true. What I questioned was whether buying six flashlights from a company called Cheaper Than Dirt! constituted hunting gear.

(I told Perry I wrote this, and he said I need to quit telling people he shops at Cheaper Than Dirt! He said that's like if he told people I buy all my jewelry off QVC.)

(It's fascinating that he didn't want to get into a debate over whether or not he bought six flashlights at one time because . . . GUILTY. He just wants to clarify he bought them from Cabela's.)

(As if any of you reading this book will care.)

This seems like a good time to tell you that Gulley and her husband also went through a Dave Ramsey stage a few years ago, where she carried cash in different envelopes designated for various expenditures. It worked beautifully for about three weeks, until she had a complete mental breakdown in the aisle at Target because she couldn't figure out if favors for her son's birthday party counted as "miscellaneous" or "household expenses."

But at least they made an effort. And I'm sure Dave Ramsey knows what he's doing, but some other friends of ours also opted to try out the cash-in-envelopes system, and someone stole all their money out of the wife's purse while she was at work. I'm no financial genius, but having all your money stolen seems counterproductive to the entire concept of financial management. Although I'm sure the criminal appreciated that it was going to be easy to manage his ill-gotten gains, thanks to those handy labeled envelopes.

I just know if I had to figure out all those envelopes, I'd get into some sort of Peter-robs-Paul-to-pay-Mary scenario where I would take money out of "grocery" to buy shoes and tell myself I'd just cut back on "entertainment" to make up the difference. But then I'd forget and never make up the difference, and there would be a shortage or an overage or whatever it is the bank calls it when you don't have money where you are supposed to have money. Essentially, I'd become a one-woman Enron corporation.

But we weren't completely irresponsible. We didn't spend more than we had, and we were careful not to get into debt, because that had been a painful lesson I'd learned in my early twenties. Those credit card companies aren't playing when they say 22 percent interest, which doesn't make up for the free blanket they give you when you sign up for a Visa. And we were certainly more sensible than a couple I know who decided during their first year of marriage that they were sad they couldn't afford to go on vacation, so they sold their car, bought ski clothes, and flew to Colorado with the proceeds.

I bet their parents were so proud.

I do think I have at least a tad of financial sense, thanks to my dad. Charles Marino has never met a dollar he didn't immediately invest into some type of sensible, high-yield mutual fund. When I was a child, there were nights you could barely sleep from the sound of pennies yelling from being pinched. The man still owns a rust-colored velour jogging suit he bought in 1976. AND WEARS IT. Even though, in all fairness, he did buy me a pair of Guess overalls in 1984 that cost $80. And $80 in 1984 is the equivalent of like $400 in today's economy. Which is a lot to pay for your thirteen-year-old to look like a jaunty farmer.

My point is that finances in marriage can be a dicey proposition. It's hard for two people from two different backgrounds to reconcile how to manage a joint checking account. To this day, Perry still doesn't see how a new living room rug is something we need, and I don't believe anyone should buy Williams-Sonoma peppermint bark in bulk quantities just because it's on sale.

So, like everything in life that isn't fun, dealing with finances requires some compromise. And a little bit of understanding. And occasionally sneaking in packages from the car when Perry isn't home, and when he asks if something I have on is new, replying, "What? This? I've had it FOREVER. I can't believe you don't remember."

(I'm not advocating deception. I prefer to call it creative consumerism.)

I also tend to round things down to fifteen dollars. Any time Perry asks me how much anything costs, I just say, "Fifteen dollars." He knows this isn't the case since we aren't living in 1975, but he goes with it because it makes us both feel better. A girl I used to work with did the same thing with her husband, and I was at her house one time when a new couch got delivered. "Well, great," he groaned. "Another hundred dollars out the door."

Sure.

Because couches cost $100.

If you buy them from someone's garage.

The thing is that in all the checking accounts and retirement accounts and grown-up responsible financial things, Perry and I have made a commitment to honor God first. We try our best to remember that all things come from him and belong to him. And he has never failed to provide for us even when conventional Mr. Drysdale wisdom would say it doesn't make sense.

I'll never forget the look on my dad's face several years ago when I announced that Perry and I decided I should resign from my job and pursue writing full time. It was like we'd just declared that we believed fairies would henceforth be delivering bags of money to our doorstep, and I just knew my dad was envisioning a future where he would have to let us live on his front lawn in tents that he purchased. But Perry and I knew it was a step of faith that God was calling us to take, so we—very prayerfully and soberly and freaking-outerly—walked out on a precarious financial ledge.

It was one of the hardest years of our marriage. Perry had to have surgery, and we had bad insurance, my car got broken into, and a band of gypsies depleted our savings account. (Not really, but that sounds more fun than telling you how we had to get our roof fixed.) It wasn't fun times.

But we saw God provide what we needed time and time again. It was Proverbs 30:8 in action: he gave us neither poverty nor riches. And the upside of only getting your daily bread is it eliminates a lot of arguments about whether or not you need to get new kitchen countertops, because you don't think much about those things when you're busy buying five boxes of Hamburger Helper because they're on sale for fifty-nine cents each and you've forgotten that you think Hamburger Helper is gross.

And ultimately it's these times that can make or break a marriage. You can let it tear you down and make you bitter over other people who appear to have more, or you can band together and realize it's just money. It comes and goes, but never once has it bought anyone real, lasting happiness.

A fact that Perry and I have reminded each other of repeatedly over the years during lean times as we toast each other with a glass of wine poured from a $2 bottle right before we dig into our Hamburger Helper stroganoff.

# CHAPTER 8

# Home Improvement

OVER THE YEARS, Perry and I have attempted various home projects, because while I normally tend to be more of the "let's hire someone to do that" mentality, Perry is more of an "if you build it, they will come" guy. (Why am I referencing *Field of Dreams* in relation to home improvements? I don't know. It just seemed to fit.)

But I've always contended there is nothing that will test a marriage like a project. It doesn't matter what it is, because when you put the male mind and the female mind together in one effort, there is bound to be some disagreement on how things should be done.

One of the things we love about our house is the back house. It's basically a wooden structure, similar to a garage, located in back of our house. Hence the name: back house.

It is a building with dual identities, much like Clark Kent, that encompasses the finest features of both garage and dwelling. The garage section is just a one-car garage with a door that slides open, and when you pull in, there is another set of doors at the back of the garage that access a shed-type area. The doors are there because our house was built when the majority of people still drove horse-drawn buggies. The original owners could pull their buggy into an enclosed garage area and tie their horse in the shed. Charles Ingalls never had it so good. This should also be an indicator of the back house's condition. It has seen better days. Namely, the1920s.

The nongarage portion of the back house is the actual house part (although I use the term *house* loosely), and I suppose its original purpose was to serve as maids' quarters. But since I am now the only maid around here, we use it for other things. Plus, no one would actually want to live there—well, except maybe a few rats.

When we bought our house, Perry immediately adopted the back house. It is his domain, but sometimes, if I ask nicely, he'll let me store some stuff out there. Someday if Perry ever writes a book, he can call it *Tales from the Back House*, and I assure you it won't be about meaningful things like cute shoes or purses but will involve words like *bullet casings*, *gunpowder*, *maximum kill percentages*, and *carnage*.

A lighthearted look at a man and his great loves.

Anyway, the back house is where the magic—and the storage—happens. This place holds more fishing equipment than any one person could ever need. Roy Scheider didn't take out this much equipment when he was looking for Jaws. On the bright side, if 250 people ever show up at our house and need fishing tackle, we can provide it.

There is also a small partitioned area that used to house a

nonworking toilet, but Perry got rid of the indoor plumbing facilities to create a storage space for a few cots, some buckets, and a sleeping bag, which tells you that it is, indeed, a man's place. No self-respecting woman would get rid of the indoor plumbing.

Perry can have the back house. I'll take the front house. And at least I know I'll see him when he needs to go to the bathroom. I hope. I don't really want to think about the alternative.

One night our friends Hannah and Stewart came over for dinner. Hannah had suddenly found herself without a job due to circumstances beyond her control and had some free time on her hands. As we sat around the dinner table, we lamented the fact that it's awful to find yourself with all kinds of free time, yet no disposable income to go waste at Target.

I confessed that I'd pretty much confined myself for the last several weeks because I have no willpower when it comes to reduced Christmas merchandise, and it would only be a matter of time before I came home with mismatched manger scenes at unbelievably low prices.

We began to discuss what we could do with our free time, and she said she planned to clean out her garage. And I'm not sure what happened, but all of a sudden I heard myself exclaiming, "OH! That is a great idea! I'm going to paint our back house! It needs it so bad, plus it will be a great way to tone my arms for spring and summer!"

And thus, a terrible idea was born.

In all truthfulness, the back house had been driving me crazy. The paint is chipped and peeling, and let's be honest, you can only make fun of the RV in your neighbor's driveway for so long when you have a building on your property that is in such a state of dishabille.

We'd repainted our house when we renovated it several years ago but decided not to have the back house repainted because we had big plans to tear it down and build a great garage with an upstairs bonus room. But then we had a child, and then I quit my job, and we still haven't won the lottery—which, I'm not one to cry "discrimination," but I think might be directly related to the fact that we don't buy lottery tickets.

I saw a golden opportunity to save us thousands in home repair costs, in addition to the money we were saving from my self-imposed Target ban. I hate to brag, but I felt a little bit like I was living straight out of Proverbs 31, where it says, "She rises early to paint her back house and flees the temptation to purchase excessive Mossimo goods."

When we got home from church the following Sunday, I decided the time had come to begin my project. Perry was very supportive and found me a scraper and some type of steel brush.

"Umm, what's this? Where's the paint and the paintbrush?"

"You have to prep. You can't just paint over all the chipped paint."

"Why not?"

"It will just peel. Here, I'll show you how to scrape."

Perry then gave a brief demonstration of scraping technique while I wondered what on earth I'd just committed to. Who am I? Bob Vila? I thought this was only going to involve slapping fresh paint on some wood.

"Oh. Okay."

Then he handed me a scraper, some retro mirrored safety goggles (which not surprisingly didn't look anywhere near as cool as Tami Taylor's aviators on *Friday Night Lights*), and disappeared.

I scraped for a grand total of three minutes before I felt my forearms begin to cramp up. Which is when Perry helpfully called out, "Remember, it's a marathon, not a sprint! This whole process will probably take you a month!" and he pulled out a camera and began to take pictures as I toiled laboriously and murmured hateful things under my breath.

Marriage. For better or FOR WORSE.

But between that statement and the presence of the camera, he'd thrown down the gauntlet and, like Scarlett O'Hara, I vowed that as God is my witness, I would not be beaten, nor would it take me a month to pick cotton or paint the back house or whatever.

My progress would have been much faster if the back house weren't three-dimensional. But I decided early on that I wasn't completely committed to painting the backside because no one sees it except our neighbor who hasn't mowed his grass in three years, and his opinion means nothing to me.

As the endless painting stretched before me, the whole thing began to feel like heaven. Not so much in the "there will be no tears or sorrow" kind of way, but more in the "this will be how I spend eternity" kind of way. I had just one request. I told Perry, "If this kills me, which I have no doubt it will, please make sure I'm buried in a sleeveless dress, because I have no doubt that the silver lining in all of this is that my arms will have never looked better."

Then came a stretch of days when it was too cold to paint. At least that's what I claimed. So I took Friday off, and then Saturday, because Caroline told me, "Painting isn't for Saturdays. Saturday is a day for rest." Who knew she was Jewish?

By Sunday I knew it couldn't be avoided anymore. I had to get back in the game, or the neighbors were going to perform an intervention. It might be paranoia, but I think they'd already begun to make some calls, because while I was painting on Thursday, no fewer than three different paint companies drove by very slowly in their trucks. One of them even called out, "Do you need any help?"

I turned around excitedly in the hope that some kindly Samaritan was offering his services, but alas, it was Mr. Rodriguez of Rodriguez & Brothers Paint Company, and my intuition told me he wasn't offering anything for free. I yelled down from my ladder, "No, thank you. I've got it."

"You still have a lot of work to do!"

Thanks for pointing out the obvious. You must be related to my husband. Have a nice day.

The point is that I felt the neighbors doubted my ability to actually finish the project—doubts that weren't helped by my two-day vacation from painting—and they were starting to call in the big guns in an attempt to lead me into the temptation to pay a professional.

But I would not be moved.

Perry took Caroline down to the ranch on Sunday afternoon, so I donned my finest painting clothes and attempted to finish applying primer. I actually enjoyed myself for a while and decided that my OCD tendencies lend themselves well to painting intricate trim work and such. In fact, if not for all the paint and the manual labor, I might have made a good professional painter.

However, just as I was complimenting myself on a job well done, I looked under the eaves in time for a drop of paint to hit me right on my eyelid. I immediately panicked. Sadly, I didn't panic because I might be permanently blinded by paint, but because I was afraid it would cause my eyelashes to be green and I had a big week ahead of me and didn't really need green eyelashes.

I held my eye closed and ran in the house to rinse it with water.

After it was completely doused, I opened it just a little to survey the damage and found that, other than some green residue around my lash line, I was okay. I'd just sport the whole "smoky eye" look for a few days.

When I was a freshman in high school, I actually got paint in my eye (not from painting houses but rather from a big banner that read "Go Bruins! Bash the Wildcats!"), and I had to wear a patch over my eye for two weeks. I was a fourteen-year-old pirate wearing Keds and Guess overalls. It did wonders for my self-esteem, and it's a miracle I can even pick up a paintbrush after that tragic turn of events.

After a long day of painting, I felt good about all I had accomplished. About half the back house was primed, and I figured I could finish priming the other half by the next day. When Perry got home, I told him that it wasn't too bad, but I was getting frustrated with all the trim work on the garage door. He said, "Well don't get frustrated this early in the game. You're going to have to paint it at least two more times."

"What? Do you hate me? Why? How?"

"Because one coat isn't going to last. It needs at least two coats, maybe three."

I don't like to use profanity, so I'll just say that I wasn't pleased with this news.

But it did make me think of what Caroline had told her little friend Sadie in carpool a few days earlier about the painting project. Sadie noticed the green paint on Caroline's hands and asked if our whole family was painting the back house. Caroline said, "Well, Mama and I are painting the back house. Daddy is more like our coach."

Yes, a coach. That's one word for it. He was a coach who

needed to work on his pep-talk skills before I threw myself down in the road in front of the next paint company truck that drove by our house.

Two weeks later, I'd completely lost the will to finish. Or to live. Then Perry made the comment that since I'd let the primer sit unpainted for almost two weeks, I'd have to reprime the whole thing. And I asked him why he wanted to send us into marriage counseling over the back house.

After a little bit of research (meaning I asked enough people until someone gave me the answer I was looking for), I made the executive decision that there was no need to reprime anything. My thought was that we could just keep a can of paint nearby and touch up anything that started to peel. Which seemed like a much more cost-effective solution than the whole repriming non-sense, because there is no way we'd have been able to afford all the therapy and medication I'd need to see me through that.

Finally, Perry threatened to let Shorty (who works for Perry's landscaping company and is always looking for odd jobs where he can get paid by the hour and turn a two-hour job into a fifteen-hour job) finish the painting. But there was no way I was going to let Shorty steal my painting glory after I'd already done most of the hard work, so with fresh determination, I spent a good part of the weekend finishing the whole thing.

I learned a lot about myself along the way, and I can guarantee I'll never be the same.

Neither will my permanently green hands. Or our landscaping. Or the kitchen step stool. Or the knockoff Ugg boots I wore for most of the process.

And finally, our dog, Scout, might forever have a green stripe down his back since he stayed under my feet the entire time because he is my loyal companion. Everyone else abandoned me, which maybe didn't have as much to do with avoiding helping me as it did the fact that I was wearing maternity sweatpants, a seventeen-year-old Christmas-formal sweatshirt, and house shoes, but Scout stayed by my side the whole time.

Unfortunately, he never got the concept of wet paint and kept falling asleep right up against the house. He and I now know the wisdom contained in the immortal words of Kermit the Frog.

*It's not easy being green.*

And it's not easy doing home repairs while your husband supervises because he doesn't believe you'll ever finish the project.

In a lot of ways home improvement is like marriage. It's not glamorous. It can take a lot of hard work and effort. There are days it feels like it might be easier to burn the whole thing to the ground and start all over again. Then you remember how much you love the house or your husband and you recommit yourself to what it takes to see the whole thing through.

Even when it might involve paintbrushes and compromise and sanding and scraping all the rough edges.

And when you look back on a tough patch a few months after the worst has passed, you don't remember all the hard work and the tears. You just have the satisfaction of knowing you've made something beautiful.

# CHAPTER 9

# In Sickness and in Health

WHEN I WAS NINETEEN YEARS OLD, I made an odd discovery. I had a mole in my belly button. (Yes, my belly button. What do you call it? Your navel? Then you are much more mature than I am.) When I first noticed it, I thought maybe it was just dirt or something. And I don't mean to imply that I don't practice proper belly-button hygiene, but there was just something there that I had no recollection of ever seeing before. It was all so sudden.

But after pulling out a Q-tip and some alcohol, I determined that it was some type of growth. And so I told my mother about it, and she scheduled an appointment at the dermatologist for me because I guess that seemed like the logical choice for belly-button issues. The dermatologist checked it out and determined that it needed to be removed; however, it wasn't something he felt comfortable doing since it was in such a precarious position in my belly button. So he referred us to a plastic surgeon.

Yes. I have had plastic surgery on my belly button. I know! It's very glamorous! Quit asking me questions about it.

Truthfully, I am not alone in this. Apparently belly-button plastic surgery is a very big thing in China. But so is Hello Kitty and eating chicken feet, which means they might have question-able taste.

Anyway, it was an outpatient procedure. I went into the plastic surgeon's office, he gave me three local injections to numb the area (sweet mercy, the pain) and then cut out the mole. After he bandaged it up, I was cleared to go home and wasn't even offered any painkillers, which I took to be a sign that it wouldn't be a painful recovery. I mean, it's a belly button. That ranks lower than a gallbladder but slightly higher than a root canal.

I spent that night at my grandmother's house, and this is where I need to tell you that her house was one of those split floor plans, with the master bedroom all the way across the house from the other bedrooms. And when I woke up in excruciating pain around 2 a.m. when all the local anesthetic wore off, I couldn't even man-age to stand up straight due to all the belly button agony. I had to get on my hands and knees and crawl across the house to beg my grandmother to call the emergency doctor's line to get me some sort of pain medication. I couldn't stand up straight for the next three days. It was terrible.

I know. I am the bravest person you know.

I first relayed this cautionary tale to Perry before he went to see the dermatologist for a few suspicious spots on his skin. He looked at me in stunned silence. I just knew he was admiring my bravery in the face of such tremendous belly-button agony. He said, "Are you telling me that your belly button hurt so bad you had to drag yourself across the house?"

"Yes."

"I am so embarrassed for you right now."

Whatever. He doesn't know my life.

I'd made an appointment for Perry to go to the dermatologist because he'd been complaining about two itchy spots on the back of his neck, and I was a little concerned about the amount of hydrocortisone he was going through every month. It's not like that stuff grows on little hydrocortisone trees in our backyard.

There was no doubt in my mind that he probably had some sun damage. All you have to do is look at the color of his feet to know that God intended him to be a fair-skinned person. They are practically translucent! But he is an outdoorsman who lives in South Texas with an occupation that requires him to be outside about 98 percent of the time. Plus, we are from a generation that believed Hawaiian Tropic SPF 2 was legitimate sunscreen along with some white zinc oxide across our noses, but that was more about looking cool than being sensible.

The night before the appointment, I told him he needed to make sure the doctor did a full check of all his moles, especially one on his neck that looked a little suspicious to my untrained but highly paranoid eye. Something about it just didn't look right, and it certainly didn't help that it might have growled at me one time when I got a little too close.

The doctor looked him over and explained that the itchy patches were just spots that are sensitive to the sun. They see the sun and start to cry and complain that the sun is hurting their feelings, and then they get all dramatic and itchy. The bottom line is that they are similar to a needy friend—harmless yet mildly annoying.

However, the doctor looked at the mole on his neck and decided to send it off for a biopsy because it was giving her the evil eye. Perry came home with a little Band-Aid and a few comments about how I always send him off to get all sliced up. Which yes, yes I do.

What else was I supposed to do for entertainment? It wasn't like summer television had that much to offer. I just told him that I was trying to ensure he stays around as long as possible, because if something happened to him, I'd be stuck with a surplus of Columbia fishing shirts.

After his appointment, he just sat around the rest of the afternoon since they'd told him he should take it easy. He said he wasn't sore, but I kept telling him he needed to take some Advil in preparation for when the local anesthetic wore off. Did he need to hear the story about my belly button again? Because I am always willing to tell it.

But the truth is, I was worried about him. When you're young and brand-new and say those vows in front of your friends and family, you just throw out the "in sickness and in health" line because it's part of the ritual. Like when you tell Aunt Nancy you love the sweaters she buys you every Christmas. It's just something you say without thinking about what it might really mean or all the horrendous sweaters you're committing to for the future.

Essentially, you're taking over this person's health care. It's like you're the government but hopefully more efficient and not looking for ways to cut corners. If your spouse becomes ill, people look to you to be in charge of the whole thing. Doctor visits, medications, and lots of wine. Or maybe lots of whine. It depends on the day.

And sometimes it's just fetching Kleenex and cold medicine

while your husband suffers from a man cold. Which we all know is the very worst of all the colds. It's far superior and more serious than any type of flu a wife might contract. It requires chicken noodle soup in bed, lots of "poor baby," and Xanax. Granted, the Xanax is for the caretaker, but you get my point.

Perry's iffy mole turned out to be nothing to worry about, but during the course of our marriage we've also had more serious health scares. Although I realize it's hard to imagine anything worse than the belly-button story.

Perry has chronic back problems. It started when he was a counselor at a sports camp when we were dating but seemed to get worse after we got married. And so we finally went to see a doctor to explore surgical options. An MRI revealed that he had a bulging disc, and the doctor recommended that he get surgery to help with the pain. That sounded reasonable, and it certainly helped that at the time I was a pharmaceutical sales rep and had some sweet health insurance, which meant it would only cost us pennies. "What? No deductible? Sure, cut away!" I can't resist a bargain.

Perry's first surgery was about a year after we were married. We woke up at the crack of dawn to get him to the hospital in time. I held his hand until it was time for him to go back, and I cried as I sat in the waiting room because I was so worried about him. It's never an easy thing to watch someone you love with all your heart be wheeled back to have any sort of medical procedure. Have you not seen all those *20/20* episodes where someone dies because a doctor forgot to take out a sponge or something? Good night. It's enough to make you want to slap a Band-Aid on your appendix, pop an Advil, and call it a day.

When they finally let me go into the recovery room, I was

stunned to see Perry looking so pale and helpless. As much as I joke and as much as I tease him that he totally started falling apart the day we got married, he really doesn't do sickly. While I look at ill health as an opportunity to watch trashy television and stay in bed all day, he views it as something akin to a prison sentence.

So I fought back my tears as I stroked his hair and watched him fight nausea from the anesthesia. Ultimately, they decided he needed to stay the night, and he insisted that I go home to get some rest. So I headed home while I prayed he'd have a peaceful night's sleep and be much improved in the morning.

I headed to the hospital early the next day to pick him up. By the time we signed all the papers and listened to his post-op instructions, it was late morning. They wheeled him out to the car, and I watched the nurse help him in and shut the door. Then I pulled out of the parking lot and began to carefully navigate our way home. But that's when I saw a Chick-fil-A.

Suddenly all I could think about was a chicken biscuit. You know, the chicken breakfast biscuit you can only get before 10:30 a.m.? My desire was fueled by two factors. First, this was back before there were many Chick-fil-A restaurants located outside a mall food court. Second, I was rarely up and out early enough to make the breakfast-biscuit deadline.

So I gently asked Perry, "Do you mind if I pull through Chick-fil-A and get a chicken biscuit?"

To his credit, he didn't file for divorce on the spot. And maybe it was the pain medication, because he just looked at me and mumbled, "Okay."

I pulled through the Chick-fil-A line and ordered my biscuit, only to be informed that it was 10:37 and I'd missed the cutoff by seven minutes. SEVEN MINUTES. Dang those nurses and their post-op instructions. And since I didn't want anything else Chick-fil-A had to offer, I attempted to make a U-turn out of the drive-through line and, unfortunately, jumped a curb. With my husband who'd just had back surgery in the passenger's seat.

I am a horrible person. A horrible person who finds a chicken biscuit completely irresistible.

Did you ever read Cherry Ames books when you were younger? She was a nurse with jet-black hair and rosy red cheeks who was always on a new adventure wherever she was working—in the army or on a cruise ship or at a smallpox farm. (Not really on that last one, but it made me laugh.) I loved those books and aspired to be Cherry Ames when I grew up.

Sadly, jumping the curb in my quest for a chicken biscuit with my post-op husband in tow forever disqualified me from being Cherry Ames. There's a good chance I'm not even allowed to read the books anymore.

I finally got him home and situated on the couch with a blanket. According to Perry, the Clemson Tigers band marched through our living room to dispense his pain medication at some point that afternoon. Which is weird, because we're not even Clemson fans, not to mention that South Carolina is a pretty good haul from Texas. So I took this as an indication that maybe it was time to cut back on the meds just a tad.

Unfortunately, this wasn't the last of Perry's surgeries. Fast-forward about eight years and an additional back surgery later, and we decided to try it one more time. The difference was that this time we had a child and bad health insurance now that we were both self-employed. All of a sudden that Tylenol they wanted to charge $85 for seemed highly extravagant.

Perry had to be at the hospital by five thirty in the morning. I still haven't really figured out why you have to be at the hospital so early for surgery. Especially since the doctors don't seem to breeze through to draw those Sharpie cutting dots on your body until sometime around nine. Inconveniently, this surgery coincided with Mimi and Bops leaving on vacation and Gulley already being on vacation, so I was left without anyone to help me with Caroline until after eight in the morning. And that's how Perry ended up taking a taxi to have back surgery during our ninth year of marriage. Old Love!

That's what happens when you're on your third back surgery in four years. It's like having your fourth baby—you're lucky if anyone even shows up. And they sure aren't bringing flowers or food.

In fact, Perry told me I could just stay home and he'd take a cab back home when the surgery was over. I told him there was no way I was going to let him do that. Cab rides aren't cheap, and we have a perfectly good city bus system.

I finally arrived at the hospital around eight thirty or so and then proceeded to wander the vast medical maze for the next twenty minutes searching for Perry. Helpful hospital employees directed me to the fifth floor, and then the ninth floor, and then to the sublevel basement in the north tower. Finally I spied him lying in the pre-op room and recognized him in spite of the sweet hairnet on his head.

They wheeled him off and sent me to the surgical waiting room. I asked how long the surgery would take. They said about an hour, so I headed over to the food court because my stomach was in knots and needed the comfort that only an egg, bean, and cheese breakfast taco could bring. Oh, and a Grande latte from Starbucks.

(Do you see how I eat during these situations? There is no tragedy too big for food.)

It puzzles me that some hospitals have food courts because, while I completely understand why friends and loved ones wouldn't want to eat in the hospital cafeteria, going to grab egg rolls with a side of fried rice at Zing Tao's China Hut while Grandma is in surgery seems a little irreverent. Of course, those of us who eat tacos in glass houses shouldn't throw stones.

I finished my taco and then headed to the surgical waiting room. To say that I was the youngest person in there is the understatement of the century. Apparently the neurosurgery day ward usually caters to a much older crowd, as evidenced by the fact that *The Price Is Right* was being shown on every available television while various conversations were held about how handsome Bob Barker was when he was a young man. How old do you have to be to have any recollection of Bob Barker ever being young?

I also was able to witness a catfight between two of the elderly Blue Bird volunteers, which honestly was worth the price of our insurance deductible. It seems that Myrtle, who wasn't a day under ninety-seven, hadn't been doing the job of surgery waiting-room hostess well enough to meet the standards of Gloria, who was a spring chicken at around seventy-eight. Gloria was quick to tell Myrtle that the only way to do things was the way Gloria wanted them done.

Honestly, I didn't see much difference between the hostessing methods of Myrtle and Gloria, other than a little salesmanship. Gloria pushed the waiting-room coffee like a Juan Valdez drug lord. Anyone who came within a two-mile radius of the waiting room was offered "the best cup of coffee you'll ever have! Ever! The best coffee ever!"

Call me a skeptic, but I seriously doubted this claim. In my vast coffee experience, I have found that free coffee that has been percolating for hours isn't usually the best use of my taste buds. I did, however, take the bag of Oreo cookies that Gloria offered because I needed something to settle my stomach after that breakfast taco.

When Perry's doctor came in to let me know he was out of surgery and doing well, Gloria was quick to come and check on me. She was thrilled to tell me that her sources confirmed that my husband, "Mr. Perry the Eighth," was doing well. Now, Perry is a III, but I had no idea where the VIII was coming from. Gloria said it with a certain reverence in her tone, as well she should for a lineage that long and proud. It's like we were descendants of the English monarchy all of a sudden.

Then I got a glimpse of her clipboard and noticed that what she was seeing was Perry's name followed by III, which happened to be right next to his doctor's name, which starts with V. So what she actually was calling VIII was, in fact, IIIV. I'm not much on Roman numerals, but I feel fairly certain this is not the sign of any number that the Romans came up with back in ye olde Roman times.

Unfortunately, even after three surgeries, Perry's back still bothers him from time to time. And surgery is no longer an option unless he wants to spend the rest of his life moving like Joan Cusack does in *Sixteen Candles* and, let's be honest, it hasn't proved to be very successful in the past.

So the next time he started complaining about his back, I suggested he try acupuncture. I have two friends who rave about the effectiveness of acupuncture. Plus, it seemed like everywhere

I turned, I kept hearing about its miraculous effects. (Granted, most of this information was gathered while watching the summer Olympics in Beijing, so it could have just been NBC creating culturally relevant filler between Michael Phelps's events.)

(This is also where I learned that Chinese people eat chicken feet.)

I asked my friends for the names of their acupuncturists. The first one's name was Lupe Gonzales. For some reason, Chinese acupuncture practiced by someone named Lupe just didn't feel very authentic. Something tells me Lupe's ancestors weren't practicing ancient Chinese medicine.

When I called my other friend to find out who she went to, she told me she couldn't pronounce his name but it started with a *T*. Perfect. That was the kind of alternative medical credentials we needed.

Perry told me that if I'd call and make the appointment, he would go. I called Dr. T.'s office at one thirty the following afternoon and explained that my husband needed to come in for a treatment. Dr. T. said he could see him at two thirty and asked if we knew where he was located.

No. No, we didn't.

Dr. T. is located right under the Wendy's sign. "Look for Wendy's Hamburgers!"

Aww, honey. Good news! You can get acupuncture and then stop for a Frosty on the way home. What says *medical professional* like close proximity to Wendy's Hamburgers?

Except for maybe a medical degree purchased through an institute of learning that advertises on television.

I called Perry to let him know he needed to be by the Wendy's Hamburgers in an hour, and meanwhile Caroline and I were headed to the pool. Have fun and enjoy your nice, relaxing acupuncture.

Truth be told, I felt a little envious as I headed to the pool loaded down with various swim paraphernalia. Perry was probably lying peacefully in a candlelit room while basically getting a massage. Maybe I could come up with an ailment that required acupuncture followed by a delicious Frosty.

By the time Caroline and I traipsed in from the pool later that evening, Perry was already home sitting on the couch. I walked through the back door and asked, "How was it?"

And at that moment I saw the look in his eyes.

He looked a little like Jack Bauer after that season of *24* when he was tortured by the bad guys. Of course, technically, that was every season of *24*, but you get what I'm saying.

I looked at him and asked, "Did it hurt?"

"It was the worst pain I have ever felt in my life."

"Seriously? The worst pain? Worse than when you had that deviated septum and your nose was packed with cotton?"

"Yes. It was torture. I'm never going back."

"Wow. Kristie and Heather didn't say anything about it hurting."

"Did you ask them if it hurt?"

"Um. Well . . . no."

"Call them and ask if it was supposed to hurt. I knew we should have gone with Lupe."

I picked up the phone and called Kristie and Heather and found out that, yes, acupuncture can sometimes hurt. Especially when you're dealing with chronic pain and nerve issues. That probably would have been a good question to ask BEFORE I scheduled the appointment for Perry.

Oh, hindsight. You are funny.

Thankfully, we can laugh about it now. And truth be told, I kind of laughed a little bit about it then. Not because my husband was in pain, but because I fancy myself to be some kind of pseudo medical expert since I sold cough medicine for ten years and didn't ask what was probably the most important question.

I was much more concerned about an unpronounceable last name that seemed to scream credibility, and a Frosty.

Dr. T. told Perry that for the acupuncture to really work, he'd need to come in for about four or five sessions. I think that's how long it takes to unblock your chi.

Needless to say, Perry's chi remains blocked.

But on the plus side, I think he finally understands the level of pain I experienced after my belly-button ordeal. And there is nothing like empathy to bring a couple together.

Or to give them a reason to make fun of each other's pain tolerance.

# CHAPTER 10

# Nilla Wafers
# Aren't a Food Group

Over the course of a week not long ago, Perry and I spent almost every night rewatching *Band of Brothers*. It's so rare that we agree on what constitutes good entertainment that we are often forced to watch the same movies repeatedly if we want to watch something together. The last time we'd watched the series all the way through was the summer right after Caroline was born. I remember it clearly because I was trying to lose the rest of my baby weight, and I'd allow myself one York Peppermint Pattie every night while we watched. I would unwrap that York Peppermint Pattie, smell the foil packaging as if it were a fine wine, and then try to make it last as long as possible by eating it in about twenty small bites. I didn't find it AT ALL annoying that Perry inhaled the rest of the bag and washed it all down with a vanilla milkshake yet still managed to lose weight that summer, while I subsisted on four pieces of lettuce and the occasional cheese cube and barely managed to drop three pounds.

Of course, it feels a little strange to talk about the pain and sacrifice involved in eating only one chocolate mint treat while watching a show about World War II soldiers fighting in the harsh weather conditions with no winter clothing, limited ammunition, and very little food. But WHAT ABOUT THE LETTUCE I HAD TO EAT ALL SUMMER?

Maybe I'm part of the GREATEST GENERATION after all. Or at least the generation that has made Jenny Craig a very wealthy woman.

As we watched *Band of Brothers*, I was reminded of so many scenes I'd forgotten. Scenes that reminded me of the sacrifices those men made for our freedom. They truly are what made our country great.

But I'll tell you what else makes our country great—the fact that ESPN actually televises a hot-dog-eating contest like it's a real sporting event. Of course, in all fairness, competitive eating is totally a sport compared to, say, bowling or poker. A ninety-two-year-old grandmother can bowl or play some cards, but no way is she eating sixty-eight hot dogs in ten minutes.

Even though I'd heard about Nathan's hot-dog-eating contest, I'd never actually witnessed it until last year. Caroline spent Friday night with Mimi and Bops, so I'd spent most of my Saturday morning watching old episodes of *Beverly Hills, 90210* while Perry ran to Academy to buy some new goggles so he'd be properly outfitted for the beer scramble at the pool later that day.

(I just read back over that last sentence, and wow, being in your late thirties is exciting. It's no wonder that sometimes I confuse our life with a visit to Shangri-La.)

(Also, priorities. We got 'em.)

Anyway, I got tired of listening to Brenda whine about Dylan right about the time Perry walked in the door, so I began flipping channels and happened upon the live coverage of the hot-dog-eating contest. He sat down next to me on the couch, and we began watching what was the most grotesque eating spectacle I've seen since the last time I volunteered for lunch duty in the school cafeteria. There aren't too many other places where it's socially acceptable to dip your food in water to liquefy it before you eat it.

I was disgusted. I was horrified. I couldn't turn away.

The thing that really got me was when they showed stats under each contestant that listed other food competitions they'd won. I was compelled to read each item out loud to Perry, which I'm sure wasn't annoying at all.

"That guy ate 8.6 pounds of fried asparagus!"

"Oh my gosh, he ate eleven pounds of jambalaya in eight minutes!"

"That girl once ate forty-six crab cakes in ten minutes!"

"That guy ate ten pounds of funnel cake in six minutes!"

At that point, Perry interrupted me and said, "I could totally eat ten pounds of funnel cake in six minutes."

"In fact," he continued, "I think if eating contests were a marathon instead of a sprint, I could take all these people down."

I knew I'd married an ambitious man.

And truthfully, I think he could totally take them in any contest involving meats, various candies, or fried pastries. God has given him a gift.

When we'd been married for three months, Perry went to the

doctor because he had a cold. And obviously he needed to be under the care of a doctor because, as I believe I mentioned earlier, man colds are very serious. They trump a woman with pneumonia in both lungs any day of the week. Don't you whine about your high fever and cough—can't you see his nose is RUNNY?

Anyway, they weighed him and he discovered he'd gained thirty pounds in our first three months of marriage. Fortunately, I had not done the same, because talk about a dark place. As it turned out, I was a pretty good cook, thanks to the genes handed down from my Italian grandmother. And all those months of trying out various recipes from all the different cookbooks I'd received as wedding gifts had paid off in a big way, literally, for Perry.

I have long believed that there are certain aspects of being a woman that are inherently not fair. Like the fact that men don't get cellulite on their thighs yet wear swimsuit bottoms that come to their knees. Meanwhile, women fight cellulite from the moment puberty comes to call and are expected to wear the equivalent of their underwear every time they venture out to the neighborhood pool.

But honestly, the thing that bothers me most is how quickly most men can lose weight. After that visit to the doctor, Perry decided he needed to lose a few pounds to get a little closer to his bachelor weight. Although in all fairness, he only weighed 155 pounds the day we got married. He needed to put on a little weight because in our wedding pictures he looks a little bit like they'd let him out of hospice to attend his nuptials. Not to mention that I had no desire to wear the same size jeans as my husband. I don't require much, but I need to feel that my man can't fit in my pants.

(Insert inappropriate comment here.)

So Perry basically cut back on his Nilla Wafer intake. By which I mean he cut back to one box a day instead of two. He may have also quit eating potatoes with dinner, which wasn't much of a sacrifice because he doesn't even really enjoy a potato.

(I know. I can't really talk about it.)

(We're like two strangers sharing a home when you consider that a potato in any form is one of my love languages.)

(But seriously, how do you not care for a potato? Especially covered in butter, sour cream, and cheese? It's like a holy food trifecta.)

With his great Nilla Wafer sacrifice, Perry ended up losing about ten pounds in one week. When I exert my best weight-loss efforts, I can lose about a quarter of a pound each month. Max. And we all know that's just water weight. One good bout of PMS, and that quarter of a pound plus five of its friends are coming straight for my rear end or, worse, the dreaded inner-thigh section. I don't understand why God did this to women while men can eat their body weight in cheeseburgers and lose weight.

The following is a true story, and I'm not changing any names to protect the innocent because I am still bitter.

One Saturday night Perry and I went to a party for some friends of ours who recently got married. After we got home, Perry said he still felt hungry, so he made himself a milkshake.

At eleven thirty at night.

If I did that, my metabolism would pack its bags and leave me in the middle of the night, vowing never to return no matter how much I pleaded and begged that I would change. Then, right before we got into bed, Perry decided to weigh himself.

Who does that? I would rank weighing myself right before bedtime after a full day of meals and beverage intake right above bungee jumping at one of those carnivals they hold in a mall parking lot with workers who don't appear to have safety at the forefront of their minds.

I don't pretend to understand Perry; I just love him.

Anyway, I heard an expletive coming from the bathroom, followed by his announcement that he had put on ten pounds. I'd like to say that his pain brought me no joy, but that would be a lie. Especially because I had just spent the last twenty minutes listening to him slurp up a chocolate milkshake while I drank water with a delicious and totally satisfying bit of lemon juice squeezed into it.

That night I went to sleep with the sound of his new diet resolutions ringing in my ears.

The next morning Perry was filled with zeal that can only be found in a fresh convert to diet religion. He had seen the error of his ways and was ready to repent. He was laying his trans fats and high fructose corn syrup on the altar.

He read nutrition labels, he vowed to make Frito-Lay his arch nemesis, and he spent most of the day feeling hungry as his body adjusted to a caloric intake that was significantly less than that to which it had grown accustomed.

And because I am a supportive wife, I spent most of the day telling him why he had put on weight. It was the nightly milkshakes he'd drunk to help with his "acid reflux"; it was the powdered Hostess Donettes; it was the extra seven hundred calories a day he consumed purely in York Peppermint Patties.

I just wanted to be helpful.

Then, in a show of allegiance to his newly turned leaf, I made grilled chicken salads filled with fresh vegetables for dinner. They were a monument to healthy eating: fresh greens, sliced avocado, chopped carrots, with bright-red tomato garnish and a small side of low-fat balsamic vinaigrette dressing.

After dinner, he said he wanted to go weigh himself and see if his day of living right had made any difference. I watched him walk into the bathroom and thought to myself, *Oh, bless him. He has no idea how long it will take to see a significant difference.*

He returned to the kitchen triumphantly and announced he had already lost six pounds.

SIX POUNDS.

(Insert profanity here.)

Oh sure, you can say it was water weight or whatever, but you and I both know that the only woman in history who has ever lost six pounds in one day was Marie Antoinette. And I don't think any of us want to go that route.

Because what's the point in being six pounds thinner if no one can tell it's you?

When Perry and I were still working in youth ministry, a high school couple confided in us that they were struggling with the physical aspect of their relationship. When I told Gulley about it later (not revealing the couple's identity), she said, "Well, yeah. Of course they are. They've got those toned, tanned, high school bodies. None of us will ever look that good again."

And we agreed that it feels a little unfair that the pinnacle of your physical fitness usually coincides with a time when you're not married and don't really have the option to parade around the house naked. Maybe it would be better if we started off kind of wrinkled with cellulite and muffin tops so we could make sure we're really choosing our partner for his sparkling personality and not his physical appearance. And then the reward for staying married is that your body gets better with each ensuing year. Ten years of marriage? Have some toned thighs with muscle definition. Twenty years? Here's a set of washboard abs.

Unfortunately, that's not the way it works. Unless you spend a lot of time at the gym instead of ordering the pancake breakfast with a side of extracrispy bacon.

For most of us, our bodies will never again look as good as they did the day we walked down the aisle. Age and slowing metabolisms and bacon are not our friends. But in a weird way, that's part of the beauty of marriage. It's the journey of watching the handsome young man you married turn gray, and seeing lines form on the face that was once wrinkle free, and holding hands that don't have the tight skin of youth stretched across the bones. And the assurance of knowing you wouldn't trade those hands or that face for anyone else's.

Even someone who can't lose six pounds in one day.

# CHAPTER 11

# That Time I Almost Went on *Judge Judy*

A FEW YEARS AGO Perry began to talk about something called a Bad Boy Buggy. I wasn't sure what he meant by Bad Boy Buggy, but I assumed he wasn't talking about the car that belonged to my high school boyfriend. My assumption proved correct when he began to show me various websites depicting what appeared to be a camouflaged golf cart driving through muddy terrain with the clever tagline "They'll never hear you coming."

It's very similar to the way the Native Americans hunted the land, except they used arrows instead of a four-wheel-drive electric vehicle. Although legends say some tribes did use Bad Boy Buggies, depending on whether they had electricity in their tepees to charge the batteries.

I can't recall my exact sentiments regarding the purchase of a

Bad Boy Buggy, but I believe they might have been along the lines of "You have a hunting vehicle. It's called the truck sitting in our driveway."

The blame for this whole idea lies solely with all those hunting shows he watches on the Outdoor Channel. All of a sudden it's like it's not enough to hunt using the legs God gave you. You need a stealth vehicle to transport you and your various weaponry from location to location.

But life has a way of smiling down on Perry, and a few months later he contracted a huge landscaping job for a major golf course development. The only problem was that he needed some way to transport all their equipment and materials across the golf course without damaging the existing turf. Ironically, the answer to that solution was a brand-new Polaris Ranger XP 700, which is pretty much a Bad Boy Buggy but without the clever name.

And let me clarify that this purchase was made during the time when I was still employed by the pharmaceutical industry and we threw money around like we were the federal government. Unfortunately we didn't throw any of that money toward some granite countertops and a farmhouse sink for the kitchen before I became unemployed, but the most important thing is that we have a vehicle we can drive through a lake. And that I now make pennies a day as a professional writer and spend all day in yoga pants.

(Okay, some days I put on yoga pants. Other days I never get out of my pajamas. This is either a high or a low, depending on your philosophy of life.)

Anyway, the 2007 Polaris Ranger XP 700 served us well for the better part of two years. It fulfilled its duties as an essential part of Perry Shankle Landscaping and eventually made its way to the ranch to serve double duty as a hunting vehicle and as a means for Caroline to do her best imitation of Toonces the Driving Cat while she drove it all over God's green earth. Or brown earth, as the case may be, since we live in drought-stricken South Texas.

Then one day Perry took it to the shop to have a little minor work done. Just a few little things here and there, mainly basic maintenance.

After two days, he hadn't heard anything from them about his beloved Polaris, so he called the service department. They hung up on him. Twice. We weren't sure what was going on, but we tried to give them the benefit of the doubt because everyone knows the all-terrain vehicle service industry is a stressful business, what with all the hunting and mudding emergencies, and they could have just been very busy.

The next day Perry received a phone call from a man who introduced himself as the owner of the shop. He asked Perry a question that never really serves as a harbinger of good news: "Remember that Polaris you brought in two days ago?"

Umm, you mean the Polaris that we bought instead of granite countertops? Yes, we remember it.

Perry stated the obvious: "Yes, I remember it. Is there a problem?"

"No, there's not really a problem except that it somehow started itself up and rammed into a wall of the garage and is completely totaled."

Well of course it did. Happens all the time. If I had a nickel for every time my Volvo station wagon started all by itself and rammed into the front of our garage . . . well, I wouldn't have a nickel.

I'm not even making this up. As if I could. They tried to give us some story about the clutch coming out and blah, blah, blah, which you will never convince me isn't some sort of code for "One of our mechanics drank a case of Lone Star Light last night and thought it would be fun to see how fast they could drive your vehicle. Unfortunately, they thought the wall was just a mirage until it was too late."

We'll never know for sure what happened to our beloved Polaris Ranger XP 700, except that it wasn't good.

The next month was spent in serious negotiations with the owner as he tried every possible way to get out of having to actually replace it for us. Perry was really nice about it until the owner attempted to give him a used 2006 Polaris in bright orange. And everyone knows you're not sneaking up on anything in a bright-orange vehicle. I knew we'd reached our limit of polite when I heard Perry on the phone saying, "Well, I guess if I wanted a bright-orange 2006 Polaris, I would have bought one back in 2006. I was perfectly happy with the green one that was totaled in your garage under very mysterious circumstances."

And with those words, I began planning my wardrobe for the *Judge Judy* show, because you know if you need some smack laid down, there is no real alternative other than Judge Judy. But, alas, it never came to that.

Perry went down to the shop with a camera and a good family friend, who happens to be an attorney, to perform their own version of *CSI: All-Terrain Vehicle Repair Shop*. I think Perry even brought sunglasses so he could put them on and do his best impression of David Caruso as he said, "Or maybe [sunglasses go on] it got taken for a ride." It's amazing how that works, because all of a sudden the shop owner saw the light, and we reached an agreement.

Thus, we ended up with a brand-new Polaris Ranger XP 700. And it's not bright orange.

Too bad I can't get those mechanics to come to the house and destroy my countertops.

Oh, I'm kidding.

Kind of.

Not really.

Not at all.

# CHAPTER 12

# Root, Root, Root for the Home Team

RECENTLY A FRIEND was telling me about a mutual acquaintance of ours who's now a head football coach for a team I will not name to protect the privacy of this individual, who probably doesn't want me to write about him in my little book, considering we haven't seen each other in more than twenty years. My friend and her husband had flown out to visit him and his wife for a game, and she mentioned that this coach rode home with them afterward and turned on talk radio to listen to all the critics bashing his coaching abilities. His wife shared with them later that it is so hard to tolerate all these people talking about her husband and questioning his every move and decision.

As my friend told this story, I realized that I'd never been so grateful not to be married to a football coach. Like I told her, I get mad when one of Perry's customers calls to complain that the grass he planted doesn't look good. Some protective instinct rises up in me, and I'm all, "Do they even realize that it takes time for new grass to look good? What are they, horticulturists in their spare time?" Because I can handle it if you criticize me, but do NOT criticize someone I love.

A good marriage gives you a built-in cheerleader. You have a teammate. Someone who's on your side and will defend you and protect you. Even when it means being overly optimistic about certain issues. "Those pants look great!" or "No one will even notice your haircut!" or "That joke was funny. They just don't have a great sense of humor!"

Years ago Perry was asked to read a passage of Scripture in a friend's wedding. This wasn't anything new for him. As a former youth minister, he has actually performed entire wedding ceremonies many times, usually using ceremonial wording we've found on the Internet because we are very professional and have no idea what we're doing.

The day before the wedding, Perry was working on a big project that required a lot of heavy lifting, and he threw out his back. (I don't know why people use this expression. It's very misleading. You don't throw out anything so much as that your spine just quits working when you bend over.)

(It also makes me think of Me-Ma, who felt there was no greater conversation opener than to say, "Honey, I'm down in my back again.")

Anyway, Perry's back was no longer working properly. And we've learned over the years that it is usually at least a three-day process of lying in bed doing nothing but becoming one with a heating pad and Advil to get him back up and moving. So we called his friend Mike and explained what had happened and that it looked like we'd miss the rehearsal and the rehearsal dinner that evening but Perry would definitely be okay by Saturday evening in time for the wedding. I have no idea why we felt like we could make this guarantee when all past experience indicated otherwise.

Saturday morning dawned, and it was obvious that this back situation wasn't getting any better. We began to contemplate our options, but Perry was adamant about not letting Mike down. He'd been our worship leader with Campus Life for years and was such a dear friend. So I decided to call a friend of ours who also struggles with a bad back to see if she had any recommendations. She told me about these muscle relaxers she takes whenever her back is bothering her and assured me they were miracle workers. Like Anne Sullivan to Helen Keller.

I drove to my friend's house to pick up a couple of pills for Perry, and listen, I appreciate that you're not supposed to share prescription medication and it's against the law or whatever, but we were in desperate times. If we had to engage in some medicinal shenanigans, then so be it.

She mentioned that she usually took two at a time, so I used my pharmaceutical acumen to deduce that Perry should start by just taking one to see what happened. After about an hour, he was noticeably better and could actually sit upright for the first time in twenty-four hours. Which naturally meant that he should go ahead and take the second pill. Because I am almost like a doctor except without any training.

And here's where engaging in medical shenanigans became problematic. The second pill allowed Perry to stand upright and take a shower; however, by the time he had dried off and begun to put on his suit, we realized his fine motor skills weren't really operating at a functional level. As in, I had to get him dressed and figure out how to tie his tie, and shaving wasn't going to happen. I quickly got myself dressed and helped him out to the car before he could pass out cold on the couch.

When we arrived at the church, I had to physically keep him upright as I reminded him to put one foot in front of the other. It was like a deleted scene out of *Weekend at Bernie's*.

In hindsight, this probably would have been the time to just say, "You know what? This isn't going to work out." But that would have been entirely too logical, so we forged ahead and listened as the priest at this very formal Episcopal church explained at what point in the ceremony Perry should walk up to the lectern to read and that after he was finished he should return to his seat in the congregation.

Here's where our situation became even more problematic. The passage Perry was asked to read comes from 1 John 4:7-16. Just in case you don't have it completely memorized, I will include it here for you to read.

Dear friends, let us love one another, for love comes from God. Everyone who loves has been born of God and knows God. Whoever does not love does not know God, because God is love. This is how God showed his love among us: He sent his one and only Son into the world that we might live through him. This is love: not that we loved God, but that he loved us and sent his Son as an atoning sacrifice for our sins. Dear friends, since God so loved us, we also ought to love one another. No one has ever seen God; but if we love one another, God lives in us and his love is made complete in us.

This is how we know that we live in him and he in us: He has given us of his Spirit. And we have seen and testify that the Father has sent his Son to be the Savior of the world. If anyone acknowledges that Jesus is the Son of God, God lives in them and they in God. And so we know and rely on the love God has for us.

God is love. Whoever lives in love lives in God, and God in them.

I love John. I do. He's second only to Peter in my love for Jesus' disciples. I mean, how can you not love someone who refers to himself as "the one Jesus loved"? But let's be honest. That passage of Scripture is a little bit of a tongue twister, even for someone who isn't jacked up on illegally obtained prescription medication.

As the time came for Perry to walk up to the dais, I felt optimistic. He seemed much more coherent than he'd been earlier, and his movements appeared purposeful and not like those of a monkey after a bottle of gin. He approached the lectern with purpose and began strongly with a forceful declaration of "A reading from 1 John."

But then, as he tells it, the words in the Bible began to move around. It felt as though the Bible had come to life. And not in a good way. So he stumbled over words and lost his place, and there was a moment of silence in between phrases that probably only lasted ten seconds but felt more like five minutes from where I sat in the second row.

Mercifully, he arrived at the end of the passage, closed the Bible, and took a step back as he looked around. And then I watched in horror as he decided to stay up on the dais and took a seat in the large throne-like chair that was meant for the priest. He wouldn't have been any more conspicuous had he been a cat in a pantsuit.

When it was all over and the groom had kissed his bride, I went to collect "Bernie" with the certainty that it would probably be best if we skipped the reception portion of the evening. It seemed prudent to get Perry home as soon as possible. So we got in the car and I drove us home, while Perry asked the question I'd been dreading: "How did I do? Could you tell I was medicated?"

God forgive me.

"No. Not at all. You did great. It was just perfect." Because that's what you do for the person you've vowed to love and cherish forever. In that moment he didn't need a critic; he needed a cheerleader. And fortunately, being a cheerleader falls directly into my particular set of skills.

And then I changed the subject. "How are you feeling? Are you ready for bed?" The answer was apparently yes, because he had already fallen asleep in the passenger seat. So I helped him into bed as soon as we got home, where he remained for the next day or so until his back was legitimately better and not just numbed by enough medicine to kill a horse.

Nothing else was said about the wedding and the Scripture reading for several weeks. We didn't really know most of the other people who had been in attendance, which I felt was God's favor on us. But then the newlyweds returned from their honeymoon, and we asked them over for dinner one evening.

As we sat and talked over the delicious pizza I'd slaved over in the form of calling to get it delivered, our discussion turned to the wedding ceremony. Perry and I confessed to them how bad his back had really been and that we thought he wasn't going to make it, but we didn't want to leave them in a bind at the last minute.

And that's when the new bride and her husband began to laugh until they cried. We weren't sure what was so funny until she explained that they had just been at her parents' house earlier watching the wedding video for the first time, and her mother asked as she watched Perry read and sit down in the priest's chair, "What exactly was wrong with that young man?"

That's when Perry realized I'd been a cheerleader instead of a critic. But as I explained to him later, there was really no need to hit him with the cold, hard truth in his moment of weakness. Sometimes in marriage you just need to be on your partner's side, to be his shelter from the storms of the world. To defend him and encourage him, even when he butchers passages of Scripture at a friend's wedding.

As we navigate our way through this life, there are so many people who are ready to take shots at us and hit us in our blind spots. Your spouse should fall into the category of people you can trust to have your back and say, "Oh, it wasn't that bad." Because enough voices will tell you, "YES, it was that bad," and sometimes we all just need a soft place to land.

Even if it involves stealing a chair from an Episcopal priest.

# CHAPTER 13

# The Couple That Shops Together Has My Sympathies

I LOVE TO SHOP. No, don't argue with me. I do. I shop like some people breathe. It's just who I am. And I don't even have to buy (sometimes). I just like to look. I like to see the outfits in window displays and walk through Anthropologie and try to figure out why designers hate women enough to bring back floral-printed skinny jeans. Because let's be honest: if they don't look good on the mannequin, then they aren't going to work on a woman who actually has more to her hips than plastic makeshift bones.

However, I was a big fan of the patterned skinny jeans back in 1985. I had some floral Guess jeans that would make you cry with jealousy and longing. Or at least they would have back in 1985. Those jeans, paired with some jelly shoes, a new polo, and a ribbon belt were a lethal combination as I walked the halls of George

C. Marshall Middle School with the bilevel haircut favored by softball players everywhere.

But that was back when I had thighs the size of a thirteen-year-old girl because, well, I was a thirteen-year-old girl. Not to mention, my hair was enormous, and that helped tremendously in creating some sort of distraction from all the flowers across my rear end.

Anyway, when we got married, I was under no illusions that Perry would share my love of shopping. This is a man whose wardrobe consists of three plaid shirts, six Columbia fishing shirts, jeans, and khaki work pants. He also has a large, sombrero-like hat that he wears in the sun since he's a landscaper and spends a good part of his day outside. To quote the J. Peterman catalog, "It combines the spirit of Old Mexico with a little big-city panache." Or to quote Caroline, "Daddy looks like the man from *Curious George.*"

When we got married, my clothes took up our entire master-bedroom closet and the coat closet downstairs in our townhome. Perry's clothes took up less than half of the tiny guest-room closet. This is where I also have to tell you that he hangs all his clothes on wire hangers. I just can't even.

For a while I lived under the illusion that I was going to turn him into my very own Ken doll and create a spectacular mix-and-match wardrobe for him. Think Garanimals meets George Clooney.

But there is only so much rejection a girl can take. Only so many times you can hear, "Why do you want me to wear clown shoes?" when you bring home a pair of trendy black loafers or watch somebody gag like a cat hacking up a fur ball when they try on a beautiful green sweater you found on sale at J.Crew because they think the neck is too tight.

Guys don't understand that sometimes fashion isn't comfortable. Do they think we really want to wear the belt over the sweater and a pair of Spanx leggings that don't allow us to breathe properly until we take them off at the end of the day? No. Of course we don't. But it looks good. Like Billy Crystal as Fernando Lamas used to say, "It is better to look good than to feel good."

No woman puts on a pair of four-inch heels and thinks, *These feel heavenly. I could walk for miles.* We put them on and immediately plan out how many times we can sit down during the day and know that by the evening we will want to cut off our feet with a dull butter knife because that would be less painful.

But the majority of men dress for comfort. Although I guess the invention of the pajama jean indicates this isn't a purely male phenomenon. However, I believe few things indicate how far we've fallen as a society more than pajama jeans. Is it not casual enough to wear jeans? We have to turn them into something that feels like pajamas? The same goes for the Snuggie. For goodness' sake, just wrap yourself in a blanket. Don't try to turn it into some type of apparel you can wear around. Coco Chanel is rolling in her grave.

My grandmother wouldn't leave her house without a full face of makeup even if she was on her deathbed, and now we wear pajama pants to the grocery store. Dear America, do better.

I can't remember exactly when I gave up on my Ken doll fantasies for Perry's wardrobe. Maybe when I realized Ken might not be a straight man. Whereas Perry hasn't owned a hairbrush since he got rid of his mullet in 1989. Given this information, why did I think he would ever agree to wear a sweater vest?

Oh, I kid. I'd never want a man who wears a sweater vest.

(There was a time in college when Gulley and I attended a Christmas formal and ended up in a debate over who had the worst date. I won because my date wore a Christmas-themed sweater vest, and that is the nicest thing I can say about him.)

But every now and then, shopping with Perry is unavoidable. This usually occurs when Gap quits making the style of jeans he's been wearing for the last six years and I insist he has to go to the store with me to find some new ones. Because ain't nobody got time to bring home sixty-two pairs of jeans for her husband to try on.

This forced shopping adventure actually happened recently when Perry mentioned he was in the market for about three new pairs of jeans because he needed something nice to wear to church and out to dinner now that the weather was allegedly cooling off. Let's have a moment of silence for the fact I'm married to a man that puts denim in the category of formal wear. My friends at *Downton Abbey* would be outraged.

I knew Gap had made some changes when the shirt I bought Perry for his birthday was way too small, thanks to clothing manufacturers' decision that men need to wear shirts with an "athletic cut." And yes, perhaps athletes should wear "athletic cut" shirts if they want to, but forty-year-old dads with bad backs and a penchant for Nilla Wafers should not be expected to live up to that standard.

(In all fairness, I certainly wouldn't want to have to wear something labeled as "athletic cut." It's too much pressure. How about an "I like to watch television cut" or an "I ate mashed potatoes with gravy for dinner last night" cut? Let's try to live in the real world.)

Anyway, the men's denim section at Gap rivals the women's

section. There are boot cut jeans and straight jeans and authentic fit and easy fit and loose fit and skinny fit. And please, just say no to some men's skinny fit jeans. That is forty-seven kinds of wrong. Unless you're the worship leader of a really trendy church and wear a scarf even when it's ninety degrees outside and say "Dude" without irony.

When I told Perry he was going to have to actually walk into a store with me and try on jeans because neither of us would survive the process of my bringing home every single type of jeans in whatever various sizes he might need, he wasn't thrilled. So we waited for a rainy day when there was nothing better to do than be stuck in a "boring store" (his words), and we went out to eat breakfast first because we figured a good meal might help our nerves. (My nerves.) Then we stopped by Gap on our way home.

Y'all. Perry didn't even know where Gap was.

If something ever happens to me, I'm going to need someone to step in and do a fashion intervention for my family.

(I'm currently taking applications. People who own pajama jeans need not apply.)

We walked in, and I showed him the jeans section. He began to read the different jeans descriptions out loud: "SITS LOW ON WAIST. SLIM THROUGH LEG. BOOT CUT OPENING." And then he'd move to the next one: "SITS LOW ON WAIST. RELAXED THROUGH LEG. STRAIGHT LEG OPENING." After Rain Man read all the descriptions, he grabbed three different types of jeans in only one size and headed to the dressing room while I followed him.

And then I waited outside by the three-way mirrors like I was Kevin Arnold's mother in an episode of *The Wonder Years*. "Plenty of room in Kevin Arnold's crotch area."

Perry came out first in the Easy Fit, and I was immediately alarmed by the size of the back pockets. I can only assume that the *Easy* in Easy Fit means that it's easy to fit a bunch of stuff in your back pockets, because they were like clown pants. Which means they would have looked great with those black loafers I'd brought home a few years before. Maybe add a big red nose and a rainbow Afro to complete the look.

Next up were the Straight Fit. They were much better. And last he tried on the Boot Cut, which were my personal favorite but caused him to do some sort of move to show me how uncomfortable they could potentially be. I had no idea he was planning to perform gymnastics in his new jeans. But apparently he spends his time in jeans doing a lot of squat moves and leg lifts. He can kick and stretch just like Sally O'Malley.

And then, because I am me, I suggested he try on some more. He said he was finished, and I silently vowed that our days of shopping together were over. Just because we vowed to love each other for better or for worse does not mean we have to love each other in a shopping situation.

Especially when he saw the price tag and couldn't get over jeans that cost $54. But that's probably because he thinks all my jeans only cost $15.

(See chapter 7 on budgeting.)

So we left Gap and drove home to order them online because online orders were 25 percent off, plus I had a coupon for an additional $20 discount that I'd left in my desk drawer because I really wanted to use it to buy something for myself and not jeans for someone who doesn't even get excited about new clothing and acts like he's doing these jeans a favor by allowing them into his closet.

(Don't judge me about the coupon. I'm just being honest. It

was going to go toward the purchase of a sweater that was in need of a good, loving home because I am a humanitarian.)

About an hour after we got home from Gap, Perry grabbed his keys and said he was going to Whole Earth to buy some new socks. And, RUDE, he didn't even ask me to go with him.

Personal shoppers get no respect.

Which is why I've decided to retire. Until the next time he needs new jeans.

# CHAPTER 14

# And Baby Makes Three

LIKE A LOT OF YOU, I grew up in the age of the talk show. Phil Donahue, Oprah, Maury Povich, Sally Jesse Raphael and her red glasses. People airing all manner of personal business and throwing skeletons out of the closet with no shame.

And there were always couples with marital problems on those shows who shared that they decided to have a baby because "we thought it would bring us closer together." Or teenage girls who got pregnant in an attempt to keep their boyfriends. There were also people who were there for free paternity tests, but that's an entirely different subject.

The point is that even before I had a child of my own, I thought this was flawed logic. How could bringing in a helpless little person make two people grow closer if that's all they had going for them?

It seemed like the equivalent of declaring you'd like your house to be cleaner so you've decided to adopt a family of monkeys.

I mean, sure, I guess there are times when people initially bond over sharing a life-shaking event. Look at Jack and Rose in *Titanic*. They found true love in forty-eight hours on a sinking ship, but in the end she couldn't even make room for him on that piece of broken door. (Really, Rose? You couldn't scoot over about six inches for the LOVE OF YOUR LIFE? His heart could have totally gone on if you hadn't been such a door hog.) You have to think that long-term, Rose might have whined that Jack couldn't provide her with the luxury she'd become accustomed to, or complained that she was tired of him being an artist, and the whole thing about being from different worlds wouldn't have been nearly as romantic. Or maybe I'm just too much of a skeptic.

I really don't mean to compare having a baby with being trapped on a sinking ship. They are totally different experiences, unless you count the fact that both can make you feel completely helpless and at the mercy of something bigger than you, and possibly like you might die.

Perry and I had been married for five years before we decided to have a baby. (You can read the whole entire story in my first book, *Sparkly Green Earrings*, available in bookstores or on a garage sale table near you right now. Probably at a very discounted rate.) We were in our early thirties, and it seemed like it was time to start a family. At least that's what our parents kept telling us.

Apparently we are a fertile people because I was pregnant the very next month. And then I had a miscarriage. Perry and I were both heartbroken, but I think these things affect women differently than men. Because while we both experienced a loss, it was something that happened inside my body. Between the hormones and the sadness, something shifted in me. Depression settled in, and I spent a lot of time just wondering how soon I could go back to bed. I was a far cry from the generally happy person Perry was used to.

I had fallen and couldn't get up. If only I'd had one of those helpful pagers like they advertise on TV.

Truthfully, I look back now and realize that whole experience marked our marriage in a permanent, lasting way. I can almost draw a line between "before miscarriage" versus "after miscarriage." We'd had arguments and financial struggles and other problems in the first five years of our marriage because, well, that's marriage. But this was the first really hard, heartbreaking thing we'd experienced together. This was the first thing we couldn't just decide to buck up and be positive about.

(Why did I just use the term *buck up*? Have I watched too many *Happy Days* reruns recently?)

The morning of my scheduled D & C, Perry drove me to the hospital and was right there holding my hand before I went in and the moment I woke up after it was over. And then, because he knows my love language, he drove me through Shipley's to get a chocolate donut on the way home. I was still slightly altered and/or high from the anesthesia, but I kept reaching for his hand and saying, "I JUST LOVE YOU SO MUCH. I REALLY LOVE YOU." Because apparently medication makes me indifferent to pitch and decibel level. But I was speaking the absolute truth. I'd never loved him more because up to that point in our marriage, I don't know that I'd ever been so aware of how much he loved me.

It was the moment I realized he didn't just love me when I was fun or pretty or cooking spaghetti and meatballs for dinner. (I make unbelievable spaghetti and meatballs. It would make you fall in love with me too.) He loved me when I was hurting and depressed and crying tears that didn't seem to end and wearing the same pajamas four days in a row. This sounds so weird to say since we'd been married for five years at that point, but it was the first time I realized he really was going to stick with me for better or for worse. We were in this thing even when it got really ugly and maybe smelled a little bad. And by "it," I mean me.

We walked through a difficult six months and came out the other side stronger and better. It was like we'd transitioned to a real, grown-up version of marriage. And so when I got pregnant again, we believed we were more ready than ever to take on the monumental task of raising a human.

Yes. Like you can ever be prepared for that type of responsibility or sacrifice.

At one point about halfway through my pregnancy with our daughter, Caroline, Perry was in Colorado chaperoning about sixty high school students on a ski trip. Normally I would have been on the trip with him, but I had a host of issues with riding a bus for seventeen hours with high school kids before I ever got pregnant, so there wasn't really even a remote possibility that I was going to attempt that kind of torture while carrying a child. He'd arranged to have a few other female chaperones on the trip, but they'd all had to cancel at the last minute.

Perry, bless him, ended up being the chaperone and small group leader for ten fourteen-year-old girls during that trip. He'd call me every night after he got back to his hotel room and report that they'd put gel in his hair or that they'd used something called a "straight iron" on him. On the last night of the trip he called to tell me that someone had a pair of scissors, and he wasn't sure what happened, but the girls all started cutting one another's hair and the next thing he knew, three of them were crying in the bathroom while the other girls gathered outside the door and tried to console them with loving statements like "It will grow back" or "It doesn't look that uneven from the left side."

In short, he was slightly traumatized by the whole experience.

He arrived home from the trip on Wednesday afternoon, and I was scheduled to have an ultrasound the following Friday. It was the big ultrasound. The ultrasound that can tell you if you're having a boy or a girl. And if you think I was going to wait to find out that piece of information, then you don't know me at all.

Of course, it wasn't like I really needed the ultrasound to tell me I was having a girl, because I'd known that for a long time, thanks to the science of peeing on some Drano crystals and seeing them turn a lovely shade of seafoam green. Not to mention that I felt like I was getting some divine inspiration through Neil Diamond every time I heard "Sweet Caroline" on the radio.

On the way to the doctor's office that Friday morning, Perry looked at me and said, "I know we're having a girl." I thought maybe Neil Diamond had been speaking to him, too, because Neil just has a way (to move me, Cherry), but he said that he knew when he was on that ski trip surrounded by all the chaos and squeals of those girls that God was preparing him for life with a daughter. And as much as he didn't understand all the drama and the high-pitched voices and the nail polish and why they thought it was a good idea to cut each other's hair, he knew that a baby girl was exactly what he wanted.

And, sure enough, there was a girl on the way. When she made her arrival on August 3, 2003, our lives were forever changed—and so much for the better. But please note I said for the better, not the easier. Bringing a third person into a marriage can be a challenge even under the best of circumstances.

Especially when you feel like your husband still gets to hunt or fish whenever he wants and you're home with a toddler who screams loudly just because she likes to hear the sound of her own voice or drops a sippy cup on the floor forty-eight times because gravity is a new and exciting concept.

I remember Gulley telling me she'd never disliked her husband more than when their son was two weeks old and she was up at three in the morning changing poopy crib sheets for the fourth time that night. Then, to make matters worse, she heard a loud chomping, cracking sound and realized the dog was eating one of the wheels off the bassinet they'd borrowed from a friend, which was when she sank to the ground in tears and utter defeat. All while her spouse slept peacefully in the next room.

In his defense, he had to go to work the next day and her new job was to stay home with the baby, but that's just it. As a new mom, your life changes overnight. Your priorities change, you forget to brush your teeth, you aren't sure how you're ever going to balance all your new responsibilities, and it's overwhelming. Not to mention that your body that used to be almost purely recreational has become much like a dairy cow but not as delicate and petite.

It's a change. And life isn't just you and your husband sleeping in on Saturday mornings but instead becomes ROCK, PAPER, SCISSORS to see who gets to sleep late or who has to get up with the baby in the middle of the night or who has to change the sixth diaper that would make even a person without olfactory senses gag.

And you can't help but wonder what you used to do with all your spare time. What was life like before you had to hire a baby-sitter or sweet-talk the grandparents if you wanted to go out to dinner or to a movie together? It's a distant memory.

But Perry and I, like most couples before us, adjusted to our new normal. We made schedules and took shifts and learned to share the responsibilities that came with our new role as Mama and Daddy. And, in what is either a high or a low, we even began referring to each other occasionally as "Mama" and "Daddy."

Ultimately, Caroline has brought us closer together and made our marriage stronger because we share this remarkable little person. There are no two people in the world who love her and want the best for her like we do, and we're united in that. And sometimes when Perry is getting on my last nerve, I'll see him helping Caroline with her homework or cuddled up with her on the couch, and I'll fall in love with him all over again because I'm reminded what a good daddy he is and how he loves our girl.

I think having a child is like various tests a couple will face throughout a lifetime together. You either let the struggles and challenges draw you closer in or create resentment. The key is having a good foundation of friendship and respect and love.

And a whole lot of prayer for God to cover everything with his grace.

And maybe remembering to make room for the love of your life on the floating door when it feels like the ship is going down.

# CHAPTER 15

# I Would Do Anything for Love, but I Won't Shoot That

You know how you see those older couples who play golf together? Usually on a commercial for either adult diapers or Viagra? Perry and I will never be one of those couples. And hopefully not just because we don't play golf.

When we were dating, lo, those many years ago, I enthusiastically went to the ranch with Perry. I thought it was kind of cozy and romantic to sit in a deer blind with him and watch the sun come up as we leaned in close to each other and Perry whispered sweet sentiments in my ear, such as, "See that buck? He's too young to shoot this year."

But after about a year of dating, some of the novelty began to wear off. I do not enjoy any activity that begins at five thirty in the morning, even if it involves bacon and eggs. And hunting does not. Plus, Perry began to treat me more like a real hunting partner as my skill level grew, so instead of whispering to each other, I was told to "be quiet!" and "quit moving so much!"

Eventually I completely gave up on being a morning hunter and opted for the evening hunt instead. It was also around this time that Perry decided I was accomplished enough to hunt on my own. So he'd put me in a deer blind by myself and then drive off to his own tripod somewhere, where he could sit and commune quietly with nature instead of his girlfriend, who was apparently too loud and too fidgety. Old Love came early to the hunting scene.

This is the point when I began to pack my little camouflage hunting backpack with various *InStyle* and *Glamour* magazines, because what else was I going to do while I sat there for three hours by myself? Look at a bunch of deer milling around?

And I began to observe an interesting phenomenon. Perry always made sure he washed all our hunting clothes in scent-free laundry detergent. We had to skip the deodorant and spray ourselves down with something that can only be described as the scent of dirt. He surrounded the area with doe urine to mask any remaining scent because, according to hunters everywhere, deer have an incredibly sharp sense of smell.

However, my extensive research in the form of perusing fashion magazines while I sat in a deer blind led me to the conclusion that deer seemed to prefer the scent of Elizabeth Taylor's White Diamonds perfume, because all those perfume samples falling out of my magazines didn't seem to inhibit their activity at all. Which made it seem kind of stupid that I'd spent all that time believing I had to smell like dirt.

(Did I really just reference Liz Taylor's White Diamonds

perfume? Apparently I was reading back issues of magazines from the mid-1980s.)

Since I have a mind for science (No. I don't.), I decided to take my research even further and began to test the deer's sensitivity to noise and movement. Specifically, I began to lean out the windows of the deer blind and yell, "HEY! HEY, DEER! OVER HERE! LOOK AT ME!"

And let me tell you, those deer would look up at me and go right back to eating oats.

The people on those hunting shows have been doing it ALL WRONG.

Because I am a giver, I shared my findings with Perry. I thought he would be thrilled to know that he could now wear Old Spice and blast music while he hunted. Not that he does either of those things even when he's not hunting, but you know, he might have wanted to start.

But after I told him my scientific conclusions, he replied, "Well, clearly those deer are smart enough to realize that if you're dumb enough to hang out the window and yell at them, you're not planning to shoot them."

Whatever. Like they can reason that out.

Part of the reason I'd decided I couldn't shoot deer anymore was because of an incident that had happened the previous season. I'd agonized over shooting a doe that was out on the field of oats eating with all her doe friends, because I was afraid they'd all be so sad. But then I remembered Perry's voice telling me we really needed more venison in the freezer to get us through the long, hard San Antonio winter, so I took the shot.

The doe dropped to the ground, and all her doe friends looked up for a minute and then went right back to eating. Seriously. Like

THE ANTELOPE IN THE LIVING ROOM

they didn't even care about what had just happened to their friend. They just acted like animals. And I decided I couldn't emotionally handle shooting a deer ever again.

However, a pig was a different story.

South Texas is overrun with wild hogs. And before you go all *Charlotte's Web* (But WILBUR!) on me, you need to know that they are not pink and cute. They are hairy and have tusks and will tear up a ranch like it's their job. So you have to manage the hog population, especially since they also procreate like they're part of the Duggar family.

So one evening as I sat reading about Gwyneth Paltrow's new exercise regimen, I looked up and saw that there was a huge pack of wild hogs in front of me. I put down my magazine, picked up my gun, and aimed carefully. As soon as I made the shot, one of the biggest hogs in the pack dropped to the ground, and the rest of the pack ran back into the brush.

Looks like Mama is eating pork chops tonight.

I sat there staring at the pig lying in front of me to make sure it was really dead and I didn't need to shoot it again. But it was stone-cold dead. I went back to reading about Gwyneth and her macrobiotic meals because I knew it would still be at least an hour before Perry would be back to pick me up.

(This is the other reason I stopped hunting with Perry. He'd leave me in that deer blind until way after dark. Which, one, was scary. And, two, meant that I couldn't even read unless I pulled out my flashlight or some scary hitchhikers/serial killers showed up and lit a campfire nearby, offering me a little light to see by.)

(This is the type of scenario I began to imagine as I sat alone in the dark for what felt like hours.)

As I waited for Perry and debated whether or not I could be

like Gwyneth and learn to prefer eating air instead of real food for three meals a day, I thought about how proud of me he was going to be for shooting that hog. It had been a long time since I'd shot something on my own, and I knew he'd be impressed. Especially since it had obviously been such a perfect shot.

About that time, I began to hear the rumble of his Ford F-350 driving toward me. As I looked to see what direction he was coming from, I watched the hog I'd shot that had been lying there for almost two hours jump up, shake itself off like it had just woken up from a nap, and trot back into the thicket of mesquite trees like nothing had ever happened.

What the actual heck?

It was a hog playing possum.

And that's why I don't hunt anymore. I can't handle the stress. If an animal appears to be dead for the better part of two hours, then by all means, it should stay dead. That's like some sort of law of basic science. I'm pretty sure Marlin Perkins said it one time.

While hunting became an interest we no longer shared (or at least I no longer pretended to share), we both enjoy fishing at the coast. Well, Perry enjoys fishing, and I don't mind spending a day on a boat working on my tan while holding a fishing pole.

So for several summers we planned an annual beach vacation down to Port Aransas. Some friends had a condo they would let us use, and it was a delightful way to spend a few days. We'd usually spend the first half of the week by ourselves and then invite a few friends to join us for the last half of the week, and we'd eat fresh seafood and swim out in the waves and occasionally fish.

Then one summer Perry decided it might be fun for a group of us to go out on a deep-sea fishing excursion for the day. I agreed to this because I must have not heard him when he suggested it and just said yes because I didn't want him to think I wasn't paying attention.

But here's the thing. As I mentioned in an earlier chapter of this very book, I have motion-sickness issues.

(I have recently traced the origin of these issues back to a childhood of riding in the backseat of my dad's car. He has never met a stretch of road that he doesn't like to pretend is the last lap of the Indy 500—but with more twists, turns, and weaving in and out of traffic.)

So, in hindsight, deep-sea fishing—not really the best idea.

But I was reeled in (get it?) by the thought of all the cool fish we might catch. Maybe I'd catch a huge swordfish, even though I'm pretty sure they don't live in the Gulf of Mexico. But they might have decided to go there for vacation, and what if I was the first person to catch one?

Plus, I really wanted to go because I knew Perry really wanted me to go. And sometimes (a lot of the time) marriage is about being selfless. So I convinced myself it was going to be a great trip. *Seasickness has no hold on me. It's all about the power of POSITIVE THINKING. OPTIMISTS UNITE. Power to the (seasick) people!*

However, as a precaution, I stocked up on Dramamine, Dramamine patches, and ginger pills, which are supposed to help with the motion sickness.

Because I am like a Girl Scout. Always prepared—and a big fan of cookies.

The details of that morning are hazy, which is probably due to the fact that I'd already popped two Dramamine and was wearing a Dramamine patch on my arm. I just remember that we left well before daybreak, which should have been my first clue that I was not necessarily cut out for deep-sea fishing expeditions.

We arrived at the boat and were met by Captain Awesome and his first lieutenant, Tattoo. Honestly, I don't remember their real names, so I just made those up. (It's called CREATIVE LICENSE because I was too whacked out on Dramamine to remember anything.)

The boat began heading out toward the deep sea. And here's a critical fact that I was not previously aware of: it takes a long time to get out to the deep sea. A really long time. Fear started to overtake me as I realized that I couldn't just decide midday that I'd had enough of the fishing. I was clearly going to be stuck out at sea. Just like Gilligan.

So I popped another Dramamine to quell my rising fear.

It's a good thing that this was years before the Carnival Cruise debacle occurred, or I would have jumped ship so fast it would have made your head spin. I mean, those people were stuck out on the middle of the ocean eating only pickles and onions and pooping in paper bags. Used paper bags. Kathie Lee Gifford never sang about that on those old commercials. "In the morning, in the evening, ain't we got an engine fire and bags you can poop in?" It's not as catchy.

Anyway, we finally stopped at our destination, which was, for lack of a better term, in the middle of the dadgum ocean. I couldn't see the shore. I COULDN'T SEE THE SHORE.

Even now I can still feel the panic.

And the boat started rocking. Not rocking in a good way, like "rocking" from all the fun we were having. Oh, no. It was rocking because of the waves. Oh, sweet mercy, the waves. The sea was angry that day, my friends. But not as angry as my stomach, which immediately began a mutiny on every meal I had ever consumed in my life.

Captain Awesome and Tattoo tried to distract me by baiting my hook and handing me a fishing pole. I think the logic was that if I could start catching fish, I would forget about writing my will and screaming, "JUST KILL ME NOW" in between singing verses of old spirituals.

All of a sudden, my fishing pole almost bent in half, and the line started dragging like crazy. Everyone was yelling at me to reel, reel, REEL! So I did, and I forgot I was in total agony because I was about to bring in the largest fish ever caught in Texas deep-sea-fishing history.

And I did catch something very large. Our boat.

That's right, my friends. (Why am I talking like the Most Interesting Man in the World on those Dos Equis commercials? When he fishes, the fish jump into his boat just to be near him. Stay thirsty, my friends.) My line had gotten wrapped around our boat motor. And that pretty much sums up how the rest of our day went.

Perry and his friends Todd and Jay fished with Captain Awesome and Tattoo while I lay on the back of the boat, popping Dramamine like they were Smarties, hoping that seagulls would carry me off and drop me in the mouth of a whale to put the final nail in this nautical nightmare I was living out.

We didn't catch one fish that day. Not one.

Captain Awesome was not awesome. He was the devil. The devil who knew nothing about fishing. The devil who had bought a boat on a whim and a book called *So You Want to Be a Deep-Sea-Fishing Guide* and then had forgotten to read the book. In fact, his last words to us, as he took his money for the day, were "I'm going to go get drunk."

But no matter how much he drank, I bet he wasn't as hung over as I was three days later, when I finally woke up from my Dramamine-induced coma. Perry said at one point he thought about holding a mirror under my nose to make sure I was still breathing.

Perry and his friends were furious about the way the trip had turned out. Not because I had almost died at sea, mind you, but because we hadn't caught any fish.

Which warms my heart to this day. It's so tender.

They felt that Captain Awesome had misled them about the way he fished and the places we would go to find fish, and since Perry had read about Captain Awesome in *Texas Fish & Game* magazine (not to be confused with *Cheaper than Dirt!*, which is the catalog Perry wants me to quit saying he orders things from but I can't resist because I love the name), he wrote a letter to the editor voicing his displeasure.

He had me proofread the letter before he sent it because I may not be able to deep-sea fish, but boy can I proofread. And that's what every man really wants—a good editor. It's like that old saying: every man wants a cook in the kitchen, a tiger in the bedroom, and an editor in the home office. Or maybe I just made that up.

The letter went into great detail about our disappointment in how the day went and how Captain Awesome hadn't lived up to the hype of the article about him in *Texas Fish & Game*. It was passionate and heartfelt. A tale of our struggle with the angry sea and a belligerent captain determined to do things his way, no matter the cost. Like a modern-day *Moby-Dick*.

But my favorite line of the whole letter—in fact, maybe my favorite line ever—was the part where Perry wrote, "The real tragedy is that because of this experience my wife will never go deep-sea fishing again."

I told him to add an exclamation point to that sentence. And put "never" in all caps.

Even though I disagreed with him.

The real tragedy is that I spent four days of my life passed out from Dramamine. Days that could have been spent lying by the pool. Looking at water that doesn't move.

And the truth is, I never would have gone deep-sea fishing again anyway. Fish or no fish. Sometimes you just need to admit that you and your spouse might be better off just sharing a nice dinner together instead of trying to share a hobby.

That's why Perry doesn't watch old episodes of *Friday Night Lights* and cry with me. There are just some things about each other that you're not meant to share or understand.

# CHAPTER 16

# Don't Stop Till You Get Enough or the Feds Show Up

My best friend, Gulley, works at a preschool. And on occasion one of her fellow teachers will walk into the break room at school with an economy-sized box of granola bars or assorted chips and announce, "Please help yourself! My husband went rogue again and made a trip to Costco without me." This particular teacher happens to be older, and she and her husband no longer have any children living at home. So you can see how a box of 150 assorted granola bars might be more than the two of them could possibly eat in a year. Or ever.

She has my deepest sympathy because I, too, am married to someone who tends to frown upon buying items in quantities you can actually use before the expiration date. Perry never buys just one of anything. If it's worth having one, then in his opinion, it's worth having at least fourteen. He believes in the Michael Jackson philosophy: "Don't stop till you get enough." This applies to just about anything, and particularly knives, flashlights, and guns. Otherwise known as the redneck trifecta.

It's almost like he lived through some sort of Great Depression that causes him to buy in bulk. (I know this isn't the case because we are children of the '70s and '80s. While we may not be the Greatest Generation, we are most definitely the Walmart Generation.) At least once a week he asks me if I'm going to the store because we are "out of everything." I've learned to ask him to make a list because his definition of "everything" and mine are very different. Case in point, his list usually looks like this:

> York Peppermint Patties
> Q-tips

What? No York Peppermint Patties or Q-tips? Are we savages? What if Armageddon began and we were left trapped like rats without any means with which to clean our ears or enjoy a chocolate mint treat?

And maybe it's precisely because I have been so complacent as to let us run out of Yorks and Q-tips that Perry has become a fan of the bulk purchase. Whenever I make a grocery list, he'll always write *deodorant* or *shaving cream* and then instruct me to buy five cans of each. Because who doesn't want to spend $250 at the store with $150 of that being excessive toiletry items?

In the interest of full disclosure, I will admit I do occasionally forget to buy important things such as toilet paper. So, yes, I have contributed to his problem. Because I think we can all accept that there isn't any greater dilemma than being caught without toilet paper.

Unless it involves being without Peppermint Patties.

One day when Caroline was four years old, I decided it might be a fun activity for Caroline and me to wash my car in the driveway. I blame this lapse in judgment on the fact that our smoke alarm had gone off four different times the night before, causing me to wake up with what can only be described as deluded optimism.

In what is probably not a coincidence, Perry had to leave to meet with some clients, but before he left, he got out a bucket, some soap, and a few sponges for me to use and told me I could find anything else I needed in the garage.

Caroline and I got to work washing the car. Surprisingly, it wasn't nearly as fun as I'd remembered it being when I was sixteen. It was hot and messy, and cleaning out my wheel wells made my back hurt because I am not in the shape I was in when I could do forty high-kicks in a row while wearing white cowboy boots. Not to mention that my current car is an SUV and significantly bigger than the sweet Honda CRX I drove in high school.

Plus, due to my OCD tendencies, I couldn't just do it halfway. The car had to be spotless, and this wasn't a task for the faint of heart when you consider the atrocities I found hidden between the backseats where Caroline sits. Let's just say that goldfish crackers that have been subjected to heat and spilled apple juice don't maintain much structural integrity. I realized I was in need of some Armor All to really clean the interior, so I went into the garage, and I couldn't believe what I saw hidden on the back shelves.

I mean, I'm not one to air my family's dirty laundry, but I discovered that Perry has clearly been running a sideline business as a car wash operator behind my back. Why else would one family— a family that has washed their vehicles at home maybe twice in the last ten years—need twenty-six bottles of Armor All? Maybe you think I'm being too quick to jump to conclusions, so this is where I'll also tell you about the eleven squeegees and the orange safety cones. What other explanation could there be for this type of car-wash-supply excess? Was there some worldwide alert I'd missed about an impending shortage? I don't even understand.

In my opinion, the only time you really need to buy in bulk is if you discover your favorite lip gloss is about to be discontinued.

Several years ago I went on a trip to the Dominican Republic with Compassion International. During the trip, all my fellow seasoned travelers told me I should definitely buy some vanilla extract and coffee to take home, and so I did, because who am I to argue with food science? I bought one very large bottle of vanilla for myself and two small bags of Dominican coffee for Perry.

He is particular about his coffee, which is why I bought only two small bags. I cannot even express the various coffees we have purchased throughout our marriage in his quest for caffein-ated perfection, including one unfortunate incident that got us enrolled in Boca Java's Connoisseur Club and caused us to get approximately six pounds of coffee delivered every month, which is a little excessive, unless maybe you're Juan Valdez. We soon discovered the Boca Java Connoisseur Club is kind of like the mafia or selling Arbonne because once we were in, it was almost impossible to get us out.

I seriously thought I was going to have to cancel our credit card just to make the coffee quit showing up on our doorstep, but I finally got a representative on the phone who let me halt our coffee deliveries after I explained that Perry's medical adviser had told him to limit his caffeine intake. And by "medical adviser," I meant myself.

Anyway, I returned home from the Dominican and presented Perry with his two small bags of coffee. He seemed skeptical but agreed to give it a whirl. So the next morning he made (Brewed? Is that better coffee terminology?) his first pot. He was in love. I seriously thought he might need a moment alone with his coffee. Perhaps he and his Dominican coffee might want to get a room.

Those two small bags were depleted very quickly, but I discovered you could order it online. One evening I casually mentioned that the coffee was available online and that I'd get around to ordering more at some point. Then I forgot all about it. Until ten pounds of Dominican Santo Domingo coffee showed up on our front porch, courtesy of UPS.

Unfortunately, the shipped coffee didn't taste nearly as great as the bags I'd brought home from the trip. A fact I was reminded of every morning until our ten-pound supply of coffee beans was finally depleted. Which takes even longer than you might think, especially when you have to hear about their lack of flavor every day.

After sixteen years of marriage, I've grown accustomed to Perry's tendency to stockpile various things. (I'm using the word *stockpile* instead of *hoard* in an effort to be more sensitive to his affliction.) I've learned that every year in early January we'll receive a large shipment of Williams-Sonoma peppermint bark that he buys at half price after Christmas. I know now that if I need a flashlight, he can offer me about ten different varieties, complete with batteries. When I think we're out of paper towels, I've learned that he always has at least two more packs of twelve in the back house.

And, admittedly, this comes in handy. Especially because it never occurs to me to buy more than one of anything for any situation. We were once under a hurricane warning, and the news anchors suggested that people should stock up on essentials in case of power outages and bad weather. So I made my way to the grocery store and came home with a six-pack of bottled water, a bag of Sour Patch Kids, some Cheez-Its, and a *People* magazine. I don't know that anything has ever been a stronger test of our marriage. Perry's disappointment in my lack of basic survival skills was palpable.

But nothing could have prepared me for what happened a while back.

It is well documented that Perry loves nothing more than to hunt. It's his favorite. So naturally he enjoys loading up on various hunting supplies. I mean, this is a man who once rode the city bus to a political rally while packing heat. Which is why I didn't think anything of it when he was leaving to spend the day at the ranch and said as he was walking out the door, "Are you going to be home today? Because I'm expecting a shipment of ammo I ordered to come in, and I don't want it sitting on the front porch."

I assured him I'd be home all day and could make sure his beloved ammo was safe and sound.

When the delivery man knocked on the door a few hours later, I was surprised to see an eighteen-wheeler parked out front. We don't get many of those in our residential neighborhood. I opened the door and asked him if he could just leave it on the front porch.

"All of it?" he asked.

"Yes. Why? How much is there?" I questioned.

That's when I discovered the entire trailer of this eighteen-wheeler contained ammo Perry had ordered off the Internet, and I felt my left arm go numb because I was about to have a stroke.

Apparently Perry had come across a deal he couldn't resist on bargain-basement-priced ammunition. Perhaps Crazy Larry's Ammo Store was having a going-out-of-business sale. So I directed this poor delivery guy to where he could unload the contents of his truck while I waited for the ATF to show up and haul me off for questioning, since that seemed to be imminent.

On the upside, we are set from now until the day before forever on ammunition. It's right next to the fourteen packs of AAA batteries and the cases of microfiber towels.

But here's the thing: it's true that Perry loves to buy vast quantities of various merchandise and isn't afraid to meet someone he found on the Internet at Buc-ee's truck stop if it means he can get a good deal on ammunition. However, he is a stickler for quality merchandise. This is why he wants me to quit saying he shops at *Cheaper than Dirt!* It can't just be bargain priced; it has to meet his quality standards AND be a fair deal.

We are currently in the process of getting estimates to replace all the windows in our house. It's an old house, and this means there are exactly twenty-two windows that need to be replaced. This is not an inexpensive proposition. By which I mean that when we got our first estimate a few weeks ago, I had to hold my ears to keep my brain from leaking out.

It makes me wish we lived closer to the airport, because several years ago the federal government replaced all the windows in those older homes free of charge. Which seems to be a perfectly good use of our tax money, doesn't it? Replacing windows for people who chose to live by an airport that already existed when they moved in? It's too bad Congress doesn't feel as strongly about people who live close to train crossings. On cool winter nights we can hear the train whistles so loudly that I think I'm in a reenactment from *The Polar Express* and I start singing "Hot Chocolate."

Anyway, last week a window salesman with impeccable timing showed up on our doorstep, told me his company was working in the area, and asked if we'd like a free estimate to replace the windows in our home. I told him that would be great, and we scheduled the appointment for the following Tuesday afternoon. He said it was important that my spouse be present for the meeting. Which, frankly, seemed a little 1950s to me, but whatever. I'm just a little old housewife who doesn't know nothing about windows.

On Tuesday these two young salesguys showed up on our doorstep, complete with an iPad to give their sales presentation and show a demo window. We invited them in, and they explained that they actually work for a direct-marketing company that could sell anything but just happened to sell windows. I believe it was at this point that I began to get the feeling that this wasn't going to end well for them.

My feeling was confirmed as they launched fully into Perry's most-hated sales tactic—bashing the competition without touting the merits of the product you're actually trying to sell. He let them go on for about three minutes before he interrupted with a terse "Tell me why I would want to buy *your* windows."

Danger, Will Robinson. Danger.

These two young guys shifted gears, but then, sadly, lost us again when they said, "Our windows give you the high quality you want but at a lower price because we know you'd rather spend your money on your pretty wife."

Did we just time travel? What is happening? Check, please.

It takes a lot to awaken my feminist sensibilities, but this did the trick.

My patience was wearing thin, but Perry tends to have a longer fuse in these situations than I do. Except then they mentioned the competition negatively again: "If you have Sears come out to bid on your windows, they'll take up at least four hours of your time."

To which Perry replied, "No, they won't. Because I'll tell them they have forty-five minutes to measure and give me a price if they want this job."

That's when I realized these salesguys were lacking the ability to read social cues, because they started in on the inferiority of Pella windows until Perry cut them off with "Just give me the estimate. How much to replace our windows?"

Don Draper doodled on his iPad for a few minutes until he finally scribbled some numbers on a legal pad and scooted it across the kitchen island to where Perry and I were standing. Just the man of the house and his little woman. It took everything in me not to say, "I don't understand. Math is hard."

They explained that the first number, $13,954, would be our price if we accepted their bid right there on the spot. The second number was the price if we waited twenty-four hours. And the third number, $33,000, would be our price if we waited seven days or longer.

Have you ever seen someone's head explode? Because that's what I watched happen. Perry asked incredulously, "So you're telling me that you're going to charge me 19,000 more dollars if I want to wait a week before making a huge financial decision?"

"Well, sir, it's because we don't spend our money on marketing. We—"

Perry interrupted, "What does that have to do with how much you're going to charge me to put windows in my house? Windows cost what windows cost. And you want $19,000 more? For me to exercise due diligence and research my options?"

"Well, it's just that . . ."

"NINETEEN THOUSAND MORE DOLLARS?"

The salesguys did their best to explain the logic behind this obviously flawed marketing technique, but Perry continued, "I own my own business. I have bids sitting on my desk that are a year old, but I would still honor the price I gave the client if they called me back tomorrow, because I stand behind my product. What you're telling me is that your company knows that if I take the time to research these windows, I'm going to discover I don't want them in my house. How else can you explain charging someone NINETEEN THOUSAND MORE DOLLARS if they wait seven days?"

They couldn't explain it. I guess it wasn't just me who thinks that math is hard.

I left Perry there to finish the appointment because I had to take Caroline to the dentist. As soon as we got in the car, she said, "Well, I have never heard Daddy talk in that voice before."

"That's because Daddy doesn't like being taken to the cleaners. Daddy's a good businessman. He doesn't play around."

"Mama? I don't think those guys were very smart."

"Me neither, Baby."

It's just a shame that they weren't selling discounted Williams-Sonoma peppermint bark or cases of ammunition at incredibly low prices. Because then? Done deal.

Especially when you consider how much Perry likes to save money so he has more to spend on his pretty wife.

# CHAPTER 17

# The Twisted Gift of the Magi

Somewhere right before Thanksgiving, they always start to air those commercials where a wife walks out to the driveway and there's a Lexus or some equally pricey car with a big red bow wrapped around it.

Those commercials make me want to give someone a round-house kick to the face.

And then there are all the jewelry commercials where a husband surprises his wife with a heart-shaped pendant covered in little diamonds to "show her you'd marry her all over again." As if financing an ugly piece of jewelry at the mall can convey that kind of sentiment.

It's all a big marketing scam. It's capitalism's version of emotional blackmail to make women believe that all over America, other women are walking out to sporty luxury cars wrapped in red bows while we just opened a pair of fuzzy socks from Old Navy and a pack of bubble gum our kids wrapped up for us to let us know we're the BEST MOM EVER. With any luck the gum isn't prechewed.

Of course, maybe it's that Perry and I are notoriously bad gift givers, as in there have been times we've completely forgotten to buy each other a present to commemorate an occasion. (Don't be jealous of our romance.)

Neither of us would write down "giving and receiving gifts" as our love language because we are both particular enough that we prefer to pick out our own things. Perry would prefer that I not waste our money in an attempt to buy him some piece of fishing equipment he'll never actually use, and I prefer to not ever receive another Eddie Bauer sweater with deer on the front and pewter buttons.

Unless I time travel back to 1988. In which case, AWESOME.

So pretty early in our marriage, we each decided that we were going to opt out of the gift-giving portion of our relationship unless we genuinely had a great idea for what to get the other person. I mean, there are only so many times you can give your husband an envelope full of cash without it becoming overly sentimental and romantic.

One Christmas I actually surprised him with a lower blah-blah something-or-other for some type of gun, but I only knew to do that because I called his best friend, Monty, and asked him for help. He told me about the lower whatever thing, and the whole thing ended up with my driving an hour to the middle of nowhere and then an additional forty-five minutes past that until I ended up in some man's basement looking at weapons. Which wasn't creepy or reminiscent of *Silence of the Lambs* at all. ("It rubs the lotion on its skin.") I've never been more certain that I'd just wandered into a set of circumstances that would eventually be turned into an episode of *Law and Order* (ripped from the headlines!).

Just another day in Texas.

And that same Christmas, Perry surprised me with a pair of diamond earrings. We were like normal people that year. Or people you see in the commercials, except you never really see a commercial where a wife gets swept away by diamond earrings and the husband opens up a large box with part of a gun inside. Unless you watch the Outdoor Channel.

(Side note: If you do watch the Outdoor Channel, I would like to know your thoughts on the dating website FarmersOnly.com. Is there really a need to get that specific? Do you have to be a farmer to be on it or just have a desire to meet a farmer? This has kept me up at night.)

Anyway, most years we just stick to safe, inexpensive gifts. A pair of pajama pants from Old Navy, maybe some new bubble bath, a reindeer that poops chocolate jelly beans. We keep it classy.

But a few years ago, we had a little miscommunication about our gift-giving situation.

Perry's friend Monty builds custom guns. In fact, you could say the foundation of their friendship is based on a love of weaponry. But isn't that true of all close friendships? A few days before Christmas, Monty texted me to let me know he was sending Perry a custom-built 1911 9mm.

(I wish you knew how many times I had to clarify this name with Perry. Apparently calling it a 9mm pistol is WRONG. VERY WRONG. IT'S LIKE I DON'T KNOW GUNS AT ALL.)

(That could be because I don't know guns at all.)

Monty wanted to make sure I was going to be able to pick up the package and get it home in a timely manner. So Monty and I texted back and forth several times. Then later that night, he texted me to let me know when it would arrive. Unfortunately, Perry, Caroline, and I were all watching a movie together on the couch, and Caroline picked up my phone and announced, "MOM! You have a text from Monty! Why would he be texting you?"

And I said, "GIVE ME MY PHONE! YOU DON'T NEED TO BE LOOKING AT MY TEXTS," because I didn't want Perry to know what was going on. And, to his credit, he played the whole thing off and acted like he hadn't heard a word Caroline had said.

(Looking back, I'm an idiot for thinking he really didn't hear. Our couch isn't that big. For that matter, our house isn't that big.)

But Perry did hear. And this caused him to go into a panic. Because we'd been very clear already that we weren't going to get each other anything this year. In fact, Perry had bought a new tripod thing for the ranch a few weeks ago and announced "MERRY CHRISTMAS TO ME" as he loaded it into the back of his truck.

However, Perry knows that if I were to decide to surprise him with a really nice Christmas gift, I'd text Monty to figure out what to get. So when he heard Caroline announce I'd gotten a text from Monty, he went into a little bit of freak-out mode, thinking I was getting him some really nice present and he hadn't bought anything for me except some socks. (SmartWool socks. They're my favorite. Normally I just wear Perry's old ones, but every now and then we get fancy and he buys me a few brand-new pairs for myself. Old Love.)

So, because he is a genius, he started looking through Fashion Fridays on my blog to see what I might want. I guess he hadn't noticed all the nights I sat and licked the computer screen while looking at a pair of Frye boots, specifically the Jackie Button boots in cognac. But he saw that I'd featured them on Fashion Friday and tried to order them from Piperlime only to discover they were back ordered.

And so he called Gulley. Who instructed him to check Nordstrom. He wasn't even sure what Nordstrom was. (Proving once and for all that opposites attract.) But he looked it up online, found the boots, ordered them, and had them express shipped to get here in time for Christmas.

He even gift wrapped them.

And somewhere elves died of shock and horror when they saw how he managed to piece together five separate pieces of gift wrap in an attempt to cover the large boot box.

On Christmas morning I was absolutely thrilled and shocked to open my very own pair of new boots. And Perry was shocked and thrilled when he opened the work shirts and flannel pajama bottoms I gave him.

Or maybe just shocked.

But then I pulled out the gift from Monty, and it all began to come together. Monty and I weren't texting because I was buying Perry a custom-built gun. We were texting because Monty was giving Perry a custom-built gun.

And yet I got a really great pair of boots out of the whole thing.

Of course, I offered to take back my boots since the whole thing was a big misunderstanding. But you need to know I was shuffling my feet across our rock front porch to ensure that the soles of the boots were scuffed enough that they couldn't be returned. I'm no fool. He was going to have to pry those boots from my cold dead feet to get them back.

It was like a real live "Gift of the Magi" moment. Except totally warped because I didn't cut my hair. And Perry doesn't own a pocket watch and certainly wouldn't know where to buy fancy hair combs. And Perry got a gun from his best friend. We would make O. Henry cry and probably give up writing altogether.

Perry called Monty to thank him for the gun and told him the whole story. And I got a text from Monty a few minutes later that read, "Glad to hear you got some boots! I'll text you same time next year."

Anyone who tries to tell you that technology doesn't make life better? I have an awesome pair of boots that says they're lying.

# CHAPTER 18

# Frigidaire Will Be So Envious

A WHILE BACK, Perry and I were sitting in bed watching *24*. (This should clue you in to the fact that it was several years ago, since Jack Bauer has been gone from our lives for quite some time. I mourn him. Not like I mourn Sydney Bristow or Coach and Tami Taylor, but close.) A commercial came on, and I had a moment to reflect on how incredible Jack continued to look in spite of his exposure to biological weapons. He really was holding up beautifully other than the occasional tremor that conveniently managed to arise right when he was about to do something really important like disarm a bomb or save the president from being stabbed with a kiwi knife.

(Does anyone else remember that *24* was usually brilliant but every now and then had a horrendous story line, like his daughter being trapped in a cabin in the mountains with a mountain lion outside?)

Anyway, while I was thinking about Jack's phenomenal resilience, Perry turned to me and asked, "Have you read anything about radiant barrier paint?"

"Hi. Are you speaking English? What does that even mean? What would make you think that I've ever heard of such a thing?"

(Or that if I ever stumbled across an article about something called "radiant barrier paint," I'd take the time to read it unless I saw the words *Jennifer Garner* or *Rachel Zoe* or *Connie Britton to reprise role as Tami Taylor*?)

"It means radiant barrier paint. It's paint that makes a surface heat resistant. They use it on the space shuttle, and I'm thinking about buying some."

"Well, of course you are. I've always said that if it's good enough for the space shuttle, then it's good enough for us."

"I'm serious. I'm going to buy some and paint the entire attic with it to help keep the house cool. It'll cut down on our utility bill."

"That'll be nice, since there's a good chance you'll die if you go up in the attic for more than three minutes this time of year. I'll appreciate the economic savings."

Then *24* came back on, and that was the end of the discussion. Or so I thought.

However, I walked into the house the next day and overheard Perry on the phone with someone discussing radiant barrier paint. He was talking to a man named Jacob from Jacob's Ladder Construction (such a clever way to subtly let people know you are a Christian businessman without having to put a large ichthus on your Yellow Page ad) about getting an estimate to have our attic painted with radiant barrier paint. Let's just say that the estimate was more than I was willing to spend, but considering I was willing to spend approximately between zero and ten dollars to have my attic outfitted like the space shuttle, that's not really saying much.

Perry announced a few days later that he was going to do it himself. And since it was only 107 degrees in the shade, he decided it was a good time to go up in the attic and figure out a plan of attack. I wanted no part of any of it other than to sit on the couch and make jokes referencing *Coal Miner's Daughter* because he was wearing a headlamp, and that's just asking someone to quote Loretta Lynn.

So while he sweated up in the attic, I sat in the air-conditioning and called out helpful things such as, "There ain't nothin' in Kentucky for me except a chest full of coal dust and being an old man before I'm forty" and "Doolittle's done throwed me out" and because I was on a roll and couldn't stop myself "Who's that sow you got wallowin' in your Jeep?"

I just do what I can to be supportive.

I'm not sure what happened at that point—maybe the excessive heat in the attic caused him to realize he was crazy to even consider trying to paint it himself. That's why NASA has all those astronauts. What do you think they do when they're not leaping around on the moon? But whether it was the heat or he just got distracted by something else, he dropped the idea, and I was so grateful.

Several years passed with no mention of radiant barrier paint, and I certainly wasn't going to bring it up. In my opinion, it would be more fun to rent a shovel and hire myself out to dig a big hole than to spend money on our attic. Or maybe we could take a vacation and go out for a spin on a paddleboat, because what's more relaxing than to pedal yourself around a large lake? Other than using a handy invention called a boat motor? But then I began to discuss changing up the living room and kitchen. Specifically, I wanted to get rid of the autumn-gold color we'd had on the wall for ten years and go with a soft gray, since that's what everyone on Pinterest is doing and I'm a follower.

Perry was on board with my plan and then mentioned maybe it would be a good time to get insulation in our walls since we were going to paint and fix some existing cracks in the Sheetrock anyway. I vaguely accepted this because I was just happy he was agreeable to my plan to paint, plus I was secretly waiting for the moment to mention I also wanted built-in shelving installed in the living room. And maybe a new chandelier.

Then Gulley's grandmother got sick and I drove to Bryan to help with Gulley's kids while she and her mom tried to find an assisted-living facility for Nena. And it was while I was out of town and at the VERY LOUD community pool with the kids one afternoon that Perry called to report he'd had "a guy" out to the house to bid on insulating the walls and the attic.

I swear he's like a dog with a bone.

So I listened as he excitedly explained what a HUGE difference this was going to make in our home and that all it involved was drilling "a couple of holes" in the walls so they could pump in the foam insulation.

I could tell this was one of those things he wasn't going to let go of, so I agreed to the wall insulation but suggested that we wait on the attic since that was going to be a little more expensive and I'd rather put that money in a pile and burn it instead of spending it on our attic because, you know, what's more fun to spend money on than insulating your attic?

Everything else in the world.

But here's the thing about marriage. Sometimes there are breakdowns in communication. And sometimes you speak such different languages that you forget to ask important, clarifying questions. Questions like "How many holes are we talking about?"

Because while I naively envisioned that each wall would receive one small hole in a discreet location, what actually took place was a Sheetrock apocalypse.

The workmen came into our house with saws and drills and hoses while wearing masks. It was like the end of *E.T.* when the scientists realize E.T. is living in Elliott's house and come barging in wearing space suits. I wanted to ride off on my bike and fly across the moon to escape while wearing a red hoodie. And I don't really even like to wear red.

In my husband's defense, the insulation salesguy hadn't been completely up front with Perry either. And so we were completely unprepared for the mess and the dust and the hysteria and the tears. Of course, I was solely responsible for the hysteria and the tears. The workmen didn't even cry one time as they decimated what used to be the walls of our home.

After Perry saw me breathing into a brown paper bag, he suggested that maybe I should get out of the house for the rest of the day. And I agreed because I was curled up in a corner singing, "Turn on your heartlight."

The next two days were a blur of insulation and dust and walking back into the house to find my living room curtains tied in a knot to keep them off the floor. Curtains. Tied in a knot. Do you know what happens to curtains that have been tied in a knot? It's not pretty. The whole situation was bleak. BLEAK. There was so much Sheetrock dust in my house that I believed there was no way it would ever be clean again, and we would all become permanently asthmatic and emerge from our home covered in dust like a scene out of some postapocalyptic movie where the people walk around like zombies as they survey their new reality.

Finally they finished pumping insulation, filled the silver-dollar-size holes all over each wall with some type of white foam that I think they use in hell, and left. My walls looked as if they'd contracted some type of the pox.

I'd spent that entire day at the pool with Caroline because, seriously, workmen act uneasy when a woman is crying on her dusty couch while they do their job. But about four o'clock that afternoon, Perry called me and asked where we kept the mop and the Swiffer broom.

And by the time I walked through the door an hour later, the house was completely put back together. The floors were swept and mopped. The curtains were untied. The furniture had been dusted.

As silly as this sounds, it was one of those moments in a marriage when I loved him more than ever. Not just because he cleaned the house, but because I realized he knows me well enough to know that I needed the house to be clean. That he knows me well enough to know that I wouldn't be able to sleep that night until the house was put back together.

And there's something about being known like that. It makes you feel loved. Because knowing to clean up all that dust is just the tip of the iceberg of things Perry has learned about me over the years. He loves me more because of some of them and in spite of the rest. I know you will find this shocking, but I am no picnic to live with some of the time.

(I always laugh when someone who just knows me from the blog says I must be so fun. Yes. I am a laugh a minute when I decide the baseboards look dirty and feel that my life will end if they aren't cleaned immediately. It's times like these when I'm sure Perry looks at me while I scrub furiously and thinks, *Man, marrying her was a great decision.*)

The holes remained in our walls for the next six months. For six months our house looked like it had been overrun by aggressive termites with anger issues. This was due to a combination of some painters who flaked out on us and having a hard time finding a Sheetrock repairman who wanted to deal with our mess. I could hardly blame them. In fact, I apologized profusely to every single one of them who walked through our door.

And frankly, the holes nearly sent me over the edge. I was okay for a while, but it finally got to the point where any sort of tip of the emotional scale would end with my crying and saying, "AND WE HAVE HOLES IN OUR WALLS."

But finally, a few weeks before Christmas, we got everything patched and painted and repaired. We even got the built-ins installed, and the whole house was finally starting to look like a real place where grown-ups lived again. A place where people enjoy the finer things in life, like indoor plumbing and using utensils to eat a meal.

So you can imagine how I felt when, several nights later while eating dinner, Perry announced, "I think the next thing we need to do to the house is get the attic insulated."

Why on earth? Why will this man, the man I love and adore, not rest until our home is completely impervious to outdoor temperatures? If I wanted to live in a refrigerator, then I could opt to move to Alaska and become an Eskimo.

(I'm not completely sure that example makes sense. But let's go with it.)

And I tentatively, lovingly said, "You know, I just hate the thought of getting into all that and making a big mess now that the house is in such great shape."

He responded, "It won't make a mess."

Yes. That's what I heard about the wall-insulating process. That was a lie.

Perry went on to say, "It's just a matter of taking everything down from the attic so they can pump out the old insulation and put in the new stuff."

"I know. You've mentioned that before. Do you remember how much stuff we have stored in our attic? Do you recall that we have a saddle up there we've been keeping for a horse we've never owned or had ambitions to own?"

"Quit exaggerating. What's taking up the most space up there is all your Christmas decorations. You have about forty-two different manger scenes."

I replied, "Yes, because I love Jesus. Let's not offend our Lord in an attempt to make me feel bad."

And so we've been at an impasse. I'm not sure why we need our attic insulated when we still don't have a farmhouse sink in the kitchen or plantation shutters on all our windows. That just doesn't even make good design sense. Because you know what no one ever comes to your house and remarks?

"Your attic is so cool and refreshing."

It's not that I don't appreciate Perry's desire to turn our home into a Frigidaire; it's just that my brain shuts down every time he mentions it.

The conversation came up again the other day, and Perry began with a sincere "So, seriously, I really think this is something we should do, but only if you agree that it's worth the money."

And I replied, "Give me your best sales pitch. Tell me why I'd want this instead of a new rug for the living room." Because I like to pretend to be open minded.

He went into elaborate detail about the process. It will keep our attic temps at a cool ninety degrees even on the hottest summer days. (Which will make it so lovely for the "squirrels" that sometimes invade and snack on my Christmas decorations. I realize they probably aren't squirrels, but it makes me feel better to think so, which confirms my theory that squirrels are just rats with a better public-relations department.) I halfheartedly mumbled an assent that I was okay with getting a few estimates and going from there.

Then a few days later, a couple of friends of mine came to visit from Nashville. They are both single and own their own homes. We got into a discussion about the terrible flood that hit Nashville a few years earlier, and one friend told us how the electricity went out, causing the sump pump that kept her house from flooding to shut off. The two of them had to drive around town in the midst of this terrible flood in search of a generator at Home Depot. And I am not even kidding when I say I felt like they were the bravest two women I'd ever met.

Because you know what I wouldn't know how to find in case of a power outage? A generator. You know why? Because Perry would do that for me.

Marriage comes with its share of challenges and priorities that don't always match up. But it can also come with the security of knowing you have someone who knows how to fix things and take care of all your maintenance needs. Sure, it can drive you crazy when you just want to hang a picture on the wall and he wants to measure it down to the nearest five-eighths of an inch. A number you don't even believe to be valid because, seriously, an eighth of something? Who cares?

I tend to take for granted that I don't have to worry about pesky details like attic insulation or anything involving the heating and cooling of our home. And talking to my Nashville friends made me realize that there are components to home ownership that I don't think about because Perry is the one at our house who gets bids for a new sprinkler system and fertilizes our grass and figures out where the leak in the bathroom ceiling is coming from. That's why he cares about foam insulation. He's in charge of the practical, and I'm in charge of the pretty.

Our system may not work for everyone, but I'm a big fan of our distribution of responsibility. It allows me to focus on my love language, which comes in the form of a Pottery Barn catalog, while Perry walks the aisles at Home Depot and dreams of the day our attic will be sealed up tighter than the space shuttle.

# CHAPTER 19

# Because Innuendo Is the Sincerest Form of Flattery

WAY BACK WHEN I WAS IN COLLEGE, which is, sadly, many years ago now and not just five years ago like I tend to believe in my mind until I see an actual college student and realize *DANG, I don't look like that, do I? . . .*

(Dear fifteen-year-old self, you should have worn more sunscreen all those years you were a lifeguard. Tan now, pay later.)

(And by pay later, I mean hundreds of dollars in expensive wrinkle creams with retinol.)

(Or just fifteen dollars in wrinkle creams in case Perry is reading this.)

Anyway, back when I was in college, there was a really sweet, nice boy who had a bit of a crush on me. And I wanted to like him. I knew he was the kind of guy I should want to date as opposed to all those guys I believed I could "fix." So I gave my very best effort to be interested in him.

And then came the night he decided to surprise me with a trip out to the lake. He'd put together a picnic basket full of food. There were candles and roses. It was like a scene out of a Meg Ryan romantic comedy. (Or maybe Emma Stone, if you're one of those college students who didn't grow up on the wonder that is *When Harry Met Sally*.)

Everything was perfectly lovely, and I desperately tried to be in the moment and mentally will myself to fall in love with this incredibly romantic boy sitting next to me. But then he pulled out his guitar.

I felt something inside me start to freeze up. I had the distinct impression that I was about to find myself in a pickle. And before I knew what was happening, he began to serenade me with Keith Whitley's "Tell Lorrie I Love Her" except he changed the lyrics to "Tell Mel I Love Her."

(Oh my gosh. I am in a full blush and fighting the fetal position as I sit typing this in Starbucks at the mere memory of how awkward I felt.)

As he sat and sang that song, a million thoughts flashed through my mind. Chief of which was *I want to squash him like a bug*.

I know. I am a terrible person. You probably can't believe you're reading a book written by such a heartless, cold monster.

And sure, the argument could be made that it was the right gesture being made by the wrong boy. Maybe that was part of it. But a deeper part of me realized at that moment that I am not really a "my life is a romantic comedy" kind of girl as much as just a "comedy" girl. I don't do well with overly romantic gestures, mainly because my mind begins to race furiously as I try to figure out if I'm supposed to cry or smile, and I don't know what I'm supposed to do with my arms, and suddenly my teeth feel enormous.

I realize this may put me in the minority of women. Maybe most women love nothing more than a sappy romantic gesture involving changing the lyrics to a classic country song, but I am not one of them. I prefer my romance with a dash of practicality. Just a nice "You're the best wife ever" or "I'll drive Caroline to soccer practice tonight" works for me.

Hollywood doesn't really cater to women like me who don't fit the life-is-a-romantic-fairy-tale mold. But maybe we'd all be better off if we didn't get so caught up in what movies tell us is real love. In a movie, true love happens in about ten minutes after a montage of a couple throwing leaves at each other and chasing each other around a park while a Harry Connick Jr. song plays in the background, and men regularly say things like, "You complete me" or "My life was a vast wasteland of emptiness until I saw your beautiful smile across the room."

In romance novels and romantic movies, men always know exactly what to say, and it's never "I accidentally clogged the toilet again." They care about their wife's feelings and brush her hair gently out of her eyes as they listen to her, and they know just when to embrace her in a tender hug. And then we expect our husbands or boyfriends to do that same thing and, God love them, there's a good chance they grew up with brothers, and the way they learned to say, "I love you" was to let one rip under the covers and then trap their little brother in there. It's just not always in their emotional makeup to have the right response or say the right thing. How else do you explain all the times a man has said, "Is that what you're wearing?"

A woman watching this scenario knows he should abort

immediately: MAN DOWN! MAN DOWN! But most men will continue to dig themselves deeper and deeper into the hole as they try to explain what they meant, when all they need to say is, "I just meant that you look so beautiful, it won't be fair to the other women at the party."

I guess my point is that I didn't go into marriage with any overly romantic notions or expectations. I don't need candlelight dinners or serenades under the moon or roses delivered on a regular basis. Truth be told, I'm more of a Gerbera daisy kind of girl.

But I'm going to bring up something that might change your life forever, even though it's about to make me feel a little uncomfortable. I think it needs to be addressed because, according to the extensive scientific research I've done, it's an epidemic. Assuming that you believe drinking wine and laughing with your girlfriends counts as extensive scientific research. Maybe if we just get this phenomenon out there, we'll all feel a little bit better knowing we aren't alone.

Here's the thing. Men have an innate ability to create sexual innuendo out of anything. ANYTHING. Like when I reread the above paragraph, all I can hear is Perry's voice saying, "Oh, yeah. I'll bring something up," or "Yep, I'd definitely feel better if I got this phenomenon out there." It's like a part of their brains got stuck around the time they were thirteen years old and they've never recovered.

The worst part is that I know now when I've just said something that's about to get turned into an invitation to take it to the bedroom or, as Adam and Christina call it on *Parenthood*, "Funky Town." I can't tell you how many times I've innocently asked Perry if he brought any meat home from the ranch and immediately realize I've just made a tactical error. And heaven forbid I ask him if he can get some sausage out of the freezer for me. And you don't even want to know what he said when I brought two large jugs home to put on our bookshelves.

Just the other night we were watching TV together, and a commercial came on for a product called a pocket hose. Are you kidding me? Is this a real thing? What man is going to be able to resist making a remark about something called a pocket hose that "starts off normal size but grows larger and larger when you turn it on"?

And the thing that kills me is that even though the majority of my girlfriends all agree these conversations happen in our homes, not one of us has ever reported that we've felt a sudden urge to strip off all our clothes and head to the bedroom after our husbands tell us, "I've got some meat for you right here." I mean, is there one man in the history of the world this strategy has ever worked for?

The whole thing certainly hasn't been helped by Michael Scott from *The Office* introducing "That's what she said" into pop culture. For the love of all things, do not remark while attempting to get something to work, "I'm having a hard time trying to turn this on." You'll regret it. That's a promise.

But every now and then I'll meet a guy who appears to be the sort of husband who might read poetry to his wife under the stars, and I think, *I bet he never cracks a joke when the pocket hose commercial comes on.* And she'd probably cry if he did. Because they are clearly a sensitive-type couple, which . . . good for them. The world needs people like that. Perry and I just don't happen to be among them, and ultimately, that's why we're a good match. Because when he says stuff like that, I laugh. Or roll my eyes, depending on my mood.

I think sometimes we can get caught up in believing that other women are experiencing more romance than we are, and perhaps that's right. But there are also a lot of women out there who know their husbands are feeling amorous because they whisper, "I haven't put my retainer in yet tonight" or "I just brushed my teeth" or "Did you notice I got my burger without onions?" And that's okay. That's real life.

Which is why it's all right for us to sometimes reply, "Okay, but I'm going to leave my socks on because it's cold."

Granted, you never hear Meg Ryan or Emma Stone say that in the movies, but you also never see anyone with hair that looks as good as theirs either.

# CHAPTER 20

# In-Laws and Outlaws

REMEMBER WHEN THERE was all that brouhaha (most underused word ever) about Chick-fil-A? And all of a sudden delicious chicken got thrown into the political spotlight? And chickens everywhere were all like "What happened? We're just chickens."

Then the Chick-fil-A cows painted a new sign that said, "Get off our backs." Or maybe not. I can't remember for sure, but that would have been awesome. Truett Cathy should have called me. Because we talk on a regular basis.

Anyway, it was during this time that people decided they needed a day to show our support for Chick-fil-A, because if Chick-fil-A goes away, then there really won't be a reason to continue living.

Something you should know about my mother-in-law is that she loves to send all her kids e-mails about any type of political movement and/or petition we need to sign. So she sent us all a message that read:

> *Dear Children,*
> *As you know, Chick-fil-A has recently been under fire for their beliefs. On August 1 there will be a day we can show our support of the Cathy family by eating at their restaurant. I have never eaten at a Chick-fil-A, but I will definitely give it a try on August 1. I hope you will do the same.*
>
> *Love,*
> *Mother/Sallie*

Please go back and reread the part about how she'd never eaten at a Chick-fil-A prior to August 1, 2012. I don't even understand.

But that pretty much sums up my mother-in-law. She is not one to think that *fast* and *food* belong anywhere in the same sentence, whereas I grew up in a family that didn't think dinner had been served until we'd made our way through a drive-through lane. Perry's mom would make June Cleaver feel like a failure. Honestly, one time when Perry and I brought over fast food, she put it on her fine china and set full places in the formal dining room. She may have even lit candles. And I guarantee she had a seasonally appropriate centerpiece, because she is not a savage.

The first Thanksgiving Perry and I were dating, his mother invited me to join them for Thanksgiving lunch, and I happily accepted. Then I called her a few days later to ask if she would like me to bring anything to contribute to the meal, and she requested that I make the homemade cranberry sauce. I didn't even know there was such a thing as homemade cranberry sauce.

I just thought cranberries grew in a can with Ocean Spray printed on the front. Honestly, it doesn't feel like Thanksgiving to me until I hear the *thwack* of cranberries hitting the plate as they come out of the can. I guarantee the Pilgrims felt the same way, even though it was probably a nightmare to get those cans open using only an arrowhead they'd borrowed from the Indians.

But she gave me her recipe for fresh cranberry relish, and admittedly, it was significantly more delicious than the canned variety. That was also the Thanksgiving I discovered that not everyone believes in pumpkin pie for dessert. Perry's family's tradition was something called chocolate icebox pudding. I believe it was sometime after my first bite of pudding that I decided we should spend the rest of our lives together.

However, things aren't always that magical. Several years into our marriage, I missed the way my family always had a smorgasbord (second-most underused word ever) of all types of side dishes. I longed for more of an assortment than just turkey, dressing, fresh cranberries, and green beans. And not green beans in a casserole, but fresh and steamed. To which I ask, what's the point of eating a green bean if it's not covered in cream of mushroom soup and french-fried onions?

My mom's side of the family always had fruit salad tossed with whipped cream, broccoli-rice casserole, the aforementioned green bean casserole, and sweet potatoes covered in marshmallows, among other things. And when we had Thanksgiving with my dad's Italian side of the family, there was always spaghetti and meatballs as an alternative to turkey. I come from a people who enjoy a little variety in their culinary experience.

So I decided one year that I would create my own variety. I made a broccoli-rice casserole, complete with the ever-elegant

Cheez Whiz, to take to my mother-in-law's house for Thanksgiving lunch. And I promise, the reaction was the same as if I'd plopped a dead, cooked rat in the center of the dining room table.

"What is THAT?" my brother-in-law asked with a scowl.

"It's broccoli-rice casserole. I brought the food of my people, just like the Indians did on that first Thanksgiving," I replied as I put a serving spoon in my beloved casserole with a flourish.

"It smells weird," he said.

"Yes, that's the Cheez Whiz. It's an acquired taste."

All I know is if that's the way the Pilgrims treated the Indians at their Thanksgiving feast, it's no wonder that whole situation went so awry and eventually ended up with scalpings and such.

Then there was the Thanksgiving just three months after we got married when I brought Perry to my grandparents' lake house. The seven-hour trip included moments to treasure, such as when Perry bought an Elvis clock complete with swiveling hips at the local gas station, where the cashier remarked, "Honey, if I had a dime for every piece of Elvis memorabilia at my house, I'd be a rich, rich woman" (wouldn't we all!), and my grandfather, Big Bob, getting so upset that someone had put out his burning pile of leaves that he proceeded to walk into the kitchen, pull a bottle of vodka out of the freezer, and drain it. Big Bob didn't drink EVER, with the exception of the occasional can of Pabst Blue Ribbon, so you can imagine the effect the vodka had on him. He spent most of the day passed out in his recliner. My grandmother, Nanny, was outraged, but the picture of the family all gathered around Big Bob as he sat slumped over at the head of the table is priceless. It's like we were living in a Robert Earl Keen song.

The lesson we all learned was don't mess with a man's burning leaf pile. And maybe wait until you've been married a little longer to bring your husband home to spend Thanksgiving with the whole family.

One of my most painful experiences as an in-law was the Easter Caroline and I went to Perry's aunt's house for an Easter egg hunt. Perry didn't go with us because he had to work, so we picked up Perry's mom and headed to the festivities. I believe there is no greater act of marital love or martyrdom than attending an event involving your spouse's family without your spouse in attendance. Not to mention that we only see this aunt and her family once a year for the annual Easter egg hunt. Which may explain why earlier that day, during brunch at Perry's mom's house, when we told the kids we were going to hunt eggs at Aunt Edna's house, they all looked at us and said, "Who's that?"

Exactly.

Anyway, Aunt Edna has two daughters who are older than us, and one of them coordinates the Easter egg hunt every year. It always involves elaborate instructions that make my head hurt, and that year was the pinnacle of egg hunting gone bad. Whatever happened to just hiding some eggs in the grass? Why do I have to work to find clues instead of Reese's Peanut Butter Cups? Why am I involved in anything that involves throwing a raw egg back and forth across the driveway until the inevitable happens? What has happened to my life? I feel with all certainty this isn't how Jesus intended for us to celebrate that he is risen. The disciples never had to throw one raw egg that I recall.

The theme of the egg hunt was "pirate's treasure," and we were divided into teams of kids and adults. As my brother-in-law, Jeff, read the instructions, I listened intently, in between watching Caroline grind confetti into Aunt Edna's expensive antique oriental rugs. I heard Jeff read, "Each team will need to answer the pirate geography question found inside the egg to proceed to the next egg." And I knew with all certainty, like the kind of certainty with which you know your own name, that I would never have a better opportunity to prove my complete ignorance in front of my in-laws.

A key element to this whole story is that the cousin who designs these hunts is a genius. And I don't mean a genius in the same way Perry tells me, "You're a GENIUS!" when I forget to buy milk despite it being written in capital letters at the top of my grocery list. I mean she's a real genius. She knows a lot of stuff about math and science and computers, otherwise known as the axis of evil. I'm pretty sure she's a Mensa member. However, I wouldn't know this, because I only see her once a year. At the egg hunt, not at Mensa meetings. (Just wanted to clarify.)

So the egg hunt began at a huge *X* to mark the spot to emphasize the pirate theme. Perry's cousin opened the first egg and began to read the question. About three words in, I heard the word *archipelago* and realized, without a doubt, that I was out of my league. Like the kind of out of my league I was in back in eighth grade, when every other girl in school actually needed a bra and the only curves I ever saw belonged to my Barbie doll. The only reason I even know the word *archipelago* is because Father Time used it on *Rudolph's Shiny New Year* when Baby New Year was lost and Rudolph had to search for him in the Archipelago of Times Past or something like that. However, to my credit and great relief, I did know that *Galápagos Islands* was the answer to one of the questions because I had just seen it on an episode of *Go, Diego! Go!*

(Who says kids can't learn anything from watching television?)

The remainder of the hunt passed with locations like the Caspian Sea, Kazakhstan, the Ural River, and Cape Horn being thrown about. Oh, and something about a city in China that had me prepared to yell out, "TOKYO!" as my answer, and I'll be forever grateful that, for once, my brain worked faster than my mouth.

Unless they had asked what country is shaped like a boot (ITALY!) or which country borders Texas (MEXICO!) or which country used to be part of the Communist Bloc (I KNOW IT ENDS WITH "STAN"!), there was no way I was going to be of any use in this game. Back in sixth grade, when I was coloring in all those world maps with map colors, I had no idea that twenty-six years later I would be called on to remember that information. And let's be honest, the only thing I really learned back then is that it looked good to color the United States red, because it really set off the blue color of whatever that ocean is called on the east coast of the United States.

Oh, I kid. I totally know it's the Indian Ocean.

And maybe I didn't pay attention to all that geography back then because I intuitively knew that there would one day be a thing called Google Maps. Who's the genius now?

Finally the geographical agony was over, and I was rewarded with what appeared to be a terra-cotta pot full of dirt, although I was promised there was a plant in there that would eventually grow. They probably figured I was too dense to know the difference.

Next up, it was the kids' turn to play the pirate geography egg hunt of torture, and sadly I didn't necessarily know the answers to any of their questions either, except for one. "What city do you live in?"

SAN ANTONIO!

I think it's obvious that it's just a matter of time before I run into Perry's cousin at a Mensa meeting.

An older friend of mine once shared that the Christmas after she married into her husband's large family, she arrived at lunch and discovered that her mother-in-law had set one table for the immediate family and a separate table that she referred to as "the outlaws' table" for all the spouses. That's hard core.

But it's easy to feel a little bit like an outlaw when you suddenly become part of a new family—and not just because there are times you might want to carry a gun. It's like you journey into a new, strange land just because it's the land of the person you love. Kind of like how I adore Mexican food but wouldn't necessarily want to move to Mexico. I don't know the language and the customs. I just happen to love the enchiladas.

It takes a lot of God's grace to adjust and adapt and remember that just because they don't do things the way you were raised, they're not necessarily wrong. (Except for the way they taught your husband to hang the paper towel roll, because that's clearly backward.)

There's a reason that people list in-laws as one of the biggest things (along with money) that cause stress in a relationship. Their voices become part of the DNA of your relationship, and they can either support you and encourage you or tear you down and make you feel like you're not worthy to be there. They tell you how to raise your kids and manage your money and spend your holidays. They have an effect on you whether you want them to or not. And only you and your husband can determine how much you're going to let them affect your life together, because there are times when it feels like the only commonality is that you both love the same person and you just have to appreciate that.

(On a related note, this makes me think of that children's book *Love You Forever*. If there's a chance your mother-in-law might come to your house and rock your grown husband in a rocking chair, then you have my deepest sympathies. And perhaps some unsolicited advice that you move and change the locks.)

Fortunately, I married into a family who has embraced me most of the time, even with all our differences and the fact that I think they still don't understand how I can stay in my pajamas all day on a Saturday. Or believe that Cheez Whiz is a viable food ingredient.

We've done our best to love one another for who we are, with all our weaknesses and faults and beliefs that Tokyo might be a city in China, and the fact that my mother-in-law never ate at a Chick-fil-A for the first seventy years of her life.

# CHAPTER 21

# Skeletons and Grace

PERRY AND I WENT TO a wedding for some friends a while back because we are all about some white bride's cake, and the minister performing the ceremony just kept repeating over and over again that the most important thing in marriage is forgiveness. Forgiveness is essential. Forgiveness is what will keep you together. Forgiveness is the key to a healthy relationship.

He said it so many times that I began to suspect he'd royally ticked off his wife prior to the ceremony and was trying to send her a not-so-subtle message as he married this sweet, unsuspecting couple who had no idea he might have a personal agenda.

Because, yes, I think forgiveness is important. Marriages can't survive when bitterness and resentment take root. But he made no mention of friendship and love and grace. You can forgive someone all day long, but I think forgiveness can sometimes be offered independently of grace. Forgiveness often says, *I'll let this slide, but I'm not really going to forget that it happened,* whereas grace says, *It's over and it's finished, even though you may not deserve it.*

I think Anne Lamott said it best in one of my favorite quotes: "I do not at all understand the mystery of grace—only that it meets us where we are but does not leave us where it found us." There's something about grace that makes us want to do better, be better, because we know we've been given a pardon.

And that's what so much of marriage is—giving each other a pardon. Letting some things go and realizing neither one of you is married to a perfect person. Even though there are times you feel certain he got the better deal because you would never join a basketball league without asking him if it was okay first, or leave to go hunting for the weekend and just assume that he doesn't mind being alone for three days in a row. And not just because you don't play basketball or like to hunt.

Of course, there are also the times Perry chooses to ignore my tendency to overshop or how I can forget to go to the grocery store when we're down to half a roll of toilet paper. Grace is a two-way street.

But there is nothing in my life or my marriage that compares with the grace Perry showed me a few years ago. It changed me in a permanent way and will go down as one of the most profound lessons of my life.

When Perry and I first became friends all those years ago and eventually started dating, I never let him harbor any illusions that I was perfect. There had been countless mistakes and bad roads I'd taken in my late teens and early twenties, including the broken engagement that left me raw and scarred. In fact, I think one of the scariest parts of finally running back to Christ at the age of twenty-two was looking around during Bible study and wondering who would want me when I felt so damaged. I knew God had forgiven me, but could a good man look at me and want me to be his wife when there were other girls who seemed so much sweeter and softer and might even rise while it was still night to prepare food for their families like in Proverbs 31, when I knew that cooking a big breakfast before dawn wasn't ever going to be part of my skill set?

But then Perry came along, and we fell in love. I was honest about who I was and where I'd been, and so was he. Neither of us had been angels, but there was also that line in my mind of how much detail to share about where you've been and what you've done. Do you just give a rough overview of your past mistakes, or do you throw all those skeletons out of the closet and see where they land?

(Bones! All over the place! Big mess!)

So I spent a lot of time praying about it and felt God was assuring me that Perry knew the things he needed to know and that the rest was part of my past—dirty water under the bridge.

So we got married and had a child and spent the next twelve years living life together. Then I went to a Beth Moore Living Proof Live conference in New Orleans in April of 2009. I can't even remember exactly what she talked about. I could go back and look in an old notebook, but that would take a lot of effort, and it isn't the point of this story. Quit being so impressed with my attention to detail.

As I sat in that audience, I knew with all certainty that God was telling me I needed to tell Perry a few things I'd never told him before. Things that had happened years before I'd even met him.

And my stomach began to hurt. *Why now, God? Why, after all this time? This doesn't even make sense. I don't want to do this.*

I flew home after the weekend and spent the next week wrestling with God. I told myself I was just imagining the whole thing, because it didn't make sense. It was just one of those ideas that seemed right while I was listening to Beth Moore talk, but it didn't translate to reality. The past is the past, and I didn't want to dredge it up. It seemed pointless, and truth be told, I was a little terrified of the whole idea.

But finally one night, about seven days later, Perry and I were in bed watching TV, and I knew I couldn't avoid it any longer. I knew that to continue to ignore God in this was complete disobedience, and it was driving me crazy. I was going to have to throw any remaining bones out of my closet. *Look! Is that a tibia?*

I was a wreck. I cleared my throat to begin to talk and then decided I'd better go to the bathroom first because that's always a good stalling strategy, not to mention that I felt like I might throw up. I'd worked myself into a frenzy. I was convinced that I was about to share things that would make Perry walk to the closet and pack his forest-green Eddie Bauer duffel bag and leave me forever.

Isn't that what fear does? It grows and magnifies everything to the point where all rational thought is lost and we can only see the city limits of Worst Case Scenario, which borders Crazy Town.

Finally I gathered myself enough to look at Perry and say, "We need to talk. I need to tell you some things, and I'm really scared."

Listen. If you need to get your husband's attention, this is a highly effective opener.

He immediately sat up straighter, turned off the TV, and looked directly at me. I could tell his face was a little paler than it had been a few minutes before. My voice was cracking, and my hands were shaking. "First of all, this was all years ago," I began. And I tearfully told him everything God had put on my heart to share with him.

I made my confession, never looking him in the eye because I knew I couldn't without falling apart. And then I finally looked at him, cautiously waiting for his reaction. Waiting for the hammer to fall. Waiting for him to get up, hurl words of condemnation, and walk out of the room.

Instead he looked me straight in the eye, never wavering, and said, "And?"

I don't know when any reaction has caught me so completely by surprise or when one word was ever filled with so much grace. Perry said, "That doesn't change one thing about you to me. That's your past. I don't care about that. I love you."

And in that moment I understood at least part of why God had me tell Perry a part of my past that didn't really seem to matter after all those years. It wasn't even about our marriage. It was to give me a tangible realization that even though I thought I understood what grace looked like, I really had no idea how deep and wide the mercy of Christ is. That he looks at us when we lay ourselves bare before him, with all our ugly truths and realities, and says, "And?"

Not one thing we've done changes that we are his. That he created us and loves us with a love more fierce and loyal than any we will ever know. He isn't looking for perfection. He's looking for humble hearts that know we are nothing without his lavish grace.

In Psalm 103 we are told that God redeems our lives from the pit. Verses 11-12 proclaim, "As high as the heavens are above the earth, so great is his love for those who fear him; as far as the east is from the west, so far has he removed our transgressions from us."

I once heard someone say that those words represent the beams of the cross—reaching all the way up to the heavens with his love and stretching out to remove our sins as far as from where the sun rises to where it sets. That's how much God loves us. That's how far he goes not only to save us but also to crown us with his love and compassion (verse 4).

So, yes, forgiveness is important in a marriage. If you're married, you'll have to forgive your husband many times during your life together, and he'll have to do the same for you. But then there's grace. Which is the greatest gift of all. It's the thing that says, *I see you for who you really are, and I love you anyway.* In fact, maybe, *I love you even more now than I did before.*

It's grace that allows us to look at the flawed person before us and say, "And?" the same way God looks at us.

# CHAPTER 22

# Deck the Halls

YEARS AND YEARS AGO, when Perry and I were just two cute young kids falling in love, I dreamed of the day we would finally be married and get to share every aspect of our lives together. Specifically, I couldn't wait for Christmas as husband and wife.

As a child of divorce, I experienced some amount of anxiety and stress during the majority of my Christmas celebrations from about the age of nine on, as my sister and I were shuttled back and forth to make sure we spent equal amounts of time with our mom and our dad. I always felt like the burden was on me to make sure no one's feelings were hurt and that everyone was happy. This wasn't really something my parents put on me, but I took it on because I am the oldest child and it's what we do. We're pleasers. Everyone stay calm. I can make this holiday MAGICAL with my own two hands!

Then, as a single woman out of college, I just felt like I didn't really belong anywhere. It wasn't because my family didn't make me feel loved; it was just that I longed to be somewhere else sharing the holidays with someone special.

I'll never forget driving home from the ranch with Perry right around Thanksgiving one year. We'd been dating almost six months at that point, and as we listened to Christmas music on the sweet sound system in his 1990 Ford Bronco, I began to daydream about our future Christmases as husband and wife. My fantasy world was significantly helped when Rich Mullins's song "You Gotta Get Up" came on. Especially the verse that says:

> *Mom and Daddy stayed up too late last night*
> *Oh I guess they got carried away in the Christmas candlelight*
> *And you gotta get up . . .*
> *It's Christmas morning*

It made me all swoony. It was all so romantic. I envisioned many Christmas Eves with Perry and me snuggled up by the fire in our matching plaid pajamas as we got ready for Santa Claus and lovingly assembled a Barbie Dreamhouse.

(I have no real explanation for the matching plaid pajamas portion of that scenario. That really isn't Rich Mullins's fault as much as it was my slight obsession with the Garnet Hill catalog. All the best families wear matching pajamas.)

When our first Christmas as husband and wife approached, I was giddy with all the giddiness. I made plans for us to go eat dinner and then head to the Christmas tree lot to pick out our first official

Shankle Family Christmas Tree. Imagine an excitement level of ten and then ratchet it on up a few notches. That was me. I could have scaled ten Christmas tree lots in a single bound on pure adrenaline.

We arrived at the lot (only because I didn't know of any Christmas tree farms where we could cut down our own tree, because I would have absolutely gone that route had it been a viable option) and began to peruse the possibilities. And this is when the first problem arose. Perry came from a Noble fir family, whereas I came from a family that believed in Scotch pine. We were in a mixed-Christmas-tree marriage and had no idea. No one covered that in premarital counseling.

But I was swayed by the Noble fir. It had some appeal. So we focused our efforts in that section of the tent. And then I saw it. It was like when Charlie Brown sees his tree, except the tree that captured my heart was about eight feet tall and almost as wide as it was tall.

"This is THE ONE," I breathed with deep reverence.

Perry gave it a once-over and announced, "You are delusional. Do you know what our house looks like? This tree is enormous."

"It's not that big. And we have nine-foot ceilings. Those ceilings are begging for a good, tall tree. This is the one."

Perry shrugged his shoulders and sighed. "Okay, if it's the one you want. But I think you're forgetting about a geometric principle known as circumference."

I hugged him tightly and proclaimed, "I've never had a tree of this magnitude, and I barely passed geometry so I don't know what you're talking about."

Everything was all fine and good and deck-the-halls fa-la-la-la-la until we got home to our house that must have shrunk while we were at the Christmas tree lot and I realized there was no possible way we were going to get that tree through our front door. Or our back door. It became clear that we had two options: we could cut a hole in our ceiling and lower it down on a mat like those men did for their paralytic friend so Jesus could heal him, or we could make the drive of shame back to the Christmas tree lot and throw ourselves on their mercy.

We chose the latter because we didn't believe Jesus could heal our enormous tree. They let us choose a different tree that we wouldn't have to keep in our front yard, and then we drove back home to get the tree in the stand so we could decorate it while listening to festive Christmas music and drinking hot chocolate.

How could I have known then that Christmas tree selection day in our home would henceforth be known as the day of the year we are most likely to file for divorce?

In my defense, I totally thought the tree was leaning to the left and that it was secure in the stand when Perry went to adjust it.

But if we really want to engage in a Christmas activity that has the potential to put us on the fast track to marital counseling, then hanging the outdoor lights is the most obvious choice.

One year I made the executive decision to buy all new colored lights because Caroline enjoys a home that looks like it belongs on the Las Vegas strip, and I really wanted to go retro with the enormous bulb lights of ye olden days, otherwise known as my childhood.

I showed Perry the boxes of lights I'd purchased, and he began to waste precious minutes—minutes that could have been spent illuminating our home—reading the instructions.

Seriously. I can't even.

I didn't even know Christmas lights came with instructions.

He said, "It says that you can only string sixty lights together at one time. That means only two strands can be connected."

"And?"

"Well, that means to do the house the way you want it done, we're going to need about eleven extension cords."

"And the problem with that is?"

"To do that we'd need to go buy eight new extension cords."

This was foolishness. I boldly proclaimed, "Listen. Those directions don't know what they're talking about. All the boxes say that. It's just a suggestion. A GUIDELINE, if you will."

Perry looked at me skeptically and began to hang the lights.

Before long, he got into the whole spirit of proper outdoor illumination. The real beauty of lighting your home with Christmas lights is the moment of flipping the switch a la Clark Griswold, then basking in the glow of maximum wattage while feeling the sense of pride from a job well done.

And knowing your lights are so much better than your neighbor's. That's the true spirit of Christmas.

But that moment isn't the same if it involves plugging in eleven different extension cords. That kind of industriousness and attention to detail ruins the whole thing.

So we climbed ladders and hung lights until FINALLY! the moment arrived. We plugged in those bad boys, flipped the switch, and they all came on.

For about two minutes.

And then we were cast into total darkness. Except not really, because it was only four in the afternoon and still light outside, but that takes away from the drama of the story, so pretend with me that it was pitch-black outside.

Apparently they were not kidding about the whole sixty-lights-maximum thing. We did the only thing that could be done. We went inside and ordered sushi.

And the next day found Perry shopping for eight new extension cords in order to revamp our lighting system. I also feel like he spent some of that time wishing he weren't married to a crazy person with dreams of Christmas illumination grandeur.

The reality is (if our first fifteen Christmases together are any indication), holiday seasons as a married couple aren't necessarily as romantic as what I'd envisioned when I was single. In fact, sometimes it's more stressful because you have to think about things like budgets and the fact that one person thinks buying the pink Pottery Barn retro kitchen for your two-year-old is excessive. (In hindsight, he was totally right.)

And it's hard to get carried away in the Christmas candlelight when one of you is crying because the Polly Pocket Mall Roller Coaster is a device of Satan meant to ruin Christmas forever with its vague assembly instructions, and the other one of you is snoring on the couch offering little to no moral support.

However, there is a different kind of sweetness. I'll never forget our first Christmas with Caroline, when she was only four months old. Santa brought pacifiers and some Gerber plastic bowls that year. It was a simple Christmas morning celebration, just Perry and me with our new baby girl and a fire in the fireplace. But I remember it so clearly because I finally had the family I'd always dreamed about all those years ago, when I was driven back and forth across town in an attempt to make it all seem even and fair, feeling like I didn't really belong anywhere.

I fed Caroline her rice cereal and just let it wash over me that God had given me a home. And a husband I loved dearly along with a little bundle wearing an elf hat and Santa Claus house shoes that were way too big for feet that never touched the floor anyway. There have been Christmas gifts before and since, but other than the gift of Jesus that started the whole thing, none have ever meant as much as that Christmas when I realized that God had fulfilled his promise in Psalm 68:6 to set the lonely in families.

Even when your Christmas tree leans a little to the left.

CHAPTER 23

# The Antelope in the Living Room

A COUPLE OF YEARS AGO Perry returned home after a weekend of hunting. I knew he was home because Caroline and I walked into the house to find a set of deer antlers recently belonging to a deer sitting on the island in our kitchen. Like an appetizer. Except they were attached to a skull.

Sadly, this doesn't even faze me anymore.

Because there was a time when Perry actually decided to boil an entire deer skull in a pot. On the stove. In our kitchen. Which is located inside our house.

I know. I don't understand either. But at least now I can say I have experienced something that is certainly akin to the smell of boiling feet in a stew made of garbage.

The fresh deer antlers caused me to remember and reflect on

a little incident that happened right before Thanksgiving a few years ago. There was a time I didn't believe I'd ever be able to tell this story because the subject matter was too sensitive and we may or may not have been on our way to divorce court over the entire incident. But enough time has passed that I can bring it up. What was it that Mark Twain once said? Humor is tragedy plus time. And also, sometimes if you don't laugh, then you will cry and remember how you grew up in a family that believed golf was an adventurous outdoor activity and you accidentally married a man who is like one long *Wild Kingdom* episode.

Gulley and I had spent the days leading up to Thanksgiving in Bryan with the kids. There was all manner of fun to be had, but there was also a fair share of drama. Especially toward the end of the trip, as the stress of the kids bickering back and forth and various people being put in time-out began to wear on both of us to a degree no amount of nerve medication could cure. I'd give you all the details, but I think I blacked out sometime Monday afternoon and didn't wake up until it was time to drive home on Wednesday.

By the time we were packing up the car, Caroline was in full meltdown mode and insisting that her life was very hard and full of sadness. Which isn't something you really have patience for after days spent at places like Santa's Wonderland and Aggie football games. I told her to get over it and GET IN THE CAR.

So we began our long ride home. With just a little bit of tension in the air. Of course, Gulley and I were totally fine, but we weren't sure about the kids.

We stopped for kolaches in Caldwell, and everyone seemed to regroup and find their happy place. We picked songs on the iPod, did a little car dancing, and talked about our Christmas wishes. Then, as we were on a vast, empty stretch of land known as Highway 21 between Bastrop and San Marcos, Will announced that his tummy hurt. And that announcement was followed shortly by a high-pitched scream and the unmistakable sound of throwing up.

There was nowhere to go. No gas station. No convenience store. No fire department where we could drop the kids off and see if they were too old to be placed for adoption.

I continued to try to break the land speed record to get us all home while Gulley turned around and did the best she could to clean everything up. Fortunately Jackson had received a large Aggie bucket at the football game that Saturday. I feel certain it wasn't intended to be used that way, but on the other hand, they were passing them out on a college campus, and odds are good ours wasn't the only one that got used as a yuck bucket.

We finally arrived home, definitely worse for the wear, and I had barely gotten our suitcases in the door when I informed Caroline we needed to go to the grocery store to get a few things for Thanksgiving. I knew it was going to be awful, especially because we were going to Central Market, which is the mecca for people who consider Thanksgiving a culinary Super Bowl. And I was just a stressed-out rookie dragging my child around, trying to figure out where they keep the pomegranate molasses while she complained about the cruelty of life, because Bobby Flay had filled my head with delusions of brussels-sprouts grandeur as all chefs on the Food Network are wont to do. This is why it's so much safer for me to watch *The Rachel Zoe Project* on Bravo instead. I know how to shop for a fur vest, but I have no idea how to find gourmet food ingredients. It's not my skill set.

When we finally walked in the door from Central Market, I was past the point of stressed and frazzled in that way all mothers get after a three-hour road trip and an hour in the grocery store listening to "Can we buy these cookies?" and "I didn't mean to knock over that display of canned pumpkin!" Frankly, I made stressed and frazzled look like a free trip to a resort in the Bahamas that specializes in thousand-thread-count sheets, down pillows, and fruity drinks with umbrellas in them.

So you can imagine my reaction when I walked through my back door and immediately spied an enormous antelope head hanging right next to my new front door that still had a piece of plywood where the beveled glass was supposed to be.

No.

Just no.

(There was a piece of plywood because we'd recently had a new front door installed. And by recently I mean six months before. And the door guy broke the glass in our window and still hadn't come back to repair it. Which was fine because the plywood looked super classy.)

I stood there in shock, trying to figure out what this thing was and why it was on my wall. It didn't help that it was hung in such a way that it appeared to have been running down the block when it suddenly crashed through the front of our house.

Perry walked in the house about that time and asked, "What do you think?"

At that time he had known me for sixteen years, which makes me think it must have been a rhetorical question. I looked at him and said, "I don't know what that is, but it looks a lot like a demonic goat. It can't stay there, and I need to know why you hate our house."

This wasn't an unprecedented situation. A few years earlier Perry attended a dinner for the National Rifle Association with a group from our church while on a mission trip.

Church group, mission trip, NRA.

We are a living, breathing, right-wing cliché.

He won a wooden sign at the dinner that featured a picture of the Liberty Bell and a quote that read, "Those who are willing to trade liberty for security deserve neither." He was so proud that he was the big winner, and if you could have seen this sign, you'd know I am playing fast and loose with the word *winner*. He decided to surprise me by hanging the sign in our kitchen, leaving me to wonder what had happened to my life. Did Charlton Heston move in?

Anyway, for months, MONTHS, I'd been engaging in conversations about how we were going to reduce the number of animal mounts in our living room and find a nice vintage map of Texas to hang on the wall. We were going to decorate like real grown-ups and not like college kids who think those jackrabbits with deer antlers (the jackalope) are hilarious conversation pieces. I was going to get a new lamp, hang some new pictures. I'd pretended to be domestic and made FAUX WINDOW TREATMENTS, for goodness' sake. Apparently all these decorating conversations had just been me talking to myself.

Because there was an enormous nilgai antelope hanging right by my front door.

It was a little tense at our house for the next few days. Like the kind of tense when you give your spouse polite smiles to hide the fact that you can't believe you're married to someone who has just desecrated your home with an animal that looks like a cross between a cow and a deformed goat.

But ultimately we attempted to find some middle ground because at the end of the day we love each other in spite of all our many and vast differences. He may not love or understand my fondness for expensive denim and shoes, and I don't really love or understand his fondness for things with horns or fur hanging on the walls, but marriage is about compromise.

That is why the scene by my Christmas tree that year involved a giant antelope head looming over our tree like it was its guardian and protector.

And also why every time I walked in the living room, I would proclaim, in a theatrical voice that would make James Earl Jones envious, "And, lo, an antelope of the Lord appeared, and the glory shone round about him."

And there was peace on earth and goodwill toward men and some serious internal strategy about how to make the back house the new permanent residence of the antelope.

# CHAPTER 24

# Coming Home

ONE DAY, when Caroline was four, she was riding around on her scooter in the kitchen (which I loved because it's fantastic for the hardwood floors), and she came to a stop right next to me.

She proudly announced, "Emily and I are in our very own club. You can't be in our club."

"Why not?"

"Because it's a club for four-year-olds, and you're not four."

And since I am very, very mature and have read many parenting books that are chock-full of parenting wisdom, I replied, "Well, that's fine. Daddy and I have our very own grown-up club."

Perry piped up from the living room, "That's right, it's called MARRIAGE, and there's no escape. It's like being part of a street gang. You have to die to get out."

He is hilarious.

But what really holds us together? What are the fragile threads that bind us together in spite of all our differences? Love, commitment, friendship. I remember when I was just a teenager, I read a quote from Ann Landers that said, "Love is friendship that has caught fire. It is quiet understanding, mutual confidence, sharing and forgiving. It is loyalty through good and bad times. It settles for less than perfection and makes allowances for human weaknesses."

Yes. It's all those things and the grace and mercy of God that bind two flawed people together until death. It's not always easy, and there are hard days or years when you don't know how you're going to make it through.

But then there are the times he walks through the door at the end of the day, and I catch my breath at how handsome he still is or we laugh hysterically at the same thing or we sit on the couch and watch old music videos by the Police while he shares that a girl dumped him in eighth grade for a boy who could play "Every Breath You Take" on the drums, and I know without a shadow of a doubt that there's no one I'd rather have by my side as I go through life. There is nothing fancy about a good, solid marriage, because at the end of the day it's just two people deeply committed to the same thing.

Caroline played T-ball when she was in kindergarten. We'd sit in the stands and cheer her on wildly every time she walked up to bat, and yell like idiots when she dog-piled with all the other kids in an attempt to field the ball.

One time, both of my parents were at one of Caroline's games.

My mom had flown in from out of town, and my dad and stepmom were also in attendance. My mom and dad have been divorced for more than thirty years, and both remarried, so the relationship is cordial enough, but something in me still regresses to an anxious ten-year-old girl every time we're all together in the same location.

As we all sat there and cheered for Caroline, this profound thought came to me, and I take those where I can get them. I realized that I would be devastated if the day came many years from that point when Perry and I were the grandparents sitting in the stands watching Caroline's kids play T-ball, or whatever, if we weren't doing it together.

It broke my heart. And I don't fault my parents. That's not what I'm trying to say. They did the best they could. Marriage is hard. I realize that at least 50 percent of all marriages don't make it for the long run. Those aren't really great odds. Honestly, with stats like that, it's a sheer wonder that so many people keep taking that optimistic walk down the aisle.

I just knew at that moment that I was going to do whatever I had to do to fight for my marriage to make it for the long haul. I once heard Beth Moore say that sometimes the best part of staying married is being glad later that you did. That's what that day at the T-ball fields symbolized for me.

It was the tangible awareness that it's not just a marriage between Perry and me. It's a union that's creating a legacy for Caroline. And Caroline's future children. In this world that sometimes treats marriage like it's a disposable commodity we can throw away when it no longer seems to serve our purposes, a world that whispers to us that the grass might be greener on the other side, that's something worth keeping in mind before you throw the whole thing out. One of the prayers I continually pray for our family comes from Deuteronomy 30:6—that the Lord would circumcise our hearts and the hearts of our descendants so that we will love God with all our hearts and with all our souls. That's the legacy I want to leave. That's the legacy that's worth working through the hard times to leave for our daughter.

The thing I share with all my girlfriends as we sit and drink margaritas and eat queso once a month is that in spite of the fact that we're all married to different men with different personalities, not one of us is married to the perfect man. One is stingy with the budget. One can't remember to pick up his dirty clothes. One doesn't think gifts are important for Mother's Day.

And it's a reminder that Mr. Right isn't out there. There's just Mr. Right-for-You. He may look totally different from what's right for your best friend. Your marriage is a unique being with as much of its own DNA as you and your husband bring to the table.

I remember early on in our marriage, Perry and I were friends with a couple who did everything together, even grocery shopping. I thought something was wrong with us because we had so many separate interests. But that's just who we are. It's not wrong; it's different.

A while back, I was away on a trip and left Perry at home with Caroline. Which meant that he was also in charge of her wardrobe.

This is not a task for the faint of heart.

I tried to help him by laying out various acceptable outfits because I knew it would only be a matter of time before she tried to convince him that she could wear her gymnastics leotard with her platform disco shoes to school. And maybe a tiara for that extra something special.

He did car-pool pickup. He coordinated playdates. He came up with things they could eat for dinner.

Rumor has it they even ordered sushi one night.

And when I got home late Thursday night, he had flowers and dinner waiting for me. These were all things I never could have imagined the day I stood at the altar with him. They are the little gifts that only come as you live real life together.

Our life over the last several years has turned into an unexpected adventure. We've made some scary decisions that have sometimes felt like we were holding hands and jumping off a cliff.

Perry worked in ministry for the majority of our marriage. During that time, I worked in a job I wasn't necessarily crazy about but knew was God's financial provision for us. My income allowed him to be in full-time ministry, which nobody really gets into for the sweet cash flow.

Eventually Perry began to feel like it was time for him to move on from his work with Campus Life and transition full time into the landscape business. Less than a month later, I resigned from my sales job to pursue writing as an actual career.

We watched our roles switch.

A while back, someone asked him if he was interested in getting back into ministry, and he said, "It's Melanie's turn. She supported me all those years, and now I want to support her as she goes where God leads."

And to say that he has is such an understatement.

Over the course of a marriage, life doesn't always turn out the way you envisioned. There are twists and turns, ups and downs, good and bad. Perry and I aren't the same two crazy, skinny kids who vowed to love and cherish each other until death do us part more than fifteen years ago.

Those two fools had no idea all that life would throw our way, and if someone had told us, we never would have believed we'd be able to survive it all.

What I'm trying to say is that we have been blessed. I've been blessed with a man who can drive me crazy with his love of hunting shows, UFC, and leaving half a paper towel sitting on the kitchen counter, but who supports me, loves me, and makes me feel cherished.

It's more than I could have asked for or imagined. And, for better or for worse, Perry falls into the category of my life labeled God's Outrageous Blessings. He is my Ephesians 3:20 in the flesh.

When I look in his eyes, I don't see perfection. I don't see a love story that would necessarily be something people would watch on a big screen and dream about. I see someone who will fight for me and protect me and love me in spite of all the ways I am still a wreck. I see home.

Wherever he is.

That's my home.

# Acknowledgments

WHEN I REALIZED I was actually going to write a second book, I had to take several deep breaths into a paper bag and look to the following people to preserve my sanity.

To my sweet Caroline: When you tell me that you want to grow up and write books just like your mom, it makes all the hard work worth it. God has given you so many gifts, and there is nothing you can't do. I love you so much it hurts.

To Perry: I'd marry you all over again. And it's because you don't take yourself too seriously that I was able to tell all these stories. Thank you for that. I love you.

To Dad and Cher: Thanks for all the times you picked up Caroline from school and kept her entertained and well fed at various restaurants while I worked on the book. You have encouraged me and loved me and shown me what a good marriage looks like. Love you both.

To Amy: The best thing about a sister is that you've lived through every bit of this with me. Love you.

To my mother-in-law, Sallie: You did a remarkable job raising the man who makes me laugh every day. Thank you for your faithfulness and prayers for him over the years.

To Gulley: My marriage wouldn't be nearly as strong if you weren't around to listen to all the things Perry doesn't want to hear about.

Thanks for always loving me, defending me, and reading my terrible first drafts. We've been loving each other a long time, and I'm so grateful.

To Sophie: I can't imagine doing any of this if I didn't have you to always encourage me. We thought we met because we had the same throw pillows on our couches and each of us had an only child, but God had so much more in store for our friendship. I'm so thankful for you.

To Debbi: Thanks for being my barometer of the funny. And for helping me figure out how to make a joke and be politically correct at the same time. I'm so glad you decided to become my head of unofficial marketing and public relations.

To Bill Jensen: None of this ever would have happened without your encouragement, enthusiasm, and advice. Thanks for always listening and advising and talking football with me.

To Stephanie Rische: What a gift you are! I cannot even imagine how much time you've had to spend Googling all my absurd cultural references. You are the best editor a girl could want.

To Lisa Jackson, Carol Traver, and the rest of the Tyndale team: You all took a chance letting me write this second book before my first one ever came out. Thanks for that. And thank you for indulging me in discussions about what constitutes an antelope versus a deer. I am eternally grateful for Tyndale and the support you have given me. Not to mention that my life is significantly richer thanks to Carol's e-mails that never fail to make me laugh out loud.

To my blog readers: Y'all are the gift that keeps giving. Thanks for all the love, support, prayers, and hilarious comments over the last seven years.

And, most of all, to God: Your extravagant grace and mercy are the glue that holds my life together. I'll never get over your love for me.

you up again." I heard the car door open, and Mom get in. I had the feeling we were about to be in big trouble for fighting again. Then I got a great idea. If I could sit up fast enough, Mom might not even realize that anything had happened. In fact, if I could get my seat belt on and let her notice that Robbie wasn't wearing his, he'd get in trouble, and I wouldn't. It was a great plan. Mom was nuts about safety. "Mom . . ." I started to say as I latched my seat belt. Then I looked at the figure in the front seat. It wasn't my mother; in fact, it wasn't even a woman! The car sped from the gas station and headed down a side street. I tried to speak, but nothing came out. Then finally, I yelped in surprise, "Hey! Who are you, and how come you're driving our car?"

I saw a pair of piercing brown eyes glare into the rear-view mirror, and then the car swerved over to the side of the road and stopped. At that moment Robbie triumphantly popped up from the backseat. "See, Scott, you can't keep me down, and if you want your dumb old badge which I didn't . . ."

Robbie stopped in mid-sentence. His face went white, and his mouth opened, but no sound came out because in the front seat, he saw a man, and in that man's hand was a gun, and that gun was pointed right at my face.

## TWO

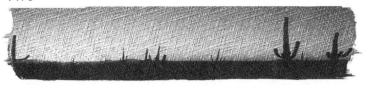

s that real?" Robbie's voice squeaked. "Who are you?"

"Shut up," the man said. His voice was real flat, as if he didn't care about anything or anyone.

I forced myself to move my eyes from the gun long enough to look at the man who was holding it. He had lots of greasy black hair that seemed to spring out from his head and he had thick, black, bushy eyebrows. His brown eyes were only slits, and they jumped angrily from Robbie to me. When they glared at me, I quickly looked away. The man swore softly and said, mostly to himself, "Just when I wonder what else could go wrong, I jack a car with kids in it."

My voice sounded scratchy. "We, uh, we could just get out, sir, and then this car wouldn't have any kids in it."

The man ignored me and looked at Robbie commandingly. "You, with the baseball hat, get up here in front next to me."

Still staring at the gun, I took a deep breath. "He's just a little kid. Leave him alone, and I'll climb up front."

The man leaned his face close to mine. I could smell alcohol on his breath. "I told you both—shut up."

The man got out of the car and opened Mom's packages in the back. He grabbed the nightgown that we had bought for Aunt Susan, made me put my hands behind my back, and wound the nightgown into a rope to tie my hands. He took a dress my mom had bought and wound it into another rope to tie my feet. Then he shoved me against the backseat and fastened a seat belt around me. When the guy had finished with me, I couldn't move at all. As he tied me up, he never said a word to me, and that made him even scarier. I couldn't help but notice the ugly, big scar running all the way down his left arm.

Somehow, as he was tying me up, he had managed to keep the gun pointed at Robbie's head. Then he barked at him, "In the front, now, right next to me. Just move my packages by the door. Do it!" he barked. "And be real careful with my stuff."

I saw Robbie's legs shake as he began to climb over the seat. "I . . . I'm coming right away."

He strapped a seat belt around Robbie, took the other seat belt and looped it around Robbie's neck. "You move— your neck could snap, okay?" The man didn't wait for an answer. He pulled a metal chain from his jeans pocket and flipped open a brown case to look at a watch. "I've already wasted too much time." Then he jumped into the front seat himself, gunned the motor, and took off for the freeway.

The car sped north on Scottsdale Road heading away

from Phoenix toward the desert. As cars passed in the other lane, I thought about trying to yell for help. But I couldn't be sure that the other drivers would hear or even if they did, that they would do anything. Besides, the gun the kidnapper had pressed to Robbie's neck kept me from trying it.

"Kidnapper!" I said softly to myself. There was an awful thud in my stomach. Everything had happened so fast that I didn't have a chance to think about how bad the situation could be. It was hard to believe this was real. I mean, Robbie and I had played cops and robbers hundreds of times, and we'd always fight because I'd say that I'd killed him so he should be dead. Then he'd shout that I'd missed him. But this was so weird. A part of me kept almost waiting for the guy to say that this was a game too, but the dry feeling in my mouth and the knots cutting into my arms and legs reminded me of just how real it all was.

It always seemed so easy on TV. Tons of times, I'd watched people get kidnapped, and they'd all been saved before the final commercial. Of course, they were the stars, and they had to live for the next show. We certainly weren't TV stars; we were just two kids. We didn't have any super powers; we didn't have any secret weapons.

The car hit a pothole, and the kidnapper grunted. I held my breath as the car's bounce made the gun shove further into Robbie's neck. This was even worse than anything I'd dreamed in my worst nightmare.

*It'll be okay,* I told myself. *By now, Mom has called every police agency there is. Someone will recognize this car any minute, and then the police will save us.*

I said this to myself over and over again until I felt a little better. I looked up to see if I could see any helicopters flying overhead, but there didn't seem to be any yet. I wished I could talk to Robbie. All the times I'd told him I never wanted to speak to him again, and now, I would have given anything to talk this over with him, but we couldn't very well talk about how to get free with the kidnapper right there listening.

When I looked out the window again, I saw another station wagon pass us. It was the identical cream color, with a beige interior just like ours. I bit my lip as I thought about how many times we had accidentally walked to the wrong car in a parking lot because so many people in Phoenix had our same kind of car. How could the police ever know which one was ours unless they could get so close they could see our license plate?

The man swerved into the other lane, and his packages hit the passenger floor. I wondered what was in them. Maybe he had more guns. Maybe he had a bomb. I tried hard to keep from totally panicking. Poor Robbie. It must be even worse sitting right next to the guy with a gun at your neck. I thought about saying something to Robbie, but I was afraid it might make the guy use the gun, and besides, what could I say that would make things any better?

I wished my hands were free. Then maybe I could signal one of the passing cars without the kidnapper seeing. I had to lean forward a little to keep my back from jamming into my tied hands, and I was beginning to feel sharp pain from the tightness of the scarf and the position in which I had to sit. I tried to move my hands, but they were tied so tightly that I could not budge them. A creeping numbness and a funny tingling began to move up my arms.

"Stop!" I wanted to yell at the other cars on the road. "How can you just drive on having a normal day when my brother and me are being kidnapped!" But of course, I didn't really yell anything, and I couldn't move my hands to make signals. *Think!* I told myself. *There must be something I can do.*

I stared at the rearview mirror to see if the kidnapper was watching me, but he wasn't, so I turned my face toward the window and silently mouthed "Help us!" to a car that passed. It sped on. I tried with each passing car to catch someone's attention, but no one noticed until, at last, a boy about my age in a blue sedan started staring at us.

The boy watched me carefully. His car was in the lane next to us, and it stayed even with us. I could tell by the way he stared that he knew something was wrong. My heart pounded when I saw him poke his mother and say something. Carefully, I mouthed the words, "Help! Kidnapped!" even more slowly. The boy watched intently. This family was going to help us! I had to make sure they understood. "Help, we're being kidnapped!" I mouthed again silently. My lips hurt from making each word so clearly. "Call the police," I carefully mouthed.

Suddenly, the boy nodded, smiled at me, then put his hands in his ears, stuck out his tongue, and made a funny face. He waved as his family's blue sedan turned off onto Dynamite Road. He thought it was all just a game.

I felt tears sting my eyes. No one was going to pay any attention to us. My arms felt like needles were shooting through them. I wished I could get loose. I began to move around. "Don't do that," came a command from the front seat, and the kidnapper pressed the gun into Robbie's neck.

"Okay, I won't move again; I promise . . . really. You don't have to stick that—that thing into my brother's neck so hard," I pleaded.

"You shut up. I'll decide where I keep my gun," said the kidnapper's cold voice.

"Okay, I'm sorry," I gulped, afraid to say more. Some big brother I had turned out to be. No wonder Robbie never listened to me about anything. I was always telling him I was almost three years older and knew much more, but what had I done to help either one of us get out of this mess?

Just then, the kidnapper made a sharp turn off the pavement and onto a dirt path in the desert. He slowed way down, but the car still jounced and bumped along the disappearing road.

*How can this nightmare just keep getting worse?* I

wondered as all the signs of the city disappeared, replaced by only desert rock, cracked earth, and cactus. But it did. We were going farther and farther away from any possibility of help.

The kidnapper seemed to know where he was going, but I didn't understand how because everything around us looked the same. From Boy Scouts I knew that it was dangerous to be out in the summer afternoon desert without lots of water, and I knew we didn't have that. Part of me said it was crazy to even think about enough water when there was some psychopath with a gun in the front seat, but I did. The car banged over a rock. My brother was so silent. He hadn't moved a muscle. "Robbie, you doin' okay?" I said softly.

"Shut up!" The man growled.

"What—what are you going to do with us?" Robbie's voice was real scratchy.

I prayed that the kidnapper would say that he was going to let us go, but he said nothing at all. The silence in the car suggested lots of terrible possibilities. The man moved his hand on the steering wheel. I don't know how I missed seeing it earlier. Maybe my eyes were too scared, but right then my stomach was doing flip flops as I stared at the big red snake tattooed on his right hand, and the way he moved his hand on the wheel, it was almost as if the snake was driving.

Then, in the quiet of the desert, I heard a noise in the distance grow louder, and I saw a gold Jeep come roaring toward us. *Oh, please,* I prayed. *Let this be some kind of a desert ranger.* The Jeep stopped in front of us, and a man with stringy, long brown hair and a big earring in one ear swaggered toward us. He was bigger than the kidnapper, and he didn't look like help for us. As he pulled open the door to the station wagon, I saw that he, too, had a big black gun.

"Hey, Slam," our kidnapper called.

Slam complained, "It sure took you long enough to get here." Then he noticed us. "What the—!" he yelled.

"Long story. Bad luck," the kidnapper replied, getting out of the car.

"Yours or theirs?" Slam asked.

"Both, I guess." There was a flat, dead tone in the guy's voice that terrified me. The two men moved away from the car a little, but kept their guns on us as they talked. Although I could only hear little pieces of their conversation, I caught some words about offing a guy, stealing money, and needing a car, and I thought I heard something about heroin as they moved back toward us.

Slam cocked his gun. "You want to do one, or should I kill 'em both?" He asked the question like it was no big deal.

"Doesn't much matter to me who kills them," our kidnapper said. "Let's load this stuff into the Jeep first."

## THREE

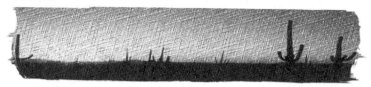

These guys were going to kill us, and we couldn't do a thing to stop them. Even if I could get loose and get Robbie out of the car, the desert was flat and wide open. Picking us off would be easy. Everything started to feel as if it were moving in slow motion. My mouth felt loaded with cotton, and my throat could barely swallow. I was paralyzed, and I was sure Robbie must be too.

Paying no attention to our frozen fear, the two men went to the back of the the Jeep with the packages the kidnapper had in our station wagon. Slam's voice rose, "You didn't bring the extra ammo? Of all the stupid—!"

"I told you. The car broke down. I could only carry the smack. Everything else stayed." The kidnapper's voice got soft and real scary. "Is that a problem?"

Slam spit on the ground, but he didn't argue. "Well then, we're not wasting what we got on them." He gestured his gun toward us.

Our kidnapper shrugged. "I don't care either way."

14

Slam started the Jeep; our kidnapper jumped in, and they roared off into the desert without a backward glance.

Almost like a robot who hadn't been programmed to move, I watched the cloud of dust that the Jeep made until it was just a speck in the distance. My throat felt as if it had a huge lump of something blocking it, but I choked out, "Robbie, you okay?"

"I think so, are you?" Robbie whispered back, still too frightened to turn around.

"They're gone!" My voice was starting to come back. I sobbed, "They're really gone. They're not going to kill us. We're free! Robbie, you hear me?"

"Free?" Robbie half-whispered. "Free!" he said loudly in joy. "We're not gonna die!"

"Robbie, can you get out of the front and untie me? He's got these things so tight, I don't have any feeling in my arms."

"Okay." Robbie moved almost as if in a trance. He undid the seat belt that had been slung around his neck, unfastened the one that had strapped him in, and opened his door. He got out of the car shaking his head and rubbing his eyes almost as if he had just awakened from some bad dream. Finally, he opened my car door and began to tug at my bindings. As I watched him work, I wondered how it could be that my ropes had been only clothes from a shopping trip an hour earlier. Somehow, it seemed as if that shopping trip must have been a whole lifetime ago.

"Sorry, I'm really trying. I can't get 'em loose. He tied

everything so tight," Robbie said, and I could see the sweat on his forehead. He tugged and pulled. "There! I got it!" he yelled.

Finally, I was free. My arms felt like two big, dead trees at my sides. I forced myself to shake my hands, and then I forced my hands to rub my arms and legs. Feeling began to return to them, and I groaned loudly. It felt the same as when I'd cracked my elbow on something, only this wasn't just my elbow; it was both of my arms and my legs. Little needles of pain shot up and down them. "Ohhhh," I moaned.

"Hey, you gonna be okay? What can I do?" Robbie shouted.

I forced myself to keep moving and stretching, and finally, the pain went away. Looking at my hands, I opened and closed my fists. Everything still worked! It was a miracle. I looked at Robbie and grinned. "I'm okay and we're alive and we're free. You can't keep the Ratliffe brothers down!"

The freckles on Robbie's nose stood out, and his face was real white. "Wow, that was the most . . . the most . . ." Robbie paused as if he didn't know words to describe exactly what it was. "That guy, he was really the worst . . . I mean when he had that gun in my neck . . ." He paused again. "Geez, am I ever glad he's gone. I hope I never see anyone like him again." Then he wrinkled up his nose. "Boy, wait until I tell Marc, and Josh, and Ricky. Ricky thinks he's so tough. He never had to face any kidnapper!"

All of a sudden, his eyes lit up. "Hey, you know what I think?" Without waiting for me to say anything, he blurted, "I bet we're gonna be on TV. I bet we're gonna be famous. I get dibs to be on TV first and tell all about what happened to us."

We were both wound up with the amazement of still being alive and being free. I jumped right in: "Nah, I'll get to be the one on TV. Your red hair will be too bright for the cameras. The TV people will all want to talk to me, but don't worry, I'll tell 'em your name."

It felt so good to be talking about normal stuff like TV and to be arguing with Robbie! He punched me lightly on the arm, whooped, and ran around the car. I knew just how he felt. Being alive at this moment was better than having no homework for a whole school year, better than hitting a home run with bases loaded. Robbie laughed and so did I. Robbie tossed his baseball hat into the air and whooped! "Wow, for a little while, I really did think those guys were gonna—"

"Yeah, I really thought—," I interrupted and then stopped myself. Robbie was still just a little kid. There was no point in scaring him with what I thought was going to happen. Besides, everything was okay now.

We grinned at each other and continued talking about the guy and his gun. Robbie was going a mile a minute, and after a few sentences, I knew he didn't even care if I listened; he just had to talk. It was fine with me. I was thinking my own thoughts. I had never even really considered what it might be like for me to die. It had just seemed like something that would happen someday when I was real old. Suddenly, I felt Robbie pulling on my shirt. "Hey, Scott, I said what do you think?"

"About what?"

"About getting out of here. It's really hot."

"Right," I said. "But before we just take off, maybe we better have some kind of plan."

"It'll be easy," Robbie said. "The kidnapper drove us into the desert; we'll just drive ourselves out. I saw a mountain to our right as we turned onto the desert road, so if we just turn the car around and keep the mountain to our left, we should be just fine." Robbie grinned a look that said, *See? Your nine-year-old brother is smarter than you thought.*

"Uh, jerk-brain, look around real good."

Robbie squinted into the distance. Rock and stone mountains seemed to go in every direction. Robbie's face grew beet red, and he didn't say anything else. Then I realized he wasn't red just because I'd shown him how silly his brilliant plan was. I was probably almost as red. We had been standing out there celebrating our luck in being alive for at least fifteen minutes, and the desert sun had been pounding into us. It had to be at least 120 or 130 degrees, and suddenly, the incredible happiness of being free was pricked by the fact that we were sort of lost in a burning hot place without any help except each other.

I stared at the ground, and then I had an idea. "How

about this. We'll follow the tracks the car made coming out into the desert until we get back out. I'll drive, and you can be my scout. I'll go real slowly, and you'll keep your eyes peeled on the road for tracks."

Sweat was pouring off Robbie's face, and without waiting for his reaction to my plan, I climbed into the driver's seat. Robbie took the passenger's front seat. "Uh-oh. I don't see any keys." That pit in my stomach was starting again. I wondered if they had taken the keys with them. No keys—no transportation. No transportation—well, I didn't want to even think about that. There was no way we could walk out of the desert, and it was much too hot just to hang around.

Suddenly, Robbie dug down behind the seat next to me, and he emerged smiling and holding Mom's keys. "I saw the guy throw them down here. Pretty good memory, huh?" It seemed to me that Robbie figured all the danger was over now that the kidnappers were gone, and that getting back home was some kind of a game. I wished I could think of it that way. "Hey, Scott," he asked, "have you ever driven a car before?"

"Uhh, sure." I lied with what I hoped seemed like confidence. There was no point to telling Robbie that I had only driven once, and that was when our uncle had let me steer. I hadn't been able to reach the pedals, so I wasn't sure whether it really counted as driving, but it would have to do. Actually, I could barely reach the pedals now and still see over the dash.

I put the key in the ignition just as I had watched

Mom do so many times, and then I put my foot on the gas. I turned the key, pressed on the pedal and hoped for the best. The motor raced; I felt a thrill, and we moved—absolutely nowhere.

Robbie looked disgusted. "I think you have to take the gearshifter thing off the P."

"Right," I said, "I knew that. I was just testing the power."

"Why?"

I didn't answer. Instead, sucking in a deep breath and hoping for the best, I moved the gearshift to D and we lurched forward. "Wow," I said almost to myself. "I'm driving. I'm really driving a car!" My heart was pounding so hard, I was almost sure even Robbie could hear it.

"Yeah," said Robbie. "But you're going the wrong direction."

I knew that. I really did. I just needed to get the feel of driving. This definitely wasn't like all the times Robbie and I had sat behind the wheel and pretended to drive. Real driving felt much different. It was scary, and I wished Robbie would just appreciate that we were moving without bumping into things. It was amazing to think that I was actually making this car head in a straight line.

Before I was at all ready to think about how to turn, Robbie stared at me and asked, "Well, are you sure you can turn this car around? If you can't, well, I could try." There was a note of impatience in his voice.

I took a deep breath. "'Course I'm sure I can turn the

car around. I just haven't driven Mom's car before, and I wanted to get used to it. Now quit worrying and just let your big brother take care of things."

It sounded good, but I knew that Robbie was right about getting turned around. I had to get us going in the right direction, or there was no point to going at all.

It was so hot that I could see wavy lines in the air. I just wished I had some idea how much you had to turn a wheel to make it move the car around. Robbie broke into my thoughts. "Okay, here's a great spot. It's flat, wide, and there's no cactus on either side. Now come on, turn the car around, so we can get going and put on the air. How can we ever get on TV and be famous if we keep going in the wrong direction?"

I began turning the wheel. The car bumped its way around the dirt path until finally the station wagon was facing the opposite way. My heart was pounding, and I had to wipe my sweaty hands on my shirt to keep them from sliding on the wheel, but we were headed home!

I turned the air conditioning on, and the car began to blow cool air. For the first time in hours, I began to feel almost normal. We would just follow this path until we got back to the freeway. I licked my lips. It had been a long time since I'd had anything to drink. I realized that the 44-ounce gulpers were still in the car somewhere, but I wasn't taking my hands off the wheel to get one, and I wasn't letting Robbie take his eyes off the path, either. I licked my lips again. The gulpers would have to wait.

The ride seemed to be getting rougher. The steering wheel was hard to hold onto as we bounced over each rock, but at least we were still moving. I just hoped we wouldn't hit anything sharp that would cause the tire to go flat. But I had to think positive. After all, we had made it all the way out here without a flat, why not all the way back?

I stared out the window, and it looked to me as if there were tracks on a dirt path over to the left. Yet Robbie was still insisting that we continue going right. I took my eyes off the road straight ahead, and I squinted to see where the tire tracks went toward the left.

"Yikes!" Robbie screamed.

Heart pounding, I rammed my foot on the brake. The car lurched, stopped, and died. "What's with you?" I started to say, and then I noticed that the front bumper of the car was almost touching the base of a large saguaro cactus.

I got out of the car to see if I'd hurt anything, and once I was in front of the car, I could see that the tracks off to the left were more like motorcycle tracks. Robbie saw me staring. "Hey, why do you always think I'm such a baby? I was following the right tracks."

"Sorry," I said.

"You're such a . . . " Robbie looked at me. I was fighting back tears, and I think he knew it. This was his chance to get me good, but I saw Robbie bite his lip. He just looked at me for a minute, then said, "Hey, it's okay.

You're doing a good job. Driving's probably tough."

I smiled. "Yeah, well you're a good navigator, and together, we're gonna get out of here." There was a kind of awkward silence. It was weird being nice to each other. It didn't happen very often. We climbed in the car, and I started it again. It was a little easier this time because at least I had already driven the car now, but when I went to back up, the car lurched, and I knew I hadn't quite figured out all the parts to this driving thing yet.

I started to hear scraping noises as we went forward, and as the car bumped and bounced along, I wondered how much we were tearing up the bottom of it. *Please,* I said silently, *don't let this car fall apart! Keep going.*

Robbie's voice started sounding tired as he continued calling, "More to the left here; move toward that path on the right." My hands hurt from holding onto the steering wheel so tightly. The game of driving had quit being fun after the first few minutes. There was just too much to worry about. Suddenly, it seemed that we were slowing down. I hoped that it was just that the road was rougher here, and I pushed the gas pedal harder, but instead of picking up speed, we slowly rolled to a stop.

"I said to go to the right," Robbie said and then warily asked, "Why are we stopping here?"

"I don't know." I took my aching hands away from the steering wheel and tried to think. Maybe I could raise the hood the way the mechanic did at the garage, but then what? What did I know about how the inside of an engine was supposed to work or what to do if it didn't?

Robbie got out of the car and looked at it. "The tires don't look busted. Maybe you should just try starting it again."

I put my hand toward the ignition, and as I did, my eye caught the instrument panel. Suddenly, I remembered  where we had been when this whole mess had started. "Robbie," I said, feeling about a million years old. "I know what's wrong." I tried to keep the fear out of my voice as I thought about being in the middle of nowhere with no help possible. "We just ran out of gas."

"Out of gas? No! Try again. We just can't be out of gas." I looked at Robbie, and under the red baseball cap, I saw him biting his lip and trying not to cry. I knew just how he felt. I didn't see how the car would start, but I could try it once more for Robbie's sake—and for my own.

Suddenly, Robbie reached across me and pulled the key from the ignition. "Hey, what are you doing?"

Almost frantically, he began rubbing the key against his T-shirt. "Something just got on the key, and if we clean if off, the car will start again. Don't you think?" Without waiting for answers, Robbie stuck the key back in the ignition.

I pressed my foot hard on the gas, and then I closed my eyes, took a deep breath, and turned the key. The motor chugged and died. I looked at the empty gas gauge and then I tried again and again. The car didn't move; it wasn't going to move. I put my arms across the steering wheel and buried my head in them. It all made sense, I thought to myself. Mom hadn't had a chance to get gas when the kidnapper had taken the car. He'd used up all that there was.

I felt all used up too. My head was too hot and too tired to think anymore. First, I'd tried so hard to think about how to keep Robbie and me from getting killed by the kidnappers; then I'd had to think about how to get out of the desert, and then how to drive a car. The hot sun poured into the car, and I just wanted to let myself go to sleep and not have to think anymore.

In the quiet, I could hear Robbie's muffled sobs. They forced me to pick up my head, and I reached out to touch his shoulder. "Hey, Rob, it's going to be okay."

"Okay?" Robbie didn't even try to stop crying. "How can you say it's going to be okay, when everything is so awful."

He was right. No wonder the kidnappers had been so willing to just leave us there. I didn't really see any way that anything was ever going to be okay again for us, but there was no point to admitting that and scaring Robbie even more. "Listen," I said, and I hoped my words would somehow come true, "it's going to be okay because we'll just spend the night here, and by tomorrow morning, a search party will find us."

"Spend the night here? No way!" Robbie's eyes got big.

He looked almost like something had snapped inside him. "I've had it! I'm not staying out here in the desert with the snakes and — and the other stuff that comes out at night, and you can't make me." His voice was coming in gulps. "And . . . and if this dumb car won't go, I'm—I'm just going to walk home!"

o!" I shouted. I knew from the little camping I'd done that we probably didn't have much chance out here, but if we started walking at night, we wouldn't have any chance at all.

Robbie opened the car door. "I'm going," he said stubbornly. "I'm just going to follow these tire tracks until I get back to the highway, and once I'm there, someone will give me a ride home."

"But we can't—"

Robbie cut me off. "Stop it. Stop telling me what I can't do. You just don't want me to have a good idea. You just don't want me to be the one who saved us." Robbie got out of the car and started to walk. I knew it would be pitch black, and he would be completely lost if I let him go, so I forced myself out of the car after him.

"Stop!" I called. "You can go after we talk, but at least listen!"

Robbie began to run from the car. "No, I'm not listening again!"

I watched him go a few feet and then took off after him. "Robbie, come on, cut it out," I called, but that only seemed to spur him on. It was so hot I could hardly breathe. "Robbie, stop. I won't come after you, I promise. Just stop where you are and listen to me, then if you want to go, you can." I was shouting at him.

He stopped running. "Okay," he shouted back, "but you stay right there. Tell me from where you are."

I took a deep breath and put my hands to my mouth to make my voice louder. Then I shouted, "Look at your watch. It's already six o'clock. How could we get out of here before it gets dark? We don't even have a flashlight. We'd be miles from the car, and all alone with whatever animals are out here. If you just wait until morning, we'll start walking out as soon as it gets light." My words tumbled out. "In the morning we'll have plenty of light, and it won't even be so hot yet. What do you think? You want to run into some animal when it's totally dark, and you can't even see what it is?"

For a second there was silence. At least Robbie hadn't turned to keep walking away. Then I saw him start back toward me. "You're right," Robbie mumbled, coming back to the car. "Guess I just didn't want to stay out here much. Sorry I yelled."

"Forget it." I licked my parched lips. "I'm real thirsty; let's find the gulpers."

We got back in the car, and Robbie dove under the seat and pulled all four gulpers out one by one. He tried to smile. "Good thing they came in these squeeze containers

28

with caps. They're almost still full. I just wish they were still cold."

"Yeah, good thing Mom wanted to support literacy! At least we have them." I was trying hard to remember what I had learned in Scouts about desert survival. I thought they had said that a person needed about a gallon of liquid a day to survive. Well, we had that now, but what if our rescue took longer?

"Boy this feels good," Robbie said, taking a drink.

I put the gulper to my mouth and took a swig of the root beer. It burned all the way down my throat, but even though it was warm and sticky-sweet, I'd never tasted anything better. I think I could have drunk the whole thing, but I made myself stop, and I pulled the other container from Robbie, telling him that we had to make it last.

Robbie looked at me, and he looked really weird. "Scott, if I ask you something, do you promise just to tell and not to laugh?"

I smiled. I don't know why. "Okay."

"Never mind."

"Come on, I promise," I said.

"Uh, well, uh . . ." Robbie moved around on the seat. "Uhhhh . . . I was just wondering if pee makes snakes come out in the desert?"

In spite of everything, I almost started to laugh, and then I realized that Robbie was serious. To tell the truth, I didn't remember any book saying anything about the subject, but I lied. "You know, there was something in my book. It said that you could pee in the desert . . ." Robbie was hanging on my every word intently, and at some other time, in some other place, this would have been a great trick to play on him, but in this awful place, I just wanted to make him feel better. "You could pee in the desert, and it didn't make any animals come at all."

Robbie looked at me. "You sure?"

"Positive!" I said.

Robbie smiled and got out of the car. "I'll be right back." He took off. It was weird. I'd had to go so bad while I'd been tied up in the car. I guess it was just fear. Anyway, the urge was gone now. I looked at the sun. As hot as it was, it was also clear that the sun had begun to set. I had camped out with the Scouts a couple of times, but Robbie had never slept outside. He had no idea how dark it could get, or what strange sounds the night made. I hoped Robbie wouldn't be too scared. Who was I kidding—I hoped *I* wouldn't be too scared! I wished with all my heart that some rescuers would magically appear and we could be back home.

My thoughts were interrupted by Robbie returning. "Boy, do I feel better. Now I'm hungry. I don't guess we've got much for dinner except the gulpers, huh?" Then his face lit up. "Hey, what about the Lifesavers Mom took away from us because we were fighting over who got the red ones?"

I took a package of them out of the glove compartment. "Good thing we fought, huh?"

I opened the roll, and Robbie and I stared at the Lifesavers, trying to figure out how to make them last. We decided, since they were our least favorite, to eat all the green and orange ones for dinner and put the rest away to have something good for the next morning. It was sort of funny. Candy and soda pop had always sounded like a great dinner, but now that we had them, they didn't make such a super meal. At least the candy and drink helped my throat, which no longer felt so dry that I couldn't swallow. I sucked the final piece of my last Lifesaver and leaned my head back against the seat. Robbie and I sat in silence. I looked at my watch. Ten minutes passed, and it felt like it must have been ten hours.

It was going to be a long night just sitting in that car. But then I thought about the kidnappers and remembered that we could have already been dead, so I told myself that it wasn't really so awful to sit there for one night. Still, it was so very quiet. I looked at Robbie, and saw him staring out the window. He had his arms on the door, and his face in his hands. He looked pretty down. "Want to play Twenty Questions?"

"Nah, maybe later," he said dejectedly.

Suddenly I got an idea. Why hadn't I thought of it before? This would be great! "Hey, watch this. A little music and a little cool air."

"What are you—," Robbie started to say. Then I turned on the motor, snapped on the radio, and flipped on the air conditioning.

"Wow! How'd you ever get that to work?" I thought Robbie looked impressed, and I was pretty impressed with myself, too. Music immediately filled the car, but

only warm air blew from the vents. "The music is great. It makes it seem, I don't know, not so empty, but geez, it's still sure hot in here. Why doesn't the air blow cool?"

I wasn't really sure. I reasoned that just because the car was out of gas didn't mean that the battery wouldn't work at least for a while, and if the battery worked, so did the radio. "I guess the battery makes the radio run and air come out, but you need gas for the air to get cool. At least it will get cooler after the sun goes down."

"Yeah." Robbie took off his hat for a minute. Sweat had made his hair stick to his head. "Let's change the station." Robbie punched a silver button on the radio. The music ended, and an announcer said, "Here are the evening's headlines. Today, in Phoenix, two young boys were kidnapped."

"Hey, that's us!" Robbie cried.

"Shhh, I want to hear."

The announcer's voice continued, "The boys' mother, Mrs. Janet Ratliffe, had just stopped for gas at the newly opened Mini-Mart on 32nd Street when a person or persons unknown stole her car. At this time, police have no suspects, nor do they know whether the purpose was to steal the car or the children."

"It was the car," Robbie broke in; "and we know all about the suspects."

"Shhh," I commanded.

"We have Mrs. Ratliffe with us on the air, and she wants to talk to her sons' abductors."

There was silence for a minute, and then Mom's voice filled the car. "Whoever you are who took my boys, please don't hurt them. Please let them go. They can't hurt you, and they mean the world to me." Mom sounded as if she was crying, and the announcer came back on. "If you have any information about these boys . . ."

"Mommy!" Robbie half-shouted the word. I snapped the radio off. I couldn't look at Robbie because I knew he was crying, and I didn't want to cry too. "Hey, it's okay, bud. Tomorrow, we'll be back with Mom, and everything will be okay. You heard the guy say that everyone was looking for us, didn't you?"

"Yeah, I just wish they could find us tonight instead of tomorrow."

I just hoped they could find us at all before it was too late. I looked out at the desert. It definitely was not a friendly place. It seemed to me that it was getting dark outside awfully fast. I tried to tell myself that it was just that the sun had been so hot, and now it was going down, but there was a strange kind of shadowy calmness outside.

Robbie must have felt it too, because I saw him squint toward the sky. "You think there are lots of animals out here at night?"

Actually, I did. In social studies last year, we'd learned

all about how it was too hot for most desert animals to be out in the day, so they came out at night, but I didn't know if I should tell Robbie that. Things were so weird. Ever since Robbie had been able to talk, I'd been waiting for him to treat me like an older brother who knew stuff. Now that he was finally doing it, I just wished there was someone older to take care of both of us out there. "Well, are there lots of animals out here?" Robbie asked again.

"Oh, some, but we'll be okay in the car. We'll have the windows up, and the doors locked. Good thing you didn't just take off walking."

"I didn't know it was going to get dark so fast. Wow, look at all those black clouds. Where'd they come from? Let's turn on the radio again and see if they're talking about us."

I ran one hand through my hair. "Robbie, the battery won't last forever. We have to wait to turn the radio on. If we keep turning it on now, we won't have it later."

Wind started blowing hard. "Please, just for a second?"

I leaned over and turned on the radio. What could a few seconds hurt. After having squinted against the sun all day, it was strange to see everything through the haze of darkness. Music blared from the radio, so I switched the station to see if there was any news on. An announcer's voice said, "Repeating. There is a flash-flood watch for the eastern Valley desert area. Do not travel in that area for the next two hours unless absolutely necessary. If you must be in that area, do not go near any desert washes."

The first few drops of rain hit the windshield, and I turned the radio off before Robbie heard any more. Robbie looked at me; I knew what he wanted to ask, but I wasn't going to offer the answer because I knew it would scare him even more than whatever he could be thinking.

# FIVE

ast year, for a grade in social studies, I did an extra credit project on flash floods in Arizona. I didn't remember all of it, but I did remember writing that lots of people died in flash floods because desert washes didn't look like river beds at all. They were a little lower than the area around them, but they were completely dry. Suddenly, heavy rain came, and in practically no time, the dry washes were raging rivers strong enough to uproot trees. People's cars even got stuck and sank, forcing the people to try to swim in a fast river or drown in their cars.

"Uhh, Robbie, I'm just going to go outside for a minute."

"How come? It's starting to rain. You're gonna get all wet, and then Mommy—," he stopped himself. I knew what he was going to say, that Mom would be mad. Boy, did I ever wish she was there to yell at us right then!

I was not going to tell Robbie that I was trying to check and see if we were in a desert wash, so I just said, "Yeah, think about it Rob. We've been so hot all day. Wouldn't the rain feel good?"

Robbie smiled. "Yeah, why didn't I think of that!" We opened our doors and got out of the car. To tell you the truth, the whole desert looked pretty flat as far as I could see. Of course, I'd never really seen a desert wash, so I wasn't sure what I was looking for, but I didn't think we were in one. Besides, I didn't think it was going to matter. The rain was barely coming down. The drops were so few and far between that the ground didn't even look wet. So much for enough rain to make a flood.

Then suddenly there was the most enormous blast in the sky. It sounded like a million guns all being shot at the same time. Robbie opened the door and dived back into the car. I stood frozen to the spot wondering what terrible thing was happening now. Maybe the kidnappers were nearby bombing stuff. Then I realized I had heard that sound before. It had just never been so fierce or loud in the city. Heart pounding, I opened the door to the car and looked at Robbie curled down on the seat. "It was just thunder," I said as if I'd known all along that the sound was no big deal.

"Oh, yeah, I knew that." Robbie sat up and tried to match my tone. "I just felt like getting in the car, that's all."

I looked at him, and smiled. He shrugged and grinned back. A wedge of lightning followed by another blast of thunder started quite a show. We rolled down the car windows, and we could feel the temperature drop. It felt so good. The desert darkness of heavy clouds made the lightning flashes something to watch. "Like our own laser show, huh, Robbie?" I said in awe.

37

"Yeah, definitely better than the show at the planetarium that Mom took us to."

"Okay sky," I commanded. "Let's have a bright chunk of lightning over there," and I pointed. Almost on cue, the lightning struck, and Robbie and I both laughed.

"Hey, let me try." Robbie shouted out the window. "All right thunder, listen up. I want the next blast when I say three. One, two—." A loud blast of thunder filled the air. When it subsided, Robbie shouted. "Hey, can't you follow directions? You were supposed to make noise after I counted to three, not two."

We both laughed. There was still almost no rain, and the wind had died down, too. We passed time by trying to conduct the lightning storm. Sometimes, it seemed as if the lightning and thunder were following our exact directions, and others, as if nature was paying no attention to our commands at all.

"Hey," Robbie said, after he seemed to get the lightning and thunder to follow him exactly. "Maybe I'll grow up to have a rock group, and I'll call it Lightning Power. My group'll be real famous, and we'll have laser stuff just like this behind us on stage. People will wait in line for tickets to our concerts for practically forever."

"I thought you wanted to be a pro baseball player," I said.

"Yeah, I do, but I could be a rock star in the off-season."

"Right. Maybe your group could do pregame shows."

"Nah. We'd be too famous for that. Besides, I'd be busy warming up my arm for the game."

"The only thing you warm on the bench is your rear!" I said.

"Ha, ha. Keep that up and I won't get you any free tickets to my games or my concerts!"

It felt pretty good just to be kidding around about stupid stuff. Then off in the distance we saw a huge piece of zig-zagging lightning that looked as if it almost hit the ground. "Wow," Robbie yelled. "Did you see that one?"

"Yeah," I answered. "I think that one was the biggest of all." There were more thunder and lightning blasts, but nothing like the huge one. Robbie and I joked as we continued to conduct our band, "Hey, turn up the volume again!" Then way off in the distance, I saw it.

"Geez," I half-whispered, pointing ahead and to the right. "That big lightning a few minutes ago; I think it started a fire." Robbie's eyes opened real wide as he looked in the direction I was pointing. Then another blast of thunder and bolt of lightning filled the sky, and we both jumped. I guess the dry desert must have been feeding the fire fast because as we stared at the orange speck, it kept growing into a brighter ball of orange and a line of smoke wound across the sky.

I drummed my fingers on the steering wheel and began to worry. If the thunder was louder than loud here, and the lightning was brighter and longer here than anywhere else, maybe fire traveled faster than it did anywhere else. I didn't think it could get to us. We were really far from it, but then I'd heard about how desert fires could burn hundreds of acres, and I had no idea how many acres we were from the fire. I tried to think, but I absolutely couldn't think of anything we could do if the fire came our way. We couldn't outrun it, that was for sure. Our car wouldn't work and no one else was there, so I decided that all we could do was hope that the fire burned itself out long before it got to us. That wasn't very comforting. We had hours to sit there before morning. The desert was always really dry in the summer. Why should the fire burn out before it got to us?

"Wow, look at all that smoke in the sky!" Robbie exclaimed, and then I felt a glimmer of hope. Smoke . . . like smoke signals . . . like someone had to come and fight the fire. Didn't they? I tried to think if firemen only fought fires in the city, but I didn't think so. I knew they fought them in forests. I'd seen it on a TV movie, so they must fight them in the desert too. The smoke in the sky would bring firefighters, and then we'd be rescued. I turned to Robbie. "Boy, isn't that fire great?"

"Great?" he said questioningly.

"Yeah, I think it's going to get us rescued."

"The fire's going to get us rescued?"

"Yeah." I explained to Robbie what I meant.

"Cool," he said. "Then we could ride back to Phoenix in a fire truck. Boy, in one day I will have done more stuff than most kids get to do ever! When I get back to school this fall, and everyone asks me about what I did during the summer, they'll have to give me the whole school year to describe it!"

Suddenly, the wind began to blow real hard. Little loose rocks and grains of sand hurled through the air. I turned on the motor, and rolled the windows up fast. Even with the windows up, I could still feel a sort of gritty sandiness inside the car. Palo Verde trees swayed so hard that it seemed as if they might break, and other pieces of desert plants swirled past them. Soon, it was so dusty that it was impossible to see much of anything through the windows. I didn't think the wind could possibly blow hard enough to knock the car over, but I wasn't absolutely sure of anything anymore. I knew one thing. Wind was certainly going to spread the fire fast. That could make the fire even more visible and bring help faster, or it could mean that no help was coming before we were part of the fire.

There was a loud thud on the car's roof. "What was that?" Robbie called. He clapped his hand across his mouth and whispered, "Do you think there's an animal walking on our car?"

Then there was another thud and another. It didn't really sound like an animal, it almost sounded like . . . I looked out the window. "Robbie, get up off the floor of the car. It's raining. That's rain you hear. Those have to be the biggest drops I've ever seen."

The feeling of grittiness went away as the rain pounded the car. I'd heard the saying about rain coming down in sheets, but I'd never understood it until now. It was so heavy and so thick that you could barely see out the window. It didn't even look like raindrops, just like someone had turned on a giant waterfall. Only a few minutes ago, the desert had seemed to stretch out forever, and now we could only see a few inches beyond the car window. The sounds of rain banged on our car loudly. It sort of felt like we were in a car wash and we'd gotten stuck in it.

The rain was so loud that neither of us said anything. All of a sudden, I felt myself shiver. This was crazy. It had been so hot out, and now I was shivering. I didn't know why. I mean it wasn't that cold in the car, but I looked at Robbie and he was shivering, too. His baseball hat was pulled down low, and I could barely see his face. "You okay?" I practically had to sit right next to him and shout to make myself heard.

He didn't answer, or if he did, I didn't hear him. Finally, he looked up at me, and I could see that his eyes were red. It was too noisy to hear if he was crying, but I could see him sighing deeply. "Well," he shouted in my ear, "at least we won't burn up in the fire!"

I'd almost forgotten about the fire. We hadn't been able to see it or anything else for that matter for quite a while, but I was sure Robbie was right. No fire could withstand this kind of downpour. We could forget about being rescued by any firemen. I tried to make myself feel better by telling myself that even if the fire had burned for longer, and even if the firemen had come to put it out, we really were much too far from it to have ever expected them to find us. Thunder banged and boomed. It felt like the whole desert was shaking. Lightning cracked the sky, and the rain kept pummeling down.

At last, the rain slowed from sheets that you couldn't see through at all to just a normal heavy rainstorm. No wonder people got caught in flash floods! If our car had been in an indented area, it definitely would have been in a river by now. "Well," I said as much to myself as to Robbie, "at least we're not going to get caught in any flash floods!"

"How do you know for sure?" came Robbie's quiet voice.

"Because with as much rain as was out there, we'd have already been in one." I put my head back on the seat and closed my eyes. It was almost nice to listen to the rain, enjoy the cooler temperature, and not worry about any other immediate danger. It was going to be a long, hot, horrible walk tomorrow. We might as well try to enjoy tonight.

"What are you doing?" Robbie looked at me. "Are you sick or something now?"

"No, just relaxing. You ought to try it, too, while you can."

The rain danced gently on the roof, and I was almost lulled to sleep, but something kept bothering me. I couldn't think what it was. I decided that maybe if I quit trying to think about anything, it would pop back into my mind. I stretched a little to make myself more comfortable, and when I put my hand down, it hit something. I opened my eyes to look at it and saw the half-empty gulper next to me. That was it! Get water while I could! I remembered my Scout leader lecturing us before a hike that the greatest danger in the desert was lack of water. Well, here was plenty of water. I just had to get out of the car and get it.

"Robbie, find me all the gulpers, and hurry!" I figured with our luck, just as I'd get organized, the rain would stop.

"Why do you want them? I already found them once,

but we put them back under the seat somewhere. I thought we were going to save them until tomorrow. Let's just get them then. I'm too tired to start climbing around the car."

"No, we need them right now!" I started to look for them myself. It was easier than arguing. Robbie shook his head, looked at me as if I were nuts, and pulled a gulper from under one of the seats. Soon, I had all four in front of me. "Take another big drink from one of them right now."

"But I'm not even thirsty!"

I pushed a gulper toward Robbie. "It doesn't matter. We've got to keep drinking stuff. I want to get more liquid in us now, so I can fill this with water for tomorrow."

He drank a few sips. "I can't. It's going to make me puke."

I knew what Robbie meant. Putting the gulper to my own lips, I tasted the sticky-sweet, warm root beer, and I promised myself that once we were out of there, I would never, ever drink root beer again. Yuck! How could I ever have thought this stuff was good? Still, I forced myself to drink as much of it as I could. Then I opened all the gulpers very carefully and poured one into another until I had two full gulpers and two empty ones.

The rain was coming down heavily, but it wasn't terrible, and the sky was actually beginning to get lighter. I opened the car door. "Where are you going?" There was panic in Robbie's voice.

"I'm just gonna get these full of water. I'll be right back."

"Okay," Robbie said to my departing back. "But stay where I can see you . . . uhh, just in case you need help or something."

"Right," I said. "I'll yell if I need anything." I closed the car door and walked a few feet from the car, looking around for a place to wedge the gulpers so that they wouldn't fall over. A bolt of thunder crashed in the air, and I dropped one of the gulpers. "Oh, no!" I shouted to no one. "I can't lose that." But even though I looked carefully in the semi-darkness, the gulper seemed to be gone. It must have wedged under a rock or something. I dropped down onto my hands and knees. The gulper had to be there somewhere! How could something bright yellow just disappear? Then I saw it under a bush. I crawled forward a little and grabbed it. Suddenly, I felt a sharp pain in my knee. I looked down and saw blood coming from it. Geez, it hurt so bad. I wasn't sure if something had bitten me or what. I just wanted to get back to the car, but I knew I had to get the gulpers secured some-

where first. Finally, I wedged one into the space between two small cacti. I managed to scratch my right hand on the cactus needles, but the gulper didn't look as if rain or wind could knock it over. Then I saw three rocks and pushed them together against the other gulper. By now, even though  the rain was not as heavy as it had been, I was pretty well drenched. My hand hurt, and my knee throbbed, but at least we would have water tomorrow, and hopefully, it would be enough.

I opened the car door and fell onto the seat. "Robbie,

see if we have any Kleenex in the back." My knee was bleeding pretty hard, and the blood had started to run down my leg. It kind of made me sick to look at my own blood like that. I forced myself to touch the wound, and felt a piece of something sharp.

Robbie handed me the Kleenex, and I saw his eyes open real big as he looked at my leg. "What . . . what happened out there?"

"Nothing . . . I mean I just cut my leg on a rock. It's no big deal."

I pressed the Kleenex to the cut, and that made it hurt even worse. When I took it away, the blood stopped for a few seconds, and I could see a sharp piece of grey rock sticking in my leg. I knew it had to come out. I tried to put my fingers around the rock and pull, but it hurt so much to even touch the cut, I just couldn't make myself do it.

"Uh, Robbie, I need your help."

Robbie looked at me warily. "With what."

"You gotta get this rock out of my knee."

Robbie shook his head. "Uhh, thanks, but no. It's too gross to reach into your blood."

"Robbie . . ."

"I'm not doin' it."

I sighed deeply. My hand hurt. My knee was throbbing, but I knew when Robbie used that voice that he was not going to do what I wanted without a major fight, and I was too tired for that. What energy I had left had to go to getting the rock out. My knee had to work tomorrow if we were going to be able to walk out of the desert. I gritted my teeth and looked away as I pulled on the rock. "Ahhhh," I screamed, but the rock was still in my knee, and I had caused blood to start flowing faster than ever. I watched it slide down my leg and onto the beige carpet.

I started to reach toward my knee again. I was breathing real hard, and I thought I might puke, when Robbie called, "Wait! Doesn't Mom keep a first-aid kit in the glove compartment?"

"How will that help?" I said with irritation.

Robbie didn't answer. He reached in and pulled out a little white and blue box with a red cross on the top. Inside were bandages and Bactine and a small tweezers. Robbie handed me the tweezers. "Maybe this will make it easier. I'm sorry, Scott; I know it must hurt, but I just can't do it."

I took a deep breath and forced myself to reach toward my knee again. This time the tweezers hung onto the rock and pulled it out. I brought it close to my face, and in the duskiness, I could see how sharp it was, almost like an arrow.

Now, all of a sudden, Robbie wanted to help. He sprayed so much Bactine on my knee that it was running down my leg and over my shorts. "Boy," he said, examining the cut, "that was a lot of blood from such a little cut." Then Robbie sprayed Bactine on my hand and almost got it in my eyes. He started undoing about five Band-Aids.

"That's okay," I stopped him.

"But, I thought you wanted me to help."

I took over and finished covering my knee wound. I was

47

exhausted. My head hurt, my knee hurt, and my hand hurt, but I didn't complain because there was no one to make any of it feel better. I kept thinking of my Scout leader. "Be prepared!" he had always said, but how could anyone be prepared for what we had gone through today? "Never give up," my Scout leader had said. "There's a solution to almost every crisis if you just keep thinking."

"Well, I can't think anymore!" I said almost defiantly. I took off my sopping-wet T-shirt and threw it in the backseat. Now if I could just get those soggy shoes and soaked socks off too. I bent down to try to untie one basketball shoe, and I finally pulled out one foot. Then, holding the basketball shoe for a minute, I got an idea. "Give me your shoes!"

"My shoes? For what?"

"I'm gonna stick them outside the car and let them fill up with water."

"Have you gone nuts?"

"No, and I'm not kidding. Come on, off with your shoes."

Robbie held up his fists. "I'm not letting you fill my shoes with water. No way!"

I sighed. "Robbie, we need to have as much water as we can tomorrow."

"Well I'm not using any water from inside my shoes. Thanks, but I'll pass. I like using glasses to drink from."

I could feel my voice rising angrily. "Robbie, I'd like to be drinking from a glass too. Matter of fact, I'd like to be in the living room right now watching *Star Trek* in the air

48

conditioning, and I'd like to be eating a big bowl of chocolate ice-cream or finishing a pepperoni pizza, then I'd like to climb into my bed tonight, and I'd like to have some ice to put on my knee, but I don't think I'm going to get any of that. Do you?"

Robbie didn't answer, and the frustration of the day kept me yelling at him. "Don't you see that we could die out here without water? We don't have any glasses. The only thing I can see that will hold water is our shoes. Pretty soon, the rain may stop and then it will be too late. That's why you're going to gladly give me your shoes right now, or so help me, I'll rip 'em off your feet!"

obbie didn't say anything to me. He just leaned over and started untying his shoes. When I had both pairs in my hands, I opened the front car door, leaned outside the car, and put the shoes right next to the door. I hoped I was doing the right thing. We had to have water, but we also had to have shoes to walk in the desert. Still, I couldn't exactly imagine anyone stealing our Nike Airs in the middle of nowhere, and they weren't food, so I didn't think any animal might want them. I hoped all my guesses were right.

It rained hard for about another fifteen minutes, and then the rain trickled to a drizzle and stopped. It was actually no darker than when the rain had begun. I guessed that now we were seeing the regular sunset instead of the storm clouds.

Robbie and I were both sitting in the front seat, and Robbie looked at me. "You know, I was supposed to pitch in tonight's game."

"Sorry." I knew Robbie had been anxiously awaiting this game all week. If the team won, they had only one more game to play and then they would win the state title. "You guys probably will lose either way and at least now, they can't blame the loss on your pitching."

Robbie folded his arms across his chest. "Thanks a lot! You just want us to lose because you're not playing."

"That's not true. The coach said that I was a great right-fielder. He just decided to let Tommy Simon play in All-Stars instead of me because he had a better batting average."

"It doesn't matter who plays right field. No one hits there."

"Oh, yeah?" I said. "Just 'cuz you can't hit in that direction doesn't mean a good batter doesn't hit deep into right."

Robbie and I might have kept arguing. We were really good at it since we did it every day of our lives, but we were interrupted by a blood-curdling screech. For a minute both of us froze. Was it the kidnappers? Were they killing someone else? Was it some animal attacking? The shriek sounded again, and this time it sounded as if it were even closer. Robbie grabbed my arm, and clung to it. I looked at the doors to make sure they were locked, and I realized that I had left the door by the shoes unlocked. With Robbie still attached to my arm, I leaned over and pressed the lock.

"Maybe we should get down on the floor," I whispered.

Robbie nodded, but he didn't move. Neither did I. I think we were both just too scared. What if the kidnappers had come back! Then the shriek sounded again, and this time, it seemed as if it were almost on us. Robbie dove for the floor. Another minute, and I was sure some man, animal, or monster would be clawing at our car door.

Then I noticed a small bird nearby. It was hard to believe such a little thing could make so much noise, but as I followed it with my eyes, my ears heard the sound move with it. "Robbie," I said.

"Shh," he whispered. "They'll hear you."

"Robbie, it's just a bird. It's just some little bird over there. Get up and look."

Robbie gingerly rose from the floor of the car and looked at me as if he didn't quite believe me. The bird shrieked a few more times and then flew off into the horizon.

Wiping his hands on his blue T-shirt, Robbie shook his head. "How could such a little thing make such an awful sound? Boy, was I scared! I can't believe it— a bird! Have you ever seen one like it before?"

I shook my head no and said that maybe it only came in the desert. Robbie and I sat silently, and we began to hear more strange noises. I guessed the animals were too hot to come out during the day, but they were starting to be heard now that it was night. In other places, it might have been interesting to try to figure out each noise, but given our situation, each new noise was just another worry to be thought about. We watched as the setting sun cast a pinkish glow to the sky, and then it was dark.

A sliver of the moon provided a little tiny bit of light, and even through the windshield, the stars seemed especially bright, but still, the desert was really, really dark.

It was a different kind of dark than the dark of our room at night. It was a lonely, lost kind of dark.

My knee was throbbing, and I thought it might help if I could stretch it out, so I asked Robbie to get in the backseat. "I think maybe we should just try to go to sleep. We can't do anything tonight, and we want to get started early tomorrow."

Robbie nodded. "I don't really think I can sleep out here. Do you think maybe we could turn the light on in the car?"

I wasn't sure it would work, but it was worth a try. I turned the key and pressed the little black light switch overhead. It didn't exactly make the car light up, but at least Robbie and I could see each other. "I don't think we can keep this light on for too long. We don't want to make the battery run out because we will still need to listen to the radio."

"Maybe we could turn the radio on for just a little while right now. It would probably help us go to sleep."

I knew we should probably wait, but I switched the radio on anyway. There was some talk show on. People were invited to call in and describe their worst day. The first caller was talking about her cat being unable to get out of a tree and her having to call the fire department.

"Boy," I said. "Can you imagine if we could call in?" I pretended to hold a phone to my ear. "Hello. Today was our worst day. You see it started when we got kidnapped and we thought we were going to be killed. We only got to live because the kidnappers decided that it wasn't worth the bullets to kill us. Then we got deserted in the desert. The good news is that we have a car. The bad news is that it ran out of gas. We don't know where we are or exactly how to get out. We don't have any food and we don't have much water. Oh yeah, and we saw a fire and sat through flash-flood warnings and a terrible rainstorm. Other than that, we're having a great day."

Robbie whistled softly. "It doesn't even sound real to me, and I was here for all of it. Boy, when we finally do get home, I wonder if anyone will believe us when we tell them about everything."

The stupid talk show rambled on. Some woman was talking about denting her husband's new car. I snapped off the radio. Dumb people.

I heard Robbie's stomach grumble and I felt my own hunger pains. "Hey, Robbie, if you could have anything to eat right now, what would it be?"

"Hmm, a large pepperoni pizza with extra cheese, and a big cold soda with lots of ice, and then for dessert, probably a double-dip, mint-chocolate ice cream cone."

"I'd have a big juicy cheeseburger and a double order of fries." My mouth was watering at the thought. "Okay, I'm going to turn off the light now and think about that food. Picture us eating tomorrow night, and maybe if we do, we can both go to sleep."

"I'm never gonna be able to sleep out here. In a little while, let's turn the light and the radio back on, okay?"

"Sure, we just have to make sure we can hear the news tomorrow morning about where they're looking for us before we start hiking out of here."

Robbie yawned in spite of himself. "You know, maybe we'll hear that rescuers have spotted our car, and we can just stay right here. The helicopters and the TV stations and everyone will come. I hope they bring lots of good stuff to eat."

I hoped Robbie was right, but I wasn't counting on it.

The light was off for awhile. Eventually, I began to hear Robbie's rhythmic breathing from the backseat. "You asleep?" I whispered, but there was no answer. I envied Robbie. I knew I would need all my strength for tomorrow, but I couldn't go to sleep. My knee hurt every time I turned, and my mind kept wondering if there wasn't some other plan I should be thinking of. Gradually, I began to be aware of another feeling. I had to go to the bathroom. The idea of wandering out into the total darkness was not a good one. *I'll wait,* I told myself. *I don't really have to go.* Pretty soon, I was squirming around the car. This wasn't going to wait until morning. With shaking legs, I started to open the car door.

Robbie stirred in his sleep. "Where 'ya going?" he mumbled.

"To the bathroom." I don't know why I answered

because I was pretty sure Robbie was talking in his sleep.

"Uhhnm, well, don't turn on all the lights."

"Lights!?" I said in frustration. "We don't even have any—," then I stopped myself. The headlights! I could turn on the headlights! I switched the headlights on and in the darkness of the desert night, they gave off a comforting gleam. At least I would be able to see what not to step on. . . . Oops, another little problem. I couldn't walk out into the desert without shoes, and my shoes were outside the car filled with water. Great. We needed the water for tomorrow. I needed the shoes for tonight. I opened the door and looked at the shoes. There was some water in each shoe, but I wouldn't say they were more than a third full, so I poured the water into Robbie's shoes and brought mine into the car. I knew he was going to be ticked tomorrow; he'd say I'd left his full of water on purpose, but I'd have to deal with that then.

I stuck my right foot into my shoe; the shoe felt squishy inside, but what did I expect? I wasn't even going to bother to lace it. Then I picked up my left shoe to put my foot in it, and I felt something slither out of the shoe. I dropped the shoe on the floor and yelled, and I felt the thing slither across my hand.

"What's a matter?" Robbie called.

"Snake," I choked out. "I think there's a snake on me!"

# SEVEN

**R**obbie sat up with a start. "A snake! How'd we get a snake in here?"

No way was I going to sit and explain how I knew there was a snake in the car while it crawled around me somewhere in the dark. It might even be a rattler getting ready to strike. I squirmed, feeling for the door handle. No way I was staying in the car with a snake. "Just get out," I yelled to Robbie. "We gotta get out of the car now."

Both the front and back doors opened at the same time, and we jumped from the car. "Ow," yelled Robbie. "I think I stepped on something." He hobbled to the front of the car and examined the bottom of his sock in the glare of the headlights. "I don't see anything on my foot. I guess the ground was just hard. It wouldn't have hurt if I had my shoes on." Then he looked at me. "Why do you think there's a snake in the car? We've had the windows shut and the doors locked. Maybe you were just dreaming."

"Well, not exactly . . ."

"Yeah, well what exactly then?" Robbie looked part asleep, part confused, and part mad. "Well . . ."

"Well, I had to go to the bathroom."

"Yeah, and . . ."

"And well . . . I went to put on my shoes, so I could go out a little ways into the desert."

"I thought we were supposed to leave our shoes outside for them to get water. What'd you do with the water that was in your shoes?"

"I put it in yours."

"Oh, thanks a lot!"

"Robbie!" I shouted. There was silence in the desert night as the two of us glared at each other. But then I decided that maybe if I went over exactly how the snake got in the car, I could think how to get it out, so I said, "I got one shoe on, see," and I pointed to my foot to show him it wasn't just my imagination. "Then I went to put the other one on. Everything happened so fast from there, but I think when I bent down to pick up my other shoe from the ground, a little field mouse ran onto it. And then suddenly, I thought I saw this big snake coming at my shoe from under the car. Then part of it rose up off the ground and the whole thing slithered into the car real fast. That's when I screamed and told you to get out."

Robbie looked at me for a minute, and then he bit his lip. "Okay, if you think that's what happened, then I guess we better find out."

We decided to walk back to the car door and open

it. That way the inside light would go on and then maybe we could at least see the snake. I put my hand on the door handle and took a deep breath. Everything had happened so fast with the mouse and my shoe that I wasn't sure if

 we'd see nothing, or if a big, poisonous snake would spring at us.

I opened the driver's car door and jumped back just in case the snake was ready to strike. Robbie stared through the passenger side window onto the now-lighted seat. "Holey moley, there's a big snake on our front seat."

"That's what I've been trying to tell you," I shouted, slamming the door shut again.

"I can't believe it," Robbie said over and over again.

"I told you it was there."

"Scott, we gotta do something. There's a snake sitting on the front seat of the car, and we're out here where there's probably a zillion other snakes just waiting to bite us or squeeze us or something." He looked sort of glassy-eyed. "What are we gonna do?"

I ran my hand through my hair. I didn't know what we were going to do. I didn't want to stay out here all night any more than Robbie did. There were lots of strange noises, and all we could see was the path lighted by the headlights. Who knew what was out there in the darkness just beyond the headlights?

"I've got an idea," Robbie said. "Why don't we turn the radio on real loud and leave the car door open? Maybe that will bother the snake's ears so much that it will crawl away from the music."

I looked at my little brother. "I don't think snakes have ears!"

"You got a better idea?"

There was a loud hooting sound in the distance and Robbie and I both jumped. "Okay, we'll try it," I said. I didn't think it would work, but I didn't have any better plan. We crept back to the car door and stared into the window, but without the interior light on, it was too hard to see anything. "So, uh, you want to open the door this time?" I said. After all, Robbie was always complaining that I took over just because I was older.

"Okay," he said. "And then you reach in and turn on the radio. And be really careful, because when we looked before, the snake was curled up on the seat right next to the radio."

"I dunno, Robbie. What if the snake is still right there? I don't think I could get my hand away if it started to strike."

Robbie sighed. "Maybe it isn't such a great plan."

Robbie and I looked at each other, each of us feeling fear and frustration. Finally, I said, "Why don't we at least open the car door and see where the snake is? Maybe it moved away from the radio."

Of course, we had no idea what to do if the snake was

still right by the radio, but there didn't seem to be any other thing to do except open the car door and see where the snake was. I put my hand on the doorknob, took a deep breath, threw open the door and jumped back in case the snake was right there. Robbie jumped too, and we almost tripped over each other. No snake emerged from the car, and keeping the open door carefully in our sight at all times, we walked back toward the car. With the light on inside, it was plain to see that the snake hadn't moved. It was big and it had black, whitish-yellow, and dark red on it. Robbie whispered, "Is that a rattler?"

"I don't think so," I whispered back; "but it could be. I don't want to find out. It doesn't look very friendly."

We decided it was just too dangerous to try for the radio, and besides, we didn't know if snakes really moved away from music or not. We climbed up on the hood of the car and sat down. That way we could stare through the front window at the snake and see if it crawled out. Meanwhile, we'd be off the ground in case the snake had any friends slithering around looking for it.

Robbie's and my eyes glared through the windshield at the snake. If eye power could have moved it, that snake would have been gone. Instead, it seemed perfectly content to be coiled up on the front seat of the car, and why not? The car seat was a lot more comfortable than the hard metal hood we were sitting on. I looked up at the sky. The stars were so bright. I could easily see both the big and the little dipper. I'd once read a book about a guy who used the stars to guide him, and I wished I could remember how he'd done it.

After a while, my rear hurt from sitting on the hood. Robbie said he was more tired than he'd ever been in his whole life, but he didn't plan to sleep until we could get back into a locked car. That worried me. I knew that we were going to have a really hard day tomorrow. We needed all our strength, and that meant we needed to sleep some tonight. But how to get the snake out and us into the car, I just didn't know. "What's that?" Robbie whispered.

There was a strange noise off to the right. "Probably nothing," I whispered back.

"What kind of nothing makes that kind of noise?"

"I don't know."

Robbie wrapped his arms around himself. "Scott, we gotta get back in the car. We really do."

I thought and thought until I thought my brain would burst. "Okay, I got it. We'll get the jack out of the car. Since it's strong enough to hold up the car, it ought to be strong enough to kill a snake, right?" I was beginning to feel my heart pump. Now this was a plan that could work.

"I'll take the jack, and I'll hit the snake. Then the snake will be dead, and I'll use the jack to push it out of the car." I raised an eyebrow. "Pretty good idea, huh?"

Robbie looked at me. "I think it's a great idea. Really. I think it was so smart of you to think of, but . . . Now, don't get mad or anything. I'm not saying this to be mean. But I think I should be the one to hit the snake."

"You?"

"Yeah, in baseball, you miss so much of the time. Scott, we can't strike out when it comes to the snake."

I started to say something mean back to him, sort of reflex action, but I had to admit that he was right about whose aim was better. Robbie was the leading hitter on the baseball team; he was better than a lot of the older guys. Still, I thought I should be the one to take the risk with the snake. After all, I was the older brother. I went around to the back of the station wagon. I was pretty sure that when Robbie saw how heavy a jack was, he'd change his mind about who should use it.

We climbed over the roof of the car and leaned over the back of it. I grabbed the station wagon's back door handle. Swinging the door open, we peered upside down into the back of the car. "Uh, Robbie, you know where the jack is?"

"Nope, I don't think I've ever seen a jack except on TV when I saw guys fixing flat tires."

Truthfully, that was the only place I'd ever seen one, too. On TV they'd just opened the trunk of the car and there'd been a spare tire and a jack. The only problem with that was that a station wagon didn't have a trunk. Maybe a station wagon didn't have a spare tire or a jack, either. I began to get a sinking feeling, but I didn't give up. Much as I hated to, I climbed off the car. Standing on the ground, I stared again into the back of the station wagon. There was a third seat that could be pulled up out of storage space in the back, and I released the levers and pulled, hoping to see a jack. I looked in the wells in the back, but zip. Nothing. No jack.

I rubbed my eyes. Why couldn't anything go right? "Come on, Robbie, let's climb back on the hood of the car, and we'll try to think of something else." When we were sitting on the car and staring through the windshield, we could easily see the snake on the front seat. It was creepy looking.

The headlights didn't seem as bright to me as they were before, and I began to worry that if we didn't think of something pretty soon, we were going to be sitting out here on the hood of the car in pitch black darkness. Staring ahead, I could see a small Palo Verde tree in the headlights. "Robbie," I said slowly, thinking as I spoke, "See that tree over there? I'm going to go get a branch off of it, and we'll use the branch to push the snake out of the car."

"Okay," Robbie said wearily.

I had only one shoe on. My other foot was barefoot. I had been walking around the car very carefully, but the Palo Verde tree was a ways away. I couldn't risk getting cactus stickers in my foot, so I decided I would have to hop to the Palo Verde tree. I was really sorry that I'd ever taken off my basketball shoes in the first place. It was a dumb idea. By tomorrow, whatever water they'd gathered would probably have soaked into the shoes anyway.

As I got a little ways away from the car, the sounds of

the desert seemed even more threatening. I made myself keep hopping because I knew that if I really stopped to listen, I'd run right back to the car. Finally, I'd hopped to the Joshua tree. It was a scraggly little thing, and the branches were pretty puny. I wished I'd had my Boy Scout knife to cut one off, but it was sitting at home next to my bed on my nightstand. I leaned down and cleared a spot so that I could put both feet down. It felt great to stand on two feet, but I worried a lot about my bare foot. I knew there were scorpions and all kinds of other yucky bugs out there, and I hoped my bare foot wouldn't make a tempting target.

I found the smallest long branch on the tree, and I began to twist it back and forth, then up and down. I was panting with effort, and the dumb branch still clung to the tree. The next thing I knew something was coming up behind me. I jumped around, screamed, and made a fist. I might only have one punch, but whatever it was, I'd give it my best shot before it attacked.

"Don't hit—it's me. It's just me!" Robbie yelled.

My heart was pounding a million miles an hour. "What—what are you doing here?" I gasped. "You scared me to death!"

"Sorry. While I was sitting on the hood, I saw something gleaming in the headlights. I got off the car to see what it was, and guess what—it was a tin can. I took my shoes, poured the water from my shoes into the can, and look, I'm here! Of course, my shoes are a gross mess, but at least I have 'em on, and we still have the water." Robbie looked proud of himself. I was proud of him too, and I told him so. Maybe I didn't give my little brother enough credit.

Together, we worked on the tree branch. It certainly didn't want to leave that tree. Finally, we got it free, and we headed back to the car. I held on to Robbie's shoulder as I hopped my way back. When we reached the car, we approached the open door very carefully. A first glance told us that the snake wasn't still on the seat, and almost in unison, Robbie and I looked down at our feet to make sure nothing was slithering toward us. Then we noticed the snake. It was still in the car; it had just moved to the floor.

"Exactly how are we gonna do this?" Robbie whispered. "That branch isn't very heavy. If we hit the snake with it, he might just get mad instead of dead."

I looked at the snake. It couldn't possibly have grown since we'd been out getting the branch. It must have just spread out a little more. I gulped. "I guess we're just going to have to use the stick to shove him out." My throat felt real dry. My hands were shaking so much that I held the branch with both hands. "Go around and open the other door, then come back over here. We'll stand here behind him, and we'll shove him out the driver's side door. I leaned into the car on the passenger side, and I noticed that the beige part of the snake almost blended in with the beige carpet on the floor. I heard Robbie take a sharp breath, and then I heard a ringing in my ears as I edged the branch closer and closer to the snake. I felt like I might pass out. The ringing got louder, and then I felt the stick touch the snake. It took all the willpower I had not to scream and pull the stick away. Instead, I made myself put the stick next to the middle of the snake, and then I pushed as hard as I could toward the open door. There was a hissing sound.

ou did it!" Robbie squealed. "The snake's out. Quick, let's get in." My breath was coming in hard pants, but I dropped the branch and jumped in the car. Robbie and I pulled the doors shut, and I sank back in the seat. I was shaking all over. "We did it! We did it!" Robbie exclaimed. "Boy, I wish I could have kept the snake's skin. That would have really been something to show people."

I was still in shock. I didn't care about the snakeskin. I was just glad it was out of the car, and we were in it! Robbie got up on his knees and pressed his face to the glass of the front windshield. "What are you doing?" I asked.

"I'm looking to see if I can see the snake crawling away. I want to know just how big it really was so I can tell all my friends."

I put my hand over my face and closed my eyes. Let Robbie look all he wanted. I don't think he realized how dangerous the snake could have been. I mean what if I'd pushed one way, and it had sprung out and struck the other? I shuddered thinking of that huge snake coiling itself around my arm. With my eyes closed, I could almost see it moving up my arm, so I quickly opened them and sat up. Robbie's face was still pressed to the windshield. "Well, you see him?"

"Nope," Robbie sounded disappointed.

"I think we better turn off the headlights. We don't want to use up the battery before tomorrow morning. We've got to be able to hear the news then."

I reached to shut off the headlights, and Robbie groaned, "I like it a lot better with some light. Exactly what is it that uses up a battery anyway?"

"I don't know. I can't know everything. I just know that if the car isn't running and you leave the lights or the radio on for too long the battery goes dead." I was tired, and I was grumpy. "I don't have any idea how long is too long. I do remember the time you didn't shut the door all the way and the light in the car stayed on all night, and in the morning, Mom had a dead battery. Remember? She had to call Triple-A to come jump start the car, and she was late for work, and we were late for school? That's all I know about batteries."

"Okay, you don't have to take my head off. I just wondered. It sure is dark out here. Did you hear that noise?"

I didn't answer. I heard lots of noises, but the snake had worn me out. I just wanted to sink into this seat and not listen. It felt so good just to sit there that I wasn't sure I was ever going to get up. Unfortunately, it only took a few minutes to make me change my mind. I remembered what had started the whole snake situation as I felt an overwhelming need to go to the bathroom. I'd been so scared that I guess I'd forgotten before, but now I definitely needed to go. I tried to tell myself just not to think about it because there was no way I wanted to get out of this car until it was light, but the harder I tried to think about something else, the more I could only think about getting out of there and going to the bathroom. I grimaced. This wasn't going to wait until morning no matter how much I wanted it to. I reached over and turned on the headlights.

Robbie sat up from the backseat. "Hey, I thought you just said we had to keep them off."

"Yeah, well, I have to go to the bathroom."

"Oh. Can't you wait 'til morning?"

"No."

"Well I'm sure that the snake must have crawled far away from here by now." I think Robbie was trying to be helpful. It didn't help. "Besides, when I asked you before, you said snakes didn't come out when you peed."

It seemed like it must have been years ago that I'd said that to Robbie instead of a few hours ago; besides, it was a lie. I didn't know anything about the subject. That was the problem with school. They didn't teach you the stuff you really needed to know. Suddenly, I had an idea. "I'm not getting off the car."

Robbie yelped, "Yeah, well you're not going in here. That's just too gross."

I opened the door to the car, climbed out and onto the hood, stood up, and took care of business. Feeling much better, I climbed back into the car. Everything out there wore a person out. Even going to the bathroom couldn't be simple. I was just about to reach out and turn off the lights again when a coyote ran in front of the car and grabbed a squealing rabbit. The coyote tore at the rabbit, and Robbie and I sat frozen. Blood spurted from the rabbit as the coyote ran off with it. "Geez," Robbie finally whispered, "you could have been right out there going to the bathroom. I . . . uh . . . I don't think we ought to get out of the car again until it's light out, okay?"

It sounded like a good idea to me. Both of us sat thinking about the bloody rabbit and the coyote. Then Robbie leaned over the seat and turned on the radio. "I know you said we gotta save the battery, but I just need to hear some people's voices, some regular old ordinary life stuff. Please?" Robbie's face looked real white.

"Okay," I said. Actually, the idea sounded pretty good to me too, and we wouldn't keep the radio on too long.

The only station that would come in was a golden oldies station, but at least it was something. "And now for your K-O-O-L news of the hour," blared the radio. "It's one A.M. on this Thursday morning." First the announcer told about a fire that had broken out in a large Phoenix building. Then he talked about the monsoon-like rainstorm that had hit the Valley. He mentioned a couple of other stories, and then he broke for a commercial. "Boy, do you think they already forgot about us?" Robbie asked.

"Of course not," I said, but I was a little worried myself. Why hadn't they said anything about us? Did that mean there was no search going on? The radio announcer continued with other stories. The news was almost over, and I was biting my lip in nervousness. Mom wouldn't let them just forget about us. "And finally," said the announcer, "there's been no further word on the two missing Phoenix boys. Police say there has been no ransom demand. Again, we are asking anyone who has seen a cream-colored Chevy Caprice station wagon, license CCJ-023, to please contact Crime Stop immediately."

I wanted to yell at the radio guy. I wanted to scream at him that no one could see our license plate. We were stuck out in the middle of the desert in pitch black darkness. I knew it wouldn't do any good to scream at a radio, so I forced myself to say, "See, Robbie, they're still looking for us."

"Yeah, which means they don't have any idea where we are."

With that discouraging thought, we listened to a couple more songs, and then we agreed that we better turn off the radio to save the battery. I said, "Maybe tomorrow morning, we'll hear that they've found out we're here, and they're on their way to rescue us. Meanwhile, we've gotta try to sleep so we can think tomorrow."

Robbie stretched out in the backseat, and I lay down

in front. We took the clothes Mom had bought and wadded them up to make pillows. It wasn't anything like being home in bed, but it sure beat being out on the hood of the car. My whole body hurt. My eyes felt scratchy under my eyelids, and my knee throbbed. I knew that I had to sleep, but as tired as I was, I just couldn't make my eyes stay closed. Pretty soon, I could hear Robbie snoring in the backseat. Finally, just as I had about given up on sleeping, I felt myself drifting off.

"No, no, don't kill me," Robbie screamed at the top of his voice. "Please just don't kill me!" I forced my eyes open. My heart hammered. The kidnappers must have come back! They had Robbie. I made myself sit up. I didn't know what I could do, but I couldn't just let them take my little brother.

"Leave him alone!" I screamed, trying to make my eyes focus in the darkness.

"What? What is it?" Robbie yelled. "Scott, answer me. Who's hurting you? What's wrong?"

My heart was still hammering. "Are you there by yourself?"

"Yeah, aren't you?" There was a strong note of fear in Robbie's voice.

"But you screamed that you were being killed."

"I did?" Robbie asked. "I don't think I screamed."

I put my head in my hands. "You must have been having a nightmare."

Robbie reached out and put his hand on my shoulder.

"I think I was just sleeping. Maybe you were having a nightmare. Hey, it's going to be light out pretty soon. Let's just turn on the radio for a few minutes. That'll help."

Soon light shone, both inside and in front of the car, but it was much dimmer than it had been. I knew we couldn't keep the lights or the radio on for very long. The battery must be starting to go. It helped a little to have the rock-n-roll oldies blaring from the radio, but it was depressing to have the announcer sounding as if the whole world was just great. The blue glow from the radio clock showed 3:17. I wondered how soon it would get light.

"Hey, remember this song?" Robbie began to snap his fingers. "You and Howard Langson did a lip sync to it in the school talent show last year. You wore that crazy green-haired wig, and everybody loved your act."

"You know, we *did* use that song." I hadn't even remembered when I'd heard it on the radio. But now that I'd been reminded I could see myself and Howard on stage. It had been lots of fun. "That green wig was really something. I wonder what happened to it." I could see me and Howard getting our costumes together. "We got two cans of fluorescent green paint, and his mom's old wig looked real different when we were through with it. Only problem was that Howard sort of forgot to ask his mom before we painted it. Boy, was he in trouble. Then after she saw the show, his mom decided that our act was worth her wig."

I grinned, remembering. "Hey, Robbie, you ought to try out for the talent show this year. You'll be old enough."

"Nah, I don't think so; nobody could top your act from last year."

"You really think so?" I couldn't believe this was coming from Robbie, who never said anything nice about anything I did.

"Yeah, everyone laughed. I mean, even the sixth-graders who thought they were the only funny ones. Boy, that night, I told everyone around me that the guy on the left was my brother."

"You did?" I was amazed. "But you never said anything about it to me."

"Oh right, I was supposed to be like Mom and run up saying how proud I was of you, and that you were adorable." Robbie put his finger in his mouth and made a gagging sound. "Give me a break."

Imagine that, I thought, Robbie actually telling people, kids at school even, that he thought I was good. Before I could say anything else, the radio announcer came on saying that it was time for another news update. The newscaster talked about the fire again. He said that the storm had knocked down a power pole in west Phoenix, and that service to the area might not be restored until the morning. Then he said, "Searching continues for two boys kidnapped at the 32nd street Mini-Mart yesterday afternoon. Police have been following every lead. Some witnesses reported seeing the car in Flagstaff and others reported the car at the opposite end of the state in Nogales. Authorities do not know if the boys are still in that car or if they are still alive, nor is there any word as to why they were taken. We'll update you as we get new information. Meanwhile, the search continues, and police are asking everyone to watch for a Chevy Caprice station wagon—"

Robbie turned off the radio and banged at the light switch, plunging us into darkness. "Nobody's ever gonna find us!"

He sounded awful. "Hey," I said, "that's why we're going to go find them. Remember? We're going to be TV stars. We can't do that if we just wait around here forever to be rescued." Robbie didn't say anything, so I said, "Rob, really, somehow, it's all going to be okay."

He sighed. "Yeah, I guess we've been doing pretty good so far. We got rid of the kidnappers and the snake."

It was funny in a sad sort of way. I was trying to make Robbie feel better, and I think he was trying to do the same for me, but both of us were scared to death about what the morning might bring.

There was silence in the car, mostly because I think neither one of us could think of anything good to say. We each stretched out on our own seat, and with a mixture of a little hope and a lot of fear, we waited for the sky to get light.

## NINE

I turned and twisted on the seat, trying to find a comfortable position. "Go to sleep," I ordered myself, but sleep would not come. I'd close my eyes and see that snake on the kidnapper's hand, or I'd hear the guy named Slam say, "You want to kill 'em?" I guess Robbie must have been having the same problem because I'd hear his light snoring for a few minutes, and then he would move around the seat. I sighed. There was nothing I could do to make myself any less scared, but maybe I could say something to help Robbie sleep and make the night pass. "Hey, guy," I teased. "If you don't sleep, you're gonna have big, black bags under your eyes tomorrow, and when we go on TV, people are all going to say, 'Isn't it amazing that they're brothers! The dark-haired one is awesome looking, and the other one is just plain ugly.'"

"Ha," Robbie said, rising to the bait. "Even with the biggest circles in the world, I'd still look better than you."

"No way!" I said.

"Yeah way, easy way!" Then the tone of Robbie's voice changed. "Scott, no kidding now, do you really think we're going to make it out of here? Do you really think we'll get home to be on TV?"

"Of course! Don't be dumb! Nothing's going to happen to us. We've got to be okay to be on television." I didn't believe my own words. In fact, I was going over and over what to do when it did get light. I wished I were one year older. Then maybe I would have finished a wilderness survival badge, and I'd have known what to do instead of just guessing. There was this TV game show on called *Wheel of Fortune.* I sort of felt like I was spinning that wheel. Only instead of a spot marked *bankrupt* where you lost your money, our wrong spin meant we lost our lives.

My mind raced. I kept hoping that when we turned on the radio when it got light, we'd hear something about searchers being in the desert, or maybe we'd even see them, but I didn't think that was going to happen. Would we have to hike out of here? If only I had some idea how far we were from the road. At least, when we walked, we could follow the tire tracks.

Finally, the first rays of light came. It was still way too dark to wake Robbie, but I noticed that it had gotten very quiet. I had this crazy picture in my mind that it was time for all the night shift sounds or animals to go to sleep, and the day shift hadn't awakened yet. The sun broke a little more, and long shadows of saguaro cacti stretched out along the desert. I saw a cactus wren swoop on top of a cactus near our car and begin its ratchety song.

Robbie sat up with a start. "Scott, watch out, a machine gun. I heard it!"

I leaned over the seat. "It's okay, Rob. See that bird up there? The one with the big dark spot on its front? That's what's making the machine-gun sound. Listen."

The bird "sang" again. "That's the ugliest bird call I ever heard!" Robbie exclaimed. "How'd you know that's what was making the sound?"

"Two reasons. First, I was watching it this morning, and I saw it. Second, when we went camping in Scouts this spring, we heard a whole bunch of cactus wrens early in the morning. Most of us were up when the racket started, but Jose Sanchez was still sleeping. It was pretty funny. He jumped out of his sleeping bag and started screaming that we were being attacked by guns. So you see, you're not the only one to be fooled."

Robbie looked at me doubtfully. I continued. "Anyway, it's just as well that you're up. I was just about to wake you for our morning news broadcast and our delicious breakfast of red Lifesavers and warm root beer."

"Yuck, breakfast sounds gross." Robbie rubbed his eyes. "Geez, I really didn't think I could sleep out here, but I guess I did."

I dug around the seat for the gulpers of root beer and opened the Lifesavers. The Lifesavers weren't too bad, but the root beer was flat and warm and all around pretty awful. I decided I'd save it for later. Right now, it didn't seem all that hot, and I wasn't that thirsty. I guess some little part of me kept hoping that rescuers would come pretty soon and keep us from having to drink the flat root beer.

"Well, Robbie," I said, feeling my stomach churn. "Now that we've had that great breakfast, are you ready for the morning news?"

"Yeah, I guess so. I wish I could be that announcer on the radio. I know just what I'd say." He pretended to hold a microphone to his face. "The sheriff's rescue unit has located the missing Ratliffe boys, and we'll have live coverage of their rescue." Robbie took a breath. "You know, it'd be really neat if the guys from the TV show *Rescue 911* were with the sheriff, and they made a show out of our rescue."

"Right," I said. At this point, I didn't care about the TV stations; I didn't care about being famous. Well, maybe I cared a little. Mostly, I just wanted to hear someone say they knew right where we were and then promise we were going to be rescued soon. I reached out to turn the silver knob on the radio marked *power,* and I saw that my fingers were shaking. What if we turned on the radio, and the news didn't say anything at all about us? What if they'd already given up? It was too awful to think about, so I forced my fingers to turn the switch.

"Hey," Robbie said, "I thought you were going to turn on the radio."

I turned the switch harder until the volume was up

all the way, but the car stayed silent. "Oh, no," I groaned, slamming the dashboard with my hand.

"What . . . what is it?"

"The battery must be dead. The radio won't come on."

Robbie pushed his baseball hat up on his head. "Then how are we ever going to hear about how the rescue's coming? How are we gonna know whether to stay here or try to walk to the highway?"

"Would you quit asking questions!" I shouted. I couldn't look at Robbie. I ran my finger around the steering wheel, wishing the car could somehow magically start. It was beginning to get very warm in there, and I knew we would have to make some decisions soon. The last report we had heard on the radio had basically said that no one knew where we were. If we stayed in our car and no rescuers were looking in this part of the desert, we'd die from the heat before being found. If we walked back to the road, it would be long and hot and we wouldn't have shade, but at least there would be some cars once we got there, and we would get rescued. I explained everything to Robbie. "I'm going to go get the gulpers I left out in the rain last night. We're going to need all the liquids we can get." I didn't tell him that I didn't know if the gulpers were even still there or if they had any water in them at all.

"Well," Robbie said, "at least I saved this can of water from our shoes." He held it out, and we both looked at the water inside. "Kinda gross, huh?" Robbie said.

Kinda wasn't even the word for it. The water was a greyish-brown color. I guess that was no surprise. The insides of both Robbie's and my shoes were pretty disgusting, and that's where the water had been. "Well, we don't have to drink that," I said. "We can just use it to cool off or something."

"Uh-huh," Robbie said, sounding as if he didn't plan to let that water get anywhere near him. "The stuff in the gulpers better not look the same way."

I got out of the car to check them and found the first good news of the morning. The gulpers were still right where I had wedged them, and the water inside looked fine. Each one was almost a fourth-full, and I poured one into the other so that we wouldn't have to carry any unnecessary stuff. My hand shook as I poured because I was trying to be so careful not to spill even one drop. It was hard to believe that it had rained so much last night because the ground under me looked as if it hadn't had rain in years. I don't know where all the rain in a desert went, but it certainly didn't stay around. I walked back to the car with the gulper of water and held it out toward Robbie. "Great news. This water is even clear, like regular water!"

I climbed back in the front seat of the car. It was time to think of a plan and get out of there. "I'm gonna sit here and try to decide what we should take with us. We want to take whatever might help us or keep us cool, but we don't want to carry anything extra." I was really talking to myself more than Robbie. "It's going to be hot and a long way to the main streets. We don't want to get too tired to get there."

Then I turned toward him. "Tell you what, while I look around the car, why don't you scout out the tracks a little way ahead. That way we'll know where we're headed. When you get back, we'll take a little drink of water, grab our gear, and get out of here!"

Robbie opened the car door. "Right on, Robbie the amazing tracker to the rescue." He seemed glad to be doing something useful. I started thinking of what we would need. Robbie had his baseball cap, which was good, but I probably needed to figure out something to cover my head. Then I'd have to see if there was some way to hook the gulpers onto something so we didn't have to carry them in our hands the whole way. I got out of the car to search the back of the station wagon, and just as I opened the back door, I heard Robbie scream.

*Oh God,* I thought, *what now?* "Robbie! Robbie!" I yelled. But there was no answer from Robbie except another scream and then silence. I grabbed the branch we'd used against the snake. It wasn't much of a weapon, but it would have to do. Then I ran to face whatever the terrible thing was.

When I got around the front of the car, I could see Robbie kneeling on the ground. There was no other person or animal around him. "Robbie," I yelled, coming toward him. "What's wrong. Did you fall? Did you get bitten by something?"

Robbie still didn't answer, and as I got closer to him,

I could see a sort of glassy look in his eyes. "Robbie," I shouted, "you tell me what's wrong this minute!"

"Wrong? Wrong?" Robbie asked in a high-pitched, unnatural voice when I was right in front of him. "Scott, do you see any tire tracks? How can we follow the tracks out of the desert when there aren't any tracks to follow?"

It couldn't be. This was impossible. The tracks had to be there. I ran ahead of Robbie. After all, tracks didn't just disappear overnight. They had been there last night when we ran out of gas. We hadn't moved the car, so where were the tracks? I ran faster away from the car. Maybe they were just a little ways up. The car tracks were our only chance to know which way was out.

Totally out of breath, I sank down into the dirt. Robbie was right; there were no tracks. Then the reason hit me. The storm. There had been so much wind, so much blowing dust, and then so much heavy rain. The tracks had either been blown or rained away or both. It didn't much matter. What mattered was that our only road map out of here had been wiped out. I put my hand above my eyes to shade them from the glaring sun and looked out across the desert. For as far as I could see, there were only cacti and rocks. One direction didn't look any different from another. There were some scrawny dirt paths that went off in different ways at different places, but there was no way to know if we should follow one of them.

I continued to sit in the dirt. I noticed that my new, blue baggy shorts were torn in the knee and filthy. I wiped my runny nose across the shoulder of what had been my favorite white T-shirt when things like that mattered.

I had to face the truth, and the truth was that no car tracks meant that we had no chance. We'd tried so hard, but trying hadn't been enough. I sat there feeling the burning sun and wondered what it would be like to be dead. I thought maybe I should just tell Robbie to come back to the car with me, and we'd lie down and go to sleep. Maybe we'd be dead without ever waking up; then it wouldn't hurt so bad to die. My legs felt so heavy; I couldn't make them stand up. *In a minute,* I thought; *in a minute.*

Suddenly, something was tugging at me. "See, I told you the tracks were gone. Why are you just sitting there? What are we gonna do, huh? What are we gonna do?"

"I don't know, and I don't care!" I said. I could taste the tears running down my cheeks. "Why don't you just go figure it out for yourself?"

In a very small voice, Robbie said, "Okay, I'll try." He leaned over. "Hey, you want to wear my baseball hat for a while? It always makes me feel better."

I looked at my little brother. He was a pretty sturdy kid, but he looked real young and real scared. That baseball hat was the most special thing he owned. All I had to do to start a fight with him was to touch it. From the beginning of second grade, when his best friend had gone to St. Louis and brought it back from a Cardinals' game, that hat hadn't been out of his sight. Now he was offering it to me.

"Scott, 'member Coach in the Dodger game? We were

down by eight runs at the bottom of the sixth, and everyone wanted to just get the game over and go home. 'Member what coach said?"

I remembered. How could I forget that huge guy standing over us, chomping gum and saying angrily, "I can't stand a quitter. Anyone who gives up now is off the team. What's the matter with you guys anyway? You think life was meant to be easy? You think you're just supposed to win? Ha! Life's tough. You be tougher. You get out there on that field, and you play every minute like you're winners. Got it? We lose—well then we lose. You quit fighting every minute to win, and you better not even come back to the dugout because you're not part of my team."

Robbie was staring at me and biting his lip. "Well, do you remember? He said—"

I interrupted. "I remember. Okay, so we won't quit, but I don't see how we're gonna get a home run."

## TEN

**W**e decided that there was no point to walking since we had no idea where to walk. We'd just have to stay with the car and hope someone found us. It would be easier to spot it than to spot two kids wandering nowhere. It seemed like a long walk back to the car, but once we got there, I decided that I'd promised Robbie I wasn't going to quit, and I'd do my best not to.

"Okay, first thing is that I gotta try to remember what it said in my Scout badge book about wilderness survival." Little bits started coming back to me. "We have to try not to sweat."

Robbie looked disgusted. "Geez, we're lost in a huge desert with no one around, and you're worrying about not smelling. You think Jennifer Watkins is going to come with the rescue people?" He tried to imitate her voice. Are you afraid she'll say, 'Oh, Scott, I'm glad you're safe, but you smell too bad for me to kiss.'"

I smiled in spite of myself. "I do not like Jennifer

87

Watkins. How many times have I told you that? I just think she—"

"You just think she should be your girlfriend."

"Wrong about that and way wrong about why we can't sweat. It doesn't have to do with Jennifer. The survival book said that to stay alive in the desert you can't get dehydrated." I sighed, "If we had lots of water, that would be easy. Since we don't, I'm not sure what we'll do."

"Right now, I think I'd rather have air conditioning than water. Boy, that sun is hot." He wiped his forehead. "I wish we at least had a little shade. Let's get in the car."

"We can't stay in the car. It'll be too hot."

"It can't be hotter."

I was too tired to argue with him. "Get in," I said, shrugging.

"I will," he replied defiantly.

It didn't take Robbie long to get out of the car again. "Okay, you're right, but why?"

"Remember all those warnings on TV about not leaving your dog in the car in the summer because when it's a hundred degrees outside, it can be a hundred and thirty in the car?"

"Great," Robbie said. "The car is the only shade we have for as far as we can see, and we can't use it. What are we supposed to do, make shade?"

"That's it, Robbie!" I shouted. "You're brilliant."

"I am?" He looked confused.

"Yeah, that's what we have to do. We have to make shade."

"Uh-huh, make shade. Scott, I was only kidding. It's not exactly like we can grow a tree right here. We don't have any way to make it shady. I mean, we could ask the sun to set early today, but I don't think it would."

I walked over to the car and pulled open the door. "We need to start looking at every single thing in this car to see how it could help us. Let's start with the backseat."

"Geez, it's hot in here," Robbie said.

"Yeah, well, grab anything you see, and we'll get out."

"Look," Robbie said, pulling a big, white beach towel from under the seat. "And I think there's another one jammed in here." We climbed out of the car with two big white beach towels.

"So . . . what do we do with them?" Robbie asked.

I looked at them carefully and stared at the desert around us. My eyes stopped on two large saguaros off to the right that were real close together. "Robbie, get the towels. I've got an idea." I walked over to the cacti and heaved one towel up toward it. The towel fell to the ground. "Darn!" I said. I picked it up and tossed it again. This time the end of the towel caught on some of the needles on one of the arms of the cactus. Then I took the end of the towel still dangling on the ground and tossed it at the other cactus until it had caught, too. "Look, we have shade!" I said proudly.

Robbie came over to stand under the towel. "Wow," he said. "Let's see what else is in the car!" We returned to the car and pulled out everything we could find onto the ground next to the hood. It wasn't long before we had quite a pile. "I never knew our car had so much junk," Robbie exclaimed.

"Good thing," I answered. "We're going to have to turn it into our survival gear." We had gotten two carpeted floor mats from the floor of the front seat and a seat cushion from the driver's seat. We had also found two unwrapped cookies that had been wedged under the front seat, part of one roll of Lifesavers, a sharp tool to pry off hubcaps, a pad of paper and a pencil, and all the packages that Mom had bought at the mall. Also, while tearing through the car, we'd finally located the jack and the spare tire. They too were now on the ground.

I looked at everything, and I wondered how to use it all. I opened one of the bags and the white skirt and blouse that Mom had bought tumbled onto the ground. I picked them up and threw the skirt at Robbie. "Put this on."

"No way," Robbie squealed. "Get serious."

"I am serious. It's like the camel drivers in the movies. Remember, they always wore those white head things and long white robes? This is the closest we've got."

"Uh-huh, how come you aren't wearing a skirt?"

"Because you're my little brother, and we only have one skirt. I'm trying to help you."

"It's okay, Scott. You go ahead and take it. In fact, you know how Mom always complains that we don't share enough? Well, I really want you to get to wear this skirt." Robbie grinned.

"Okay, fine, I will." I stared at the skirt for a minute and pulled it on. It reached the tops of my basketball shoes. Then I took the blouse and wound it around my head like a turban.

Robbie laughed. "Wait until the TV crews get a look at you. You'll never live this down at school."

I had to admit that it was really weird to be wearing a skirt. Still, I wasn't kidding when I'd told him about the camel drivers, so if Robbie wanted to laugh, let him. I had more problems to worry about than Robbie's smirks. I bent down and picked up the hubcap tool and tried to get the hubcap off the car. I don't know what I was doing wrong, but nothing would make it come loose. I was so mad that I finally stood up and kicked the dumb thing. "Ouch!" I yelped as my foot fully felt the pain of the kick. "Darn! I guess we'll have to do without them."

"What do we need hubcaps for?"

"I was going to try to make them into a signal for any planes that might fly by. I thought the metal might reflect the sun, but nothing's gonna get the hubcaps off the car. Let's go work on making ourselves a better shady spot."

I tried to remember what else the book had said about surviving. It said something about staying cooler if you didn't sit right on the ground. You needed to be up a foot or so. I wondered if we could get one of the seats out of the car, but I didn't see how. Then I looked at the arms of the saguaro. I didn't really think they'd hold us, and besides, they were covered with cactus needles. Ouch! It hurt just to think about it. I walked back over to the car and looked again at all our stuff, wishing it would somehow turn into something great to get us out of here. Unfortunately, nothing had changed. I stared at the spare tire, and then walked over to it. I stood it on edge and began rolling it. "Hey," Robbie said, "where you going with that? You think you're going to just roll out of the desert? Get it? Roll out of the desert?"

I ignored him and rolled the tire until I could plop it down in the shady spot I'd created under the saguaros. Unfortunately, there was no way two people could fit on the tire, and no way that I knew how to get one of the other tires off the wheels. I couldn't even get the dumb hubcaps off.

The sun was making my head hurt, but I tried to think what else I could use. There was nothing big, so I started taking little rocks and even some broken cactus and piling them on top of each other. "Hey, Robbie," I called. "I could use some help here." There was no answer. It was easier to keep finding little things to pile on top of each other than to go get Robbie. Bit by bit the pile was growing higher. When it was finally as high as the tire, I headed back over to the car.

"Robbie," I yelled. "What are you doing?"

"Over here," he grunted.

I walked around the car. Robbie had gotten three hubcaps off the car and was working on the fourth. "Nice going!" I said, and I really was impressed. "Take them over to the shady spot, then come back for more stuff."

Robbie grinned. "Thanks. They weren't so easy to get off, but I did it!"

I pushed his baseball hat down on his head. Maybe we really were going to make it after all.

Eventually, we had the hubcaps and the floor mats, the gulpers, and the seat cushion. We put the gulpers in the shade, and I threw the carpeted floor mats and the seat cushion on the make-shift seats I had made. I put the hubcaps in front of us in the sun. I glanced down at my arm. My watch read 9 A.M. I couldn't believe it. How could it already feel so hot so early? All we had left to get was the Lifesavers and the cookies, and then we had to wait for what I hoped wouldn't be too long to get rescued.

As we got closer to the car, I decided we should put up the hood, so anyone from far away could see the car was in trouble. I went to the front of the car and tried to open the hood. Staring at it, I yelled to Robbie, "Hey, come here. You see any way to get this thing open?" Robbie looked, but he couldn't find any kind of handle either.

"Maybe this'll help," Robbie offered, and he banged on the hood. "Yow! My hand is burning!" he yelled, but the hood remained shut.

"Oh, never mind," I said. "Maybe the dumb thing is just broken."

Robbie looked at me. "Hey, I got another idea. Why don't we open all the doors. Then they'll have even more stuff to see."

As I was opening the car doors, I glanced inside the car, and I saw the black lever marked "hood release." I felt like an idiot. In no time, we had the hood open, and then I got another idea. I took part of the nightgown that was supposed to have been for Aunt Susan. Opening the window washer container next to the radiator, I dipped the nightgown into it. While it was still dripping with soapy water, I tore the material into strips. "Put this around the back of your neck. We can't drink the water, but we can use it to help us stay cool." I put some strips of the wet blue lacy material around my neck, and Robbie began to snicker. "If only Jennifer could see you now!"

I threw a strip around his neck. I was not going to talk about Jennifer. "Let's go sit in the shade," I said.

"Wait. Look what I thought of while you were getting the hood up." Robbie proudly pointed to the side mirrors which he had tilted upward to catch the sun's reflection. "Airplanes have to see them, don't you think?"

"Nice going, Robbie! Give me five!" I said.

Robbie looked extremely pleased with himself. "We're awesome, and we're gonna get rescued. I just know it."

# ELEVEN

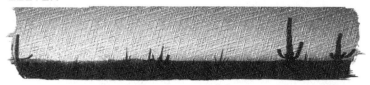

We walked over to the shady area we'd made and sat down. The seats weren't the most comfortable in the world, but they weren't that awful. "So, now what?" Robbie said.

"Now, we wait." It was really hot. My shirt was already starting to stick to my skin. I tried not to think about it. When we'd moved to Arizona, I'd heard that it was hot enough during the summer to fry an egg on the sidewalk. I didn't know if that was true, but even in the city it felt like you were always sitting under a very hot heat lamp. At least there, you had air conditioning and swimming pools.

"So, how long have we been sitting here?"

I looked at my watch. "Ten minutes."

"Is that all? Are you sure your watch didn't break?"

Just then a lizard scurried past us. It ran so fast that it didn't even look like its front legs were touching the ground. "Wow, that was a humungous lizard," Robbie said. "I saw a little one outside our window the other day, but I've never seen one that big."

"Yeah. You know Gabe Morton? Well, once he went to catch one, and he said that he grabbed its tail, and the tail came off in his hand, but the lizard still kept running."

"Really?"

"That's what Gabe said." I wiped my forehead with my arm. "Tell you what, let's think about places we could be that are cool."

"Okay. How about Alaska?"

"Well, what about it?"

"I don't know. I've never been there."

I sighed. "Robbie, like this. Pretend we were in a swimming pool back in Phoenix. We jumped in the deep end, and the water was so cold that we yelled. There were goose bumps all over our skin, and we had to swim real fast to try to get warm. But even though we swam a lap, we were still shaking, and our teeth were chattering. Can you feel it? Can you see us there?"

"No, I'm still hot."

"Yeah, me too." I looked down at my watch; practically no time had passed. I wondered what they were saying about us in Phoenix. What were they doing to try to rescue us? Even the backs of my ears felt as if they were on fire.

Robbie interrupted my thoughts. "Okay, I got a cool place for us to be. We're up on the ski slopes in Flagstaff. It is so cold. It's blowing and it's snowing. We're on the chair. We get just past mid-point, and the chair stops. We sit there, and the wind and snow sting our faces. We'd give anything to get off that chair and warm up."

"That's good," I said. "You're describing last Christmas. Boy, we were freezing. I'd sure settle for a little of that icy snow right now."

Robbie nudged me. "Look quick!" He pointed, and off to our right, I saw a roadrunner zip along. It was so fast. It ran almost directly in front of us, and we both noticed that it had a firm clamp on the head of a lizard. The body was still hanging from the bird's mouth.

"Sick!" Robbie exclaimed. Then he wrinkled his forehead. "I wonder what other bugs and stuff are out here. I sure hope we don't run into our friend, the snake from last night."

I was worried about that myself, but I figured most of the animals probably slept during the day and came out at night when they didn't have to be out in the sun. I sure hoped I was right because our only weapon was a car jack, and I wasn't sure that'd be much help. I mean, suppose one of us got a poisonous bug on us; we couldn't very well hit it with the jack. I'd never seen a real scorpion, but I knew there were supposed to be scorpions in the desert. They had long curving tails filled with poison at the end, and some people died from scorpion stings. Suddenly, it felt like a spider was crawling up my leg. I jumped up and brushed myself off, but I didn't see anything.

"What's wrong?" Robbie said.

"Uhh, nothing. I just wanted to stretch. You know it's hard to keep sitting." Robbie stared at me, and then he copied Mom's I-don't-believe-you-one-bit look. He raised one eyebrow and moved his lips as if he was eating sour candy.

I wished there was something else we could do to get ourselves rescued, but I just couldn't think of anything. I crossed my fingers and hoped that wherever we were was a frequently used part of the desert. Pretty soon, Robbie got up too. He started collecting a lot of little rocks, and then he put them all down next to our "chairs."

I grabbed a handful of the rocks.

"Hey," Robbie complained. "Get your own!"

"I will," I said; "but we'll need yours too. That pile of rocks just reminded me of something I read. When you're lost you're supposed to make a big X on the ground by where you are so they can see you from the air."

In a few minutes, we had gotten enough rocks to make the X. Then we started laying the rocks out. When we were done, Robbie shook his head. "That doesn't exactly look like an X to me."

I had to agree. It was hard to see the whole X when we were so close to the ground. I stood up, took the heel of my shoe, and scraped an X into the dirt. "Now, let's fill it in with the rocks."

The sun beat down on our necks as we made it, and it felt good to sink back into our shady spot. Robbie wiped his forehead with his arm. "Boy, I sure hope they use that X to find us because it was so hot to make it!"

"I don't care what they use. I just hope they get here pretty soon."

The two of us sat under the towel. There didn't seem to be anything else to say or do, and it was really boring just sitting there. I kept looking at my watch. It seemed like we had been sitting for hours, but each time, my watch showed only a couple of minutes had passed.

Robbie started fiddling with some of the extra rocks we'd collected. "Hey," he nudged me, "let's play a game. Let's try to get the rocks into the hubcaps."

"Nah, I don't feel like it."

"Oh, come on. What else is there to do. It's boring and it's hot just to sit here."

After about fifteen minutes, we had exhausted our supply of rocks. From looking at the hubcaps, it was easy to see why Robbie was the baseball pitcher instead of me. I had no intention of collecting the rocks so that I could get beaten again, and Robbie's face was almost as red as his hair. I guess he decided it was too much work to go round them up again too.

"I wonder . . ." Robbie paused. "I wonder if I'll ever get to pitch in a baseball game again."

"Sure," I said, trying to joke. "Who ever heard of an eight-year-old's pitching arm giving out?"

"Don't treat me like such a little kid. You know what I mean! And you know I turned nine three weeks ago! I'm not staying here anymore. It's too awful just to sit here and get hotter and hotter and hotter. I'm walking out of here. We tried it your way, and nothing has happened. We haven't heard any rescue planes or helicopters. We haven't seen any Jeeps out looking for us. Face it. No one is coming. If you're too chicken to try to find your way out, you can just stay, but I'm leaving!"

"But Robbie—" He didn't listen. He stormed away from the car and the shady spot. He didn't even take any of the water with him. I didn't know what to do. There was no way he could survive if he kept walking, but it might kill us both if I tried to stop him. Tears of frustration trickled down my face. "Robbie," I yelled, "please come back here! Please, we agreed that we would stay right here. You don't know where you're going."

Robbie yelled back over his shoulder, "No, you agreed with yourself. You always want to be the one to decide." Robbie continued to walk onward. I'd have to go after him. I couldn't just let him walk to his death. I forced myself to stand up and walk out from the shady area. I took one of the gulpers and began to walk in Robbie's direction. I could probably catch Robbie. I could probably tackle him and get him to the ground. But I wasn't big enough to put him over my shoulder and make him come back. I walked a few steps. The sun seemed even stronger than it had been an hour ago. Robbie looked back over his shoulder, saw me coming, and began to run.

This was crazy! Maybe I was only making things worse by going after him. Maybe, if he didn't have to prove that I couldn't stop him from leaving, he'd just decide to come back on his own. Biting my lip, I went back to the shady spot, slammed the gulper down, and to my horror watched as the lid popped off and some of our precious water spilled out. Defeated, I sat down and stared in the direction he was going. When he looked back and saw I wasn't chasing him, he stopped running. Unfortunately, he didn't turn around, and pretty soon, he was no more than a disappearing dot. "Oh, Robbie," I called softly. "How could you do this?"

Even if by some chance I did get rescued, how could I ever live with the fact that I'd let my little brother just disappear into the desert somewhere? My throat felt like it was on fire. I reached over for the gulper and took a sip, swishing the water around my mouth to make it last longer before I swallowed it. I had to fight with myself to keep from drinking the whole gulper. Only a sip or two. I made myself cap it and put it down.

I'd hoped with everything in me that Robbie would just turn around and come back, but he hadn't. I put my hand across my eyes. I knew that I had to go out after him and try to get him water and shade. I tried hard not to let myself think that my trying to rescue Robbie would probably mean that no one would ever find either one of us.

I decided to carry the gulper with me. This time I checked it carefully to make sure that it was tightly fastened and no water would spill out of it as I carried it. Then I began to walk in the direction that I'd seen Robbie go. My skin felt like it was being burned alive. It seemed almost like I'd crawled into a giant oven, and someone had shut the door, then turned the temperature up to high. At least I was gaining on the figure in the distance. Then I realized why. It was coming toward me. I continued walking to the approaching figure. It had to be Robbie. After all, I'd seen him go off this way, and the two of us were the only ones who seemed to even know about this spot except the snakes, the coyotes, and . . . the kidnappers.

## TWELVE

My heart was pounding as the figure came closer, and my eyes were stinging as the sweat dripped down toward them from my forehead. When it got still closer, I tried to yell, but it came out only a croak: "Robbie."

By the time he reached me, he said he felt real dizzy. "I'm sorry, you were right. Too hot. No water."

I put the gulper to his lips. He started to drink greedily, but I pulled the gulper away. "This is all the water we've got. It has to last! Come on—lean on me, and we'll go back to the shade." I put Robbie's arm around my shoulders and half-pulled, half-dragged him back to our spot. By the time we got there, I was feeling pretty dizzy myself. Robbie didn't say anything the whole way. I could hear him panting as we went. I felt so tired, I wasn't sure I could make it, but finally we got to our shaded spot. I dumped Robbie on one seat and collapsed on the other. My breathing was coming so hard that it felt like my heart was going to jump right out of my chest.

I put the gulper to my mouth and took another big swig. Then I handed it to Robbie and made him do the same. He handed the bottle back empty. The only liquid we had left was the greyish stuff from our shoes. I dipped my fingers into it and ran them around my face. Then I wetted a little piece of the blue lacy strip around Robbie's neck and wiped off his face.

"Ahhhh," Robbie screamed.

"It's water, it's just water." I shouted, my heart pounding. "Calm down."

"My arm, my arm!" Robbie grabbed at his left arm and began to rock with pain.

"What's the matter?" I screamed at him.

"I don't know. It hurts so bad!" Robbie continued to clutch his arm and moan.

I pried his fingers from his arm, and could see a big red spot that was swelling even as I watched. In the middle of the red was an almost white spot and what looked like a little puncture hole. I couldn't see a stinger, but I was pretty sure something had bitten or stung Robbie. In Boy Scouts we had learned that there were thirty-six different kinds of scorpions in Arizona, and one of them was real poisonous. *Think!* I told myself. What else did I remember about scorpions? I couldn't think of anything. Meanwhile, Robbie kept moaning, "It hurts so much."

I tried to think what I knew about any kind of bites. All I remembered was that Mom used baking soda paste if we ever got a bee sting, but that didn't help much because we didn't have any baking soda out there. Ice helped too, but we certainly didn't have any of that. I thought about something I had heard about soothing pain with aloe from the right cactus, but who knew what kind of cactus that was?

"Hey, Robbie, it's okay," I said, hoping my voice didn't sound as scared as I was. "Really, it's just a little bite or something. It'll go away."

Robbie was crying. "It was a scorpion, huh. I know it was. Did you see it? Oh, Scott, I know I got poisoned."

"Nah," I lied. "I know what a scorpion bite looks like, and this isn't one. It was probably just a dumb old ant or something. It'll stop hurting in a few minutes."

I looked at the swelling spot on Robbie's arm again. It didn't look like any ant bite I'd ever seen, but I had never seen a scorpion bite at all. I crossed my fingers and prayed that this bite was nothing. Trying to keep my voice calm, I said, "Hey, just take it easy. No point to getting all worked up over a dumb ant bite. I'm pretty sure that's all it is. Just a stupid little stinging ant. Hey, your arm'll feel better pretty soon. Just lean back," I said to Robbie. "Try to think about something else."

"Easy for you to say," Robbie muttered. "Besides, this hurts too much to be from some little old ant." Then he didn't say anything more. He just bit his lip and continued to rock back and forth holding his left arm. I wanted to say something to make it better, but I couldn't think of anything else to say, so I just patted Robbie's shoulder and hoped I was right about its being an ant.

It got real quiet. I'm not sure if we slept or not. I was feeling pretty dizzy. The sun was making everything dance in wavy lines, and I didn't know if only a few minutes or a few hours had passed when I heard Robbie say "Scott . . ." His voice was barely there. "Hey, Scott, even though we fought, I'm glad you were my brother."

Stringy cobwebs were clinging to my brain. It was hard to think, but still an alarm blared in my head. "Don't say *were*, Robbie; I *AM* your brother!"

Robbie didn't answer. It took so much effort to move, but I made myself shake his arm. "Robbie," I called, but his head had dropped down on his chest. "Not *were*, AM!" I screamed, but I don't know if it was more than a whisper. "Please, please, you can't die!"

My eyes were just slits by now, and I tried to shake my head so I could make my eyes clear and see right, but they wouldn't work. Somehow, I managed to grab for the can of gray water. Maybe if I could just cool Robbie off. I took the can and poured some water over Robbie's head. He stirred, but only a little. "Come on, Robbie, don't do this!" I forced the can to Robbie's lips and poured a little of the liquid down his throat. He gagged, and spit it out. I tried to see whether the spot on his arm was better, but my eyes wouldn't focus right.

I knew I wasn't much better off, and so I forced the little liquid left into my own parched and swollen lips. I fought waves of nausea as it went down, and then I retched.

I think the minutes crept on into hours, but my eyes were too fuzzy to see my watch. My head buzzed, and my legs felt too rubbery to ever stand up again. I was so tired. I had never been this tired in my whole life. I just wanted to sleep, but I had to do one last thing. Fumbling, I felt for the pencil and paper on the ground. When I found them, I forced my fingers to pick them up. I couldn't see well enough to read what I was writing, but I felt the pressure of my fingers moving the pencil as I wrote, "Dear Mom, We tried so hard to live. We really did love you." It was so hard to make my hand lift a stick next to me and put the paper under it, but I did it. At least, some day, if someone ever found us, Mom would get the note. I tried to lean over and hug Robbie goodbye, but my arms wouldn't move anymore. I thought I saw a snake slithering toward us, but it didn't matter. I just needed to sleep. I let my head fall to my chest, and pretty soon, I realized that I no longer felt the burning of my throat or the awful thickness of my tongue. I didn't feel hot any more. Somehow, the sun had sunk into a kind of strange darkness.

## THIRTEEN

**M**y alarm clock was buzzing. I reached out to shut it
off. "Mom," I tried to say, "I still have more time to sleep;
turn off my alarm!" but for some reason, my tongue
seemed to take up so much of my mouth that I couldn't
say the words. The buzzing sound got louder. Stupid
alarm! Why wouldn't it turn off? All I wanted to do was
sleep. My eyes felt like they were glued shut. I tried to
push them open, but they wouldn't obey. What was
wrong with my dumb body anyway! I lifted my hand
to force my eye open, and my hand felt as if it weighed
a million pounds. Finally, it got to my face, and pulled
my unwilling eye open. Now, if I could just find my
alarm clock and turn the buzzing off so I could sleep.
My vision was so blurry; but wait, this didn't look anything like my bedroom. Where was I anyway? My whole
body ached.

There were cacti . . . and then . . . then I realized
where I was. The desert. Everything came rushing back
to me. "Robbie," I croaked.

There was no answer from the slumped body next to me. My fuzzy brain took a minute to realize that even though my room and my alarm had been only a dream, the buzzing sound was real, and it was still going. If it wasn't my alarm clock, what was it?

I looked up in the sky. A plane. I stared into the blueness to make sure that this wasn't another dream, but there was definitely a small airplane up there circling around. An airplane that was probably looking for us! I tried to get up. If only I could just stand up and wave my arms and shout. The airplane buzzed in the sky as it flew to the south of us. I forced myself to really sit up from my slumped position. "Robbie, hang on. We're gonna be rescued." My tongue was so swollen that I didn't know if it made the actual words or not, but Robbie had to know. I pushed my hand over to him and tried to shake him. Robbie didn't answer. He almost seemed as if he were . . . I couldn't think it. It was just too awful. I wouldn't let myself think at all. I knew Robbie would be okay. I just had to hurry up and get us rescued. I put my hands on the seat I'd made and tried to push my body to a standing position, but I felt so weak. My legs were like rubber, and just as I thought I was standing up, my knees buckled and I fell. Lying on the ground, I watched the plane grow to be only a speck and heard the buzzing get further and further away. The plane hadn't seen us. Our last hope, and I hadn't been strong enough to make it see us. I began to cry, but no tears came. My throat was so parched that I sounded more like a moaning animal than a kid.

The ground was burning hot, and I knew I should drag myself back onto the seat I'd made in the shade. But it just all seemed like so much work, and pretty soon I'd be dead anyway. I lay there feeling both asleep and still vaguely awake. How could the plane have been right up there and still not have seen us! Then I heard the buzzing grow louder again. I rolled from my stomach to my back and stared into the sky as the little plane dipped down and flew almost directly overhead. "Please, please, please," I prayed. "Please see us here and help us."

No one seemed to hear those cries because the plane circled us once again and then flew away. Then I realized that something brightly colored was falling toward me. In the quiet of the desert, it smacked the ground about three feet from me. Too weak to get up and walk to it, I forced myself to crawl over the rocks to reach the bright color. Every time my already hurt knee made contact with the ground it throbbed so much that I yelped in pain, but I kept going. As I got closer, the fluorescent yellow and orange became even brighter. Finally, I sank down right next to it. I was panting like a dog and trembling all over. I forced my hand, almost clawlike, to grab what looked like a velcro black wallet with orange and yellow fluorescent stripes on it and long pink and orange fluorescent streamers attached to it. It took all my strength to tear the velcro apart. Inside was a piece of paper with bold black marker on it. If only my eyes could read it. I rubbed my eyes with the back of my hand, trying to make the words come into focus, but they were just a black blur!

Desperate, I tried moving the paper at different angles. Still, the words wouldn't come into focus. Finally, shutting one eye and squinting with the other, I read, "Help is on the way. Stay calm. Maricopa County Sheriff's Office." I grabbed the paper to my heart. I had never read more perfect words. "Help is on the way!" I repeated it again and again in my brain. We were going to be saved! "Robbie," I tried to call. "Hold on. Just hold on. We're not gonna die!"

# FOURTEEN

I guess I must have blacked out again for a few minutes, because the next thing I heard was a loud noise in the sky again. I couldn't get my eyes open, but I began to feel a tremendous wind blowing, and the noise grew even louder. The next thing I knew someone was leaning over me. I grabbed his arm. "You real?" I croaked.

"I sure am," a deep voice screamed into my ear above the loud noise of the plane. "And you're going to be just fine. You just relax and let us take care of you."

"Brother," I gasped. "My brother . . ." It was so hard to make the words sound like words.

"It's okay. My partner is with your brother right now. I'm going back to the helicopter to get some water. I'll be right back."

I reached for his arm. I was afraid he'd disappear—a hallucination or my imagination. When I touched only air, I began to really wonder. Was this really help, or was I just imagining it because I wanted it so badly? Then I heard the crunch of footsteps and felt a wetness on my chest and a cool wet cloth go under my neck and around my forehead. "I'm going to give you a tiny sip of water," the deep voice said. "Swish it around in your mouth." He put something to my lips and lifted my head. I wanted to gulp gallons of water; one sip seemed almost mean.

"More," I croaked.

"Let's just see . . ." he began to say and then the sound of his voice was drowned out by another helicopter landing. Everything was blowing, and the helicopter's blades and engine were making so much noise that I couldn't hear anything. Swirling dirt and dust kept me from even thinking of opening my eyes, and then I felt myself being placed onto a gurney. A voice got right next to my ear and screamed, "We're going to lift you up now. We'll load you into the rear of the MediEvac helicopter over there, and then we'll get you to the hospital. There's a nurse on board. She'll look after you. Nod if you can hear me."

I nodded my head. I felt a strong hand grip mine for a minute, and the voice yelled into my ear again, "Son, you're a brave boy. You're going to be okay!"

I felt myself being lifted into the air, and then once I was up to the helicopter, I felt my gurney being set onto some sort of track and wheeled in. I heard it click into place. "Robbie," I tried to croak.

A woman's voice said, "They'll have him on board in a minute. Now, just let yourself relax. We're going to begin to cool you down."

I forced my eyes open. The ceiling was so close to my face. I felt new cool, wet towels being placed on me. The nurse leaned over me, checking something. "Please." I tried to make my unwilling mouth form words. "Robbie, hurt. Bitten, stung."

The nurse stopped what she was doing and took my hand. "Do you know by what?"

"No, but . . ." It was so hard to make the words form, but I had to do it. "His left arm . . . upper part."

"I can't understand you," the nurse said. "Try to say it again."

I forced my unwilling mouth and tongue to work. I thought I said it over and over, but maybe I only got the words out once before the nurse patted my arm. "That will help," she said. "Now, you relax. I'm going to start an IV."

I heard another gurney roll onto tracks in the helicopter. I felt the door slam shut, and then the noises of the helicopter drowned out everything else. I let myself lay back on the softness of the gurney and sleep. Someone else could be in charge now. "Robbie," I whispered. "We made it. We're safe! You just gotta have stayed alive."

## FIFTEEN

"Look, his eyes are opening," said a voice that seemed to me to be coming from far, far away.

"Uh-huh," said another, deeper voice. "He seems to be regaining consciousness."

Everything was so blurry that I couldn't see, and it hurt too much to try to keep my eyes open, so I closed them again. I wanted to ask where I was, what was happening, but though I could get my mouth open, my tongue seemed to take up my whole mouth, and I couldn't make any words work. All I knew was that I didn't feel so hot anymore. I stopped trying to think or to speak, and I just let the coolness spread over my body.

I don't know how long I stayed like that, but the next time I opened my eyes, I saw my mom's face floating right above mine. I had never realized just how pretty she was. People said that I had her blue eyes, but the way she was looking at me, hers were much better. They were so kind-looking and filled with love.

"Oh, Scott. You're going to be okay. I was so scared.

You must have been too, but you were so brave. When the Search and Rescue Team found you, they said you had done everything just right to save your lives."

My eyes began to focus. I was alive! Oh, God. I was alive! Then I remembered about the plane and the deputy and the helicopter. As the room came into view, I realized I was in a hospital. There was a tube attached to my arm. Was my little brother okay too? My swollen tongue managed to get around a word. "Robbie?" I croaked.

"The doctors say Robbie will be fine too. He's in the next bed. He had kind of a rough go of it when he first got here. But you know your brother. You can't keep him down for long." Mom smiled. "He woke up about an hour ago, pointed to his baseball cap, and when I gave it to him, he managed a grin, and then fell immediately back to sleep."

"But—the bite on his arm? Was it a scorpion? Was it poisonous?"

"Just a bee sting. I know it hurt him a lot, but Robbie isn't allergic to bees so he was okay."

I tried to smile. "We're both gonna live?"

There were tears coming down Mom's cheeks, and I felt her reach over and take my hand. "Of course, you are! Of course, you are." She wiped her tears away with her other hand. "You just rest now. After you're stronger, I'll explain everything."

As much as I wanted to know more, I couldn't keep my eyes open. I had to go back to sleep.

I don't know how long I slept, but when my eyes

flicked open the next time, I saw I was still in a hospital. It hadn't been just a wishful dream. My head was much clearer now, and my heart pounded with relief. In spite of everything, we really had made it. I turned my head and saw that Robbie was awake in the next bed. "Hey, Robbie!"

"About time you woke up!" he said, and he gave me a thumbs-up sign.

"Well, it looks as if the two of you are finally both really awake," came the booming voice of a white-coated man. He took his stethoscope and came over toward my bed. "I'm Dr. Handson."

"Have we been asleep for a long time?" I asked.

"Oh, you've both been fading in and out for awhile. Robbie gave us a scare for a little bit there, but he's a tough young man, aren't you, Robbie?"

Robbie grinned. "Yeah, I guess I am!"

The doctor examined me and then Robbie. "Well, I'd say that both of you boys certainly are doing much better. You sure had a lot of people worried about you!"

"We were pretty worried ourselves," Robbie piped in.

The doctor chuckled. "You're very popular individuals; did you know that? First, you had practically every police force in the state trying to find you, and now you have practically every newspaper, radio, and television station waiting to do an interview with you."

"We do? Wow, Scott, just like we said in the desert. Remember? Hey, how do I look?"

At that moment, Mom walked in the room with a cup of coffee. The doctor looked at her and smiled. "Your boys are both doing just fine. They'll bounce back from all this fast. A couple more days, and it will seem as if this whole thing never happened."

I didn't know about that. I didn't think I would ever forget the terrors of those days in the desert. Robbie, however, had other things on his mind. "Well, when are we gonna be on TV?"

The doctor replied, "Son, you already have been the lead story on TV and the front page of the newspaper."

A nurse came into the room. "Sorry to interrupt, but the deputies who found these boys heard that they're conscious, and want to know if they can come in."

"Oh, please, could they come in?" Mom asked the doctor. "I owe those deputies more than I could ever say."

The doctor said it would be all right, and two men in Maricopa County Sheriff's Department uniforms walked into the room holding their hats. "How are you guys doing?" asked the tallest of them.

"How'd you find us? What did you do with us? How'd you keep us alive? Were we almost dead when you found us?" Robbie began firing questions at them before I could say anything at all.

The taller deputy grinned. "Well, you are feeling better. You certainly weren't this talkative when we found you. Good thing or we'd have been too busy answering questions to rescue you!"

The other deputy turned toward Robbie. "Amazing how fast kids recuperate. These sure don't look like the two boys I put on the helicopter."

"Helicopter! We were on a helicopter? Oh, wow, and I didn't even know it. Tell me all about it!" Robbie insisted.

Looking at the two deputies, I said, "I had just about given up hope when I saw the plane in the sky, and then I didn't think the plane had seen us. It seemed to be heading away from us. Then it circled back, and it dropped that note."

"What note?" Robbie said. "I didn't see any note."

I looked at Robbie. "You were kinda out of it at the time. That was after you got stung."

"Huh," said Robbie, but instead of waiting for answers, he burst in again. "Did the plane see us because of the mirrors on the car? I was the one who put them up like that. Did you see the hubcaps? I was the one who got them off the car, but it was Scott's idea to do it."

At the rate Robbie was asking questions, we were never going to find out what happened to us. I leaned over toward him. "Robbie! Let him tell us what happened."

"I am," Robbie said. "I want to know too. So how did you find us?"

"Actually," the taller deputy said, "we had no idea where the kidnappers had taken you. We set up a hotline and had news bulletins on radio and TV asking anyone who might have seen either of you or your mom's car to call."

"Did lots of people call?" Robbie asked.

The shorter deputy with a sort of big belly answered. "We were getting reports from all across the state. One person would call and say he was sure he had seen you in the northwest corner, and then we'd get another call from someone sure that you'd just been seen crossing the border into Mexico. Though all the law enforcement agencies in the state were cooperating, we didn't get the break we needed until yesterday afternoon when we heard from a nurse in Tucson."

"Tucson?" I said, "But we weren't ever even close to Tucson."

"Right," said the taller deputy. "But the men who kidnapped you were. Yesterday, alleged drug dealers in Tucson were involved in a shootout with police. One died immediately, and the other was taken to the hospital. Right before he died, he told a nurse that he'd left a couple of kids in the desert outside of Scottsdale. She wasn't sure that she understood him or that he wasn't hallucinating. Anyway, she got called to an emergency code, and she forgot what he'd said."

Even sitting in the bed with covers, I suddenly felt myself shiver. It was just too awful to think someone knew where we were and didn't know it was important.

Robbie jumped in. "Wow, so what made her call you?"

The shorter deputy said, "Later in the day, she took a break, and while she was sitting in the nurse's lounge, someone turned on the TV. One of the news bulletins came on, and as she heard it, she suddenly thought of the dying drug dealer's words, and she began to wonder if he could have been talking about the two of you."

The deputy who'd been silent up to now broke in. "When the nurse called, she didn't sound too sure of herself, and we thought it was just one more tip to be checked out, but we followed up on it by asking a Cessna search plane to fly over the area. It was only a matter of minutes before we got a message back that they'd located the vehicle, and then they'd seen the shelter you'd made and you."

Mom had tears running down her face. "They called me right away. Those minutes until the helicopter landed and a second group of paramedics arrived were so . . ." Mom couldn't finish.

"Hey, Mom, it's okay; we're okay now," I said.

One of the deputies cleared his throat. "Well, we'll be going now, but in a few days, we'd like to talk a little with you boys about your kidnappers."

"Sure," Robbie jumped in. "I can tell you lots of stuff. One even had a tattoo, and it was a snake, and it was awful."

Before we could really thank the deputies and before they could leave, another man entered the room and introduced himself as the chief administrator of the hospital. "Dr. Handson says you boys are well enough to participate in a brief interview, and the press is all over this place." He turned to Mom. "Would it be all right for the boys to hold a very short press conference so that we could get this hospital back to normal?"

"You've all been so wonderful to us. As long as the

doctor says it's all right for the boys, we'd be glad to have the press conference."

Robbie tossed back his covers. "TV, here we come!"

"Not so fast, partner," the administrator said. "We'll have some nurses take you in wheelchairs."

"Ahh, I can walk!" Robbie exclaimed, but the doctor said Robbie might faint, and he would be taken to the press conference in a wheelchair. "No way I'm gonna faint! I've been waiting my whole life to be on TV."

We made quite a group trooping down the hall: the administrator, Mom, the deputies, and the two nurses who were pushing our wheelchairs.

"Now, there are quite a few reporters in there. I don't want it to scare you boys," warned the administrator.

"Thanks, but it would probably take quite a bit to scare us anymore," I said.

"Besides," Robbie chipped in, "we have this little bet about which one of us is going to be better on TV."

With that, the door to the temporary press room opened, and we were wheeled in. I couldn't believe the table of microphones, the cameras, and the photographers who began snapping flash photos of us. The whole room was packed. I wasn't sure what I expected, but this was unbelievable. With my eyes still trying to focus after a flash, I felt someone stick a microphone right under my nose and heard him ask me how I felt.

"I feel really glad to be alive," I said, and to my surprise, tears welled up in my eyes.

A reporter stuck a mike in front of one of the deputies.

"It's been so hot out. How do you think these boys managed to survive the dangers of the desert?"

The deputy looked right into the TV cameras. "They really used their heads. They survived because they used liquids well, created a shelter for themselves, tried to make signals, stayed with their vehicle, and never panicked."

Another reporter shouted, "How did you boys know to do all that?"

I started to open my mouth to explain, when I heard Robbie shout, "It was easy!"

"It was?" asked the reporter, and all cameras turned toward Robbie.

"Sure," he nodded and smiled. My mouth dropped open as I prepared to listen to my little brother explain how he had made all the decisions to save the day. I had to admit that he did have a flare for TV. He waited until all the reporters had gathered around him, and then he leaned forward to speak directly into the microphones. "You see, my brother, Scott, over there, he figured everything out. He learned how to drive the car, how to get more to drink, how to make shade, and how to do all the other stuff that kept us alive."

The cameras turned toward me. "That so?" called a reporter.

I couldn't believe what I'd heard Robbie say. I was in such a state of shock that he'd used his TV time to talk about me that I could hardly speak. "Well, we did work together to keep each other's spirits up," I said.

Then a reporter turned to Mom. "And how do you feel, Ma'am?"

Mom's eyes misted and her voice sounded kind of scratchy. "I feel such great joy and such appreciation to everyone who reached out to help my sons. I'm so proud of the way they handled themselves, and believe me—I'll never leave the keys in the car again, not even for a second." Mom leaned over and hugged Robbie and me.

Finally, the press conference was over. We were back in our hospital beds, and I had to admit that I was feeling much more tired than I'd thought I would. Dr. Handson looked at Mom and ordered her to go downstairs and get something to eat. "Oh, I really don't want to leave the boys. I can just get another cup of coffee at the nurses' station."

Dr. Handson remained firm. "The boys are fine now. You are going to get some nourishment for yourself besides coffee. They'll be well looked after by the nurse." He winked at her. "Listen, I have a feeling it will take all your strength to keep up with the mischief these two create, so you'd better take care of yourself."

Mom smiled, and I wondered if she was thinking about the hose we'd brought in the house or some of our other stunts this summer. "They certainly can create their fair share of mischief, that's for sure." Then her eyes filled with tears. "I'm just so glad they're back. . . . For a while, I almost thought . . ." Dr. Handson went over and patted her shoulder. "The boys are fine, I promise. Now, down-stairs with you for some food; the nurse and I will monitor the boys." Mom blew us a kiss, and she said she'd be right back. The doctor and nurse checked us over again, and then they left the room with strict instructions that we were to stay put. I turned to Robbie, and yawning, I said, "Pretty amazing, huh?"

Robbie leaned over on his side. "I'd say. Do you realize that in three days' time we got kidnapped, almost shot, left in the desert, drove a car, almost died, rode a helicopter, and we just had as big a press conference as the President of the United States."

It was all pretty unbelievable, and in its way so was something else. "Hey, Robbie, I . . . uh . . . I just want to say thanks for the stuff you said in the desert and the stuff you said on TV about my saving us. That was really something."

Robbie looked worried. "Yeah, well, that doesn't mean I'm gonna say nice stuff about you all the time. Because I can't. I don't even want to try!"

I smiled, "No problem." And just before I drifted off to sleep, I whispered, "You just wait until you see who really looks the best on TV."

"Oh, it'll for sure be me!" Robbie declared, and then he grinned. "But we can fight about it for the whole rest of the summer!"

# ABOUT THE AUTHOR

An award-winning writer and teacher, Terri Fields has lived in Arizona for the past twenty-nine years. She has been named to the All USA First Teacher Team of twenty-three of the nation's most oustanding teachers. Fields is also the author of fourteen published books and is currently working on her latest survival adventure novel, *Missing in the Mountains*.

On her office wall, she keeps a map with pins in it showing all the states and countries from which kids have written to her about her books.

Terri and her husband, Rick, have two children, Lori and Jeff.